VIOLENT RELATIONSHIPS

BATTERING AND ABUSE AMONG ADULTS

ISSN 1534-1615

VIOLENT RELATIONSHIPS

BATTERING AND ABUSE AMONG ADULTS

Barbara Wexler

INFORMATION PLUS® REFERENCE SERIES
Formerly published by Information Plus, Wylie, Texas

GALE®

THOMSON
™
GALE

Detroit • New York • San Diego • San Francisco • Cleveland • New Haven, Conn. • Waterville, Maine • London • Munich

Violent Relationships: Battering and Abuse Among Adults
Barbara Wexler

Project Editor
Ellice Engdahl

Editorial
Paula Cutcher-Jackson, Kathleen Edgar,
Debra Kirby, Prindle LaBarge, Elizabeth Manar,
Charles B. Montney, Heather Price

Permissions
Debra J. Freitas

Product Design
Cynthia Baldwin

Composition and Electronic Prepress
Evi Seoud

Manufacturing
Keith Helmling

LIBRARY OF CONGRESS CATALOGING-IN-PUBLICATION DATA

ISBN 0-7876-5103-6 (set)
ISBN 0-7876-6075-2
ISSN 1534-1615

Printed in the United States of America
10 9 8 7 6 5 4 3 2 1

TABLE OF CONTENTS

CHAPTER 1

Domestic violence is a centuries-old phenomenon that occurs in almost every society—and is accepted in many. This chapter traces the history of wife abuse and compares traditions from different societies, including the United States.

CHAPTER 2

Using statistics from the landmark *National Violence Against Women Survey* and other important studies, this chapter attempts to draw a general profile of spousal abuse. The shifting definition of spousal abuse is discussed, and various abuse trends are explored by such demographic characteristics as race, ethnicity, income, and sexuality.

CHAPTER 3

The causes of spousal abuse are numerous and varied. Also discussed in this chapter are intergenerational abuse, risk markers and predictors of violence, and the importance of such factors as victim-offender relationship, age, marital status, income, race/ethnicity, and learned gender roles.

CHAPTER 4

One of the most commonly asked questions about abused women is, "Why do they stay in the relationship?" Citing research from different studies on the subject, this chapter attempts to answer that very complex question. It also discusses resources and strategies that women use to cope with or escape from abusive relationships.

CHAPTER 5

This chapter explores two of today's most highly charged issues: rape and sexual harassment. Among the topics discussed here are the varying definitions of, and approaches to, rape; the different types of rape, including marital rape and acquaintance rape; the increasing popularity of "date rape drugs" such as Rohypnol and GHB; shifting definitions and perceptions of sexual harassment; and sexual harassment in the military and the federal workplace.

CHAPTER 6

Reducing domestic violence is nearly impossible without changing the behavior of the batterer. That premise is the focus of this chapter, which explores different abuser types, varying approaches to batterer intervention, and program dropout and recidivism rates.

CHAPTER 7

The judicial system's attitude toward spousal abuse has improved dramatically in the past 20 years; some of the results are discussed here. Also discussed are the factors involved in reporting and prosecuting cases of domestic abuse, the police response to domestic violence calls, the effectiveness of arrest in deterring future domestic assault, protective orders, stalking, and several landmark court cases that emphasized the responsibility of the judicial system to protect battered women.

CHAPTER 8

This chapter begins with a discussion of key domestic violence legislation, including federal statutes and the domestic violence gun ban. It also considers such legal issues as keeping families together, obstacles to prosecuting abusers, mandatory prosecution, and protection orders. Finally, it summarizes some of the important legal cases that have helped to define judicial responsibility and have influenced policies and practices to protect abuse victims.

CHAPTER 9

As this chapter points out, when a woman commits murder, the victim is often her spouse or intimate partner. Among the topics covered here are courts' increasing leniency toward abused women who kill their husbands; factors that influence this form of murder; and legal issues that often affect the outcome of the trial, such as self-defense, equal force, and imminent versus immediate danger.

CHAPTER 10

Responses to survey questions on domestic violence posed by pollsters from Roper Starch Worldwide to the Florida Department of Corrections reveal varying public views on the definition, prevalence, and causes of this problem. Women's opinions about mandatory reporting of abuse and findings by researchers on abuse prevention are also presented here.

PREFACE

Violent Relationships: Battering and Abuse Among Adults is one of the latest volumes in the Information Plus Reference Series. Previously published by the Information Plus company of Wylie, Texas, the Information Plus Reference Series (and its companion set, the Information Plus Compact Series) became a Gale Group product when Gale and Information Plus merged in early 2000. Those of you familiar with the series as published by Information Plus will notice a few changes from the 2001 edition. Gale has adopted a new layout and style that we hope you will find easy to use. Other improvements include greatly expanded indexes in each book, and more descriptive tables of contents.

While some changes have been made to the design, the purpose of the Information Plus Reference Series remains the same. Each volume of the series presents the latest facts on a topic of pressing concern in modern American life. These topics include today's most controversial and most studied social issues: abortion, capital punishment, care for the elderly, crime, health care, the environment, immigration, minorities, social welfare, women, youth, and many more. Although written especially for the high school and undergraduate student, this series is an excellent resource for anyone in need of factual information on current affairs.

By presenting the facts, it is Gale's intention to provide its readers with everything they need to reach an informed opinion on current issues. To that end, there is a particular emphasis in this series on the presentation of scientific studies, surveys, and statistics. These data are generally presented in the form of tables, charts, and other graphics placed within the text of each book. Every graphic is directly referred to and carefully explained in the text. The source of each graphic is presented within the graphic itself. The data used in these graphics are drawn from the most reputable and reliable sources, in particular from the various branches of the U.S. government and from major independent polling organizations. Every effort has been made to secure the most recent information available. The reader should bear in mind that many major studies take years to conduct, and that additional years often pass before the data from these studies are made available to the public. Therefore, in many cases the most recent information available in 2003 dated from 2000 or 2001. Older statistics are sometimes presented as well, if they are of particular interest and no more-recent information exists.

Although statistics are a major focus of the Information Plus Reference Series, they are by no means its only content. Each book also presents the widely held positions and important ideas that shape how the book's subject is discussed in the United States. These positions are explained in detail and, where possible, in the words of their proponents. Some of the other material to be found in these books includes: historical background; descriptions of major events related to the subject; relevant laws and court cases; and examples of how these issues play out in American life. Some books also feature primary documents, or have pro and con debate sections giving the words and opinions of prominent Americans on both sides of a controversial topic. All material is presented in an even-handed and unbiased manner; the reader will never be encouraged to accept one view of an issue over another.

HOW TO USE THIS BOOK

People have suffered abuse at the hands of family members and caretakers throughout human history. Women have suffered a great deal of this abuse as in most cultures they were, and in many places still are, considered little more than the property of their husbands or fathers, who could do whatever they pleased to them. While this idea gradually fell out of favor in the United States during the 19th century, many American women continued to suffer, for the most part silently. Only in the

1960s did Americans begin to recognize that the abuse of women by intimate partners was a major social problem and to take steps to reduce its prevalence. Since then, scientists have researched many troubling questions that this abuse raises, such as: Why do men abuse women that they are close to? Why do women stay with men who abuse them? What are the physical and mental effects of abuse? At the same time, activists have established shelters to help abuse victims, and politicians have enacted laws to protect them. This book examines the many controversies that surround these efforts. In addition, as society became more aware of the abuse of women by their partners, it became more sensitive to the possibility of other forms of abuse, most notably the abuse of men by their female partners, the abuse of people by their same-sex partners, and the abuse of the elderly and the infirm by their caretakers. These issues are also discussed in this volume.

Violent Relationships: Battering and Abuse Among Adults consists of ten chapters and three appendices. Each of the chapters is devoted to a particular aspect of violent relationships in the United States. For a summary of the information covered in each chapter, please see the synopses provided in the Table of Contents at the front of the book. Chapters generally begin with an overview of the basic facts and background information on the chapter's topic, then proceed to examine sub-topics of particular interest. For example, Chapter 3: The Causes of Wife Abuse begins with a description of the typical characteristics of abuse victims and perpetrators in the United States. It then moves on to examine research into the causes of abuse. Thus there is a section on the struggle for power within relationships and importance of traditional gender roles, followed by sections on psychological and sociological explanations for violent relationships. The latest scientific studies—both pro and con—on various sociological theories are incorporated. Other major sub-topics in this chapter include: substance abuse as it relates to domestic violence; abuse of pregnant women; abusive behavior by adults who were abused in childhood; stress as a factor in spouse abuse; the inverse relationship between partner abuse and increasing age; and personality characteristics that may predict future violence. Readers can find their way through a chapter by looking for the section and sub-section headings, which are clearly set off from the text. Or, they can refer to the book's extensive index, if they already know what they are looking for.

Statistical Information

The tables and figures featured throughout *Violent Relationships: Battering and Abuse Among Adults* will be of particular use to the reader in learning about this topic. These tables and figures represent an extensive collection of the most recent and important statistics on abusive relationships, as well as related issues—for example, graphics in the book cover the percentage of all violent crime vic-

tims whose assailant was an intimate partner; the differences between what sorts of behaviors men and women consider to be sexual harassment; why some stalking victims do not report the stalking to the police; the unique ways immigrant women can be abused; and the estimated percentage of all abuse that goes unreported. Gale believes that making this information available to the reader is the most important way in which we fulfill the goal of this book: to help readers understand the issues and controversies surrounding violent relationships in the United States and reach their own conclusions.

Each table or figure has a unique identifier appearing above it, for ease of identification and reference. Titles for the tables and figures explain their purpose. At the end of each table or figure, the original source of the data is provided.

In order to help readers understand these often complicated statistics, all tables and figures are explained in the text. References in the text direct the reader to the relevant statistics. Furthermore, the contents of all tables and figures are fully indexed. Please see the opening section of the index at the back of this volume for a description of how to find tables and figures within it.

In addition to the main body text and images, *Violent Relationships: Battering and Abuse Among Adults* has three appendices. The first is the Important Names and Addresses directory. Here the reader will find contact information for a number of government and private organizations that can provide further information on aspects of violent relationships. The second appendix is the Resources section, which can also assist the reader in conducting his or her own research. In this section, the author and editors of *Violent Relationships: Battering and Abuse Among Adults* describe some of the sources that were most useful during the compilation of this book. The final appendix is the index. It has been greatly expanded from previous editions, and should make it even easier to find specific topics in this book.

ADVISORY BOARD CONTRIBUTIONS

The staff of Information Plus would like to extend their heartfelt appreciation to the Information Plus Advisory Board. This dedicated group of media professionals provides feedback on the series on an ongoing basis. Their comments allow the editorial staff who work on the project to continually make the series better and more user-friendly. Our top priorities are to produce the highest-quality and most useful books possible, and the Advisory Board's contributions to this process are invaluable.

The members of the Information Plus Advisory Board are:

• Kathleen R. Bonn, Librarian, Newbury Park High School, Newbury Park, California

- Madelyn Garner, Librarian, San Jacinto College—North Campus, Houston, Texas

- Anne Oxenrider, Media Specialist, Dundee High School, Dundee, Michigan

- Charles R. Rodgers, Director of Libraries, Pasco-Hernando Community College, Dade City, Florida

- James N. Zitzelsberger, Library Media Department Chairman, Oshkosh West High School, Oshkosh, Wisconsin

COMMENTS AND SUGGESTIONS

The editors of the Information Plus Reference Series welcome your feedback on *Violent Relationships: Battering and Abuse Among Adults*. Please direct all correspondence to:

Editors
Information Plus Reference Series
27500 Drake Rd.
Farmington Hills, MI 48331-3535

ACKNOWLEDGMENTS

The editors wish to thank the copyright holders of material included in this volume and the permissions managers of many book and magazine publishing companies for assisting us in securing reproduction rights. We are also grateful to the staffs of the Detroit Public Library, the Library of Congress, the University of Detroit Mercy Library, Wayne State University Purdy/Kresge Library Complex, and the University of Michigan Libraries for making their resources available to us.

Following is a list of the copyright holders who have granted us permission to reproduce material in Information Plus: Violent Relationships. *Every effort has been made to trace copyright, but if omissions have been made, please let us know.*

For more detailed source citations, please see the sources listed under each individual table and figure.

Centers for Disease Control and Prevention, National Center for Injury Prevention and Control: Figure 9.1, Figure 9.2

Family Violence Prevention Fund and Domestic Abuse Intervention Project: Figure 2.10

Florida Department of Corrections: Figure 10.1, Figure 10.2, Figure 10.3, Figure 10.4, Table 10.1, Table 10.2, Table 10.3, Table 10.4, Table 10.5, Table 10.6, Table 10.7, Table 10.8, Table 10.9, Table 10.10

National Coalition Against Domestic Violence: Table 2.12, Table 2.13

National Institute of Justice and Centers for Disease Control and Prevention: Figure 2.1, Table 2.2, Table 2.3, Table 2.4, Figure 7.6, Table 7.10

Sage Publications: Figure 2.9, Table 2.10, Table 2.11, Figure 6.1

U.S. Department of Justice, Bureau of Justice Statistics: Figure 2.2, Figure 2.3, Figure 2.4, Figure 2.5, Figure 2.6, Figure 2.7, Figure 2.8, Table 2.5, Table 2.6, Table 2.7, Table 2.8, Table 2.9, Figure 3.1, Table 3.1, Table 3.2, Table 3.3, Table 3.4, Table 5.1, Figure 7.1, Table 7.1, Table 7.2, Table 7.3, Table 7.4, Table 7.5, Table 7.6, Table 7.7, Table 7.8, Table 8.1, Figure 9.3, Figure 9.4, Table 9.1

U.S. Department of Justice, Violence Against Women Grants Office: Figure 7.2, Figure 7.3, Figure 7.4, Figure 7.5, Figure 7.7, Figure 7.8, Figure 7.9, Table 7.9, Table 7.11

U.S. Merit Systems Protection Board: Table 5.2, Table 5.3, Table 5.4, Table 5.5, Table 5.6, Table 5.7, Table 5.8, Table 5.9, Table 5.10

World Bank: Table 1.1, Table 2.1

CHAPTER 1
THE ABUSE OF WOMEN—A WORLDWIDE ISSUE

Violence against women is any act of gender-based violence that results in, or is likely to result in, physical, sexual or mental harm or suffering to women, including threats of such acts, coercion or arbitrary deprivation of liberty, whether occurring in public or private life.

— United Nations Declaration on the Elimination of Violence Against Women, 1993

Throughout history, domestic violence has existed in almost all societies. Its origin can be traced back centuries to the development of patriarchal and hierarchical systems of authority in which males controlled all property. In addition, women and children were often considered to be the property of men. The growth of male-oriented societies promoted the widely accepted belief in male superiority that in turn formed the basis for women's subordination. This belief in men's domination over women, often supported by economic, social, cultural, and religious institutions, made it acceptable for men to use violence as a way to control women. In fact, until the end of the nineteenth century, the law supported a man's right to control his wife by force, and it was not until the advent of the women's liberation movement during the late 1960s and 1970s that domestic violence gained recognition as a social issue.

Today, there are social service and justice system resources, including shelters and counseling, available to victims of abuse. In the United States, victims also have legal options. Yet despite this relatively recent progress in the United States, the use of violence in family and intimate partner relationships is still regarded as a man's right in many parts of the world.

An international examination of male violence against women reveals that it is a universal constant—it appears in practically every culture throughout the world and is tolerated by many governments. Many groups, including the United Nations (UN), believe that collaborative international efforts are needed to address this far-reaching health and social problem.

EUROPEAN TRADITIONS

The subservient role of women was well established by the Middle Ages. During the fourteenth century in France, a man could legally beat his wife for failing to obey his orders as long as he did not kill or permanently maim her. The 1371 tale of Geoffrey de la Tour de Landry reflected the contemporary attitude toward "the wickedness of a nagging wife" and the proper punishment for her behavior:

Here is an example to every good woman that she suffer and endure patiently, nor strive with her husband, nor answer him before strangers, as did once a woman who did answer her husband before strangers with short words: and he smote her with his fist down to earth; and then with his foot he struck her in her visage and broke her nose, and all her life after she had her nose crooked, which so shent [spoiled] and disfigured her visage after, that she might not for shame show her face, it was so foul blemished. And this she had for her language that she was wont to say to her husband, and therefore the wife ought to suffer, and let the husband have the words, and to be her master, for that is her duty.

There were some, however, who cautioned men to treat their women with some restraint. Bernard of Siena, Italy, advised the husband in 1427 to treat his wife as he did his fowl and livestock. It is doubtful his advice was heeded, though, since Siena was also home to the Rules on Marriage, which declared:

When you see your wife commit an offense, don't rush at her with insults and violent blows, rather, first correct the wrong lovingly. [If this doesn't work] scold her sharply, bully and terrify her. And if this still doesn't work . . . take up a stick and beat her soundly. It is better to punish the body and correct the soul than to damage the soul and spare the body. You should beat [your wife] only when she commits a serious wrong. Then readily beat her, not in rage but out of charity and concern for her soul.

Wife beating was rarely viewed as the first recourse. Social and religious values were designed to teach women that it was their duty to yield to their husbands' desires. If they resisted, however, those values also taught that it was in a woman's best interest to have the badness beaten out of her. Violence, it seems, was only justified if an appeal to reason or faith was unsuccessful.

The "Rule of Thumb"

It is commonly believed that the term "rule of thumb" originated in the 1600s when an English court found that assaults on a wife were legal provided that the husband used a stick no bigger than his thumb. However, the *Oxford English Dictionary,* an accepted authority on the origin and use of language, reveals that the term does not apply to wife beating. Instead, the dictionary defines the meaning as "to measure by practice or experience," especially by carpenters.

The "rule of thumb" is mistakenly attributed to English common law (the traditional source of American law) and the famous English legal commentator Sir William Blackstone. Blackstone, however, never referred to a "rule of thumb," although he did refer to an ancient law that permitted domestic chastisement:

> The husband . . . by the old law, might give his wife moderate correction. For, as he is to answer for her misbehavior, the law thought it reasonable to entrust him with this power of chastisement, in the same moderation that a man is allowed to correct his apprentices or children. . . . But this power of correction was confined within reasonable bounds and the husband was prohibited from using any violence to his wife.

Blackstone admitted that the prohibition against violence was not well enforced, especially among the lower classes. It was not until 1829 that a husband's right to chastise his wife was finally removed from England's statutes.

The phrase "rule of thumb" remains linked with domestic abuse despite efforts to dispel this relationship. It is believed that a link was mistakenly derived from statements made by judges in North Carolina and Mississippi, who both referred to an "ancient law" that reportedly allowed a man to beat his wife with a stick no wider than his thumb. Although neither judge used the term "rule of thumb," the phrase was reinvigorated and gained more credence when the judges' decisions were reported in a 1974 article that was republished in a 1975 anthology about domestic violence.

Misinterpretation of the phrase was fueled by a 1982 U.S. Commission on Civil Rights report about domestic violence (*Under the Rule of Thumb: Battered Women and the Administration of Justice*) that reiterated the definition wrongly attributed to Blackstone. As recently as 1993, an article in *Time* magazine quoted a New York University law professor's contention that the rule of thumb governed the size of the weapon a husband could use against his wife.

AMERICAN TRADITIONS

In colonial America, English common law allowed physical "chastisement." The early Puritans, however, forbade wife beating. According to a Massachusetts Bay Colony edict, "No man shall strike his wife nor any woman her husband on penalty of such fine not exceeding 10 pounds for one offense, or such corporal punishment as the County shall determine."

Calvin Bradley v. The State (of Mississippi) resulted in the first American legal ruling on the subject of "reasonable chastisement." In that 1824 case, the court found that Bradley, convicted by a lower court of assault and battery against his wife, had gone too far in chastising his wife. "If the defendant now before us could shew from the record, in this case he confined himself within reasonable bounds, when he thought proper to chastise his wife, we would deliberate long before an affirmance of the judgment," the court noted. While criticizing Bradley for bringing shame to his family, the court ruled:

> Family broils and dissensions cannot be investigated before the tribunals of the country, without casting a shade over the character of those who are unfortunately engaged in the controversy. To screen from public reproach those who may be thus unhappily situated, let the husband be permitted to exercise the right of moderate chastisement in cases of great emergency and use salutary restrains in every case of misbehavior, without being subjected to vexatious prosecutions, resulting in mutual discredit and shame of all parties concerned.

Forty years after that ruling, the North Carolina High Court ruled similarly in *State v. Jesse Black.* The 1864 case involved a man who abused his wife after she called him names. In its ruling the court said:

> A husband is responsible for the acts of his wife and he is required to govern his household, and for that purpose the law permits him to use towards his wife such a degree of force as is necessary to control an unruly temper and make her behave herself; and unless some permanent injury be inflicted, or there be an excess of violence, or such a degree of cruelty as shows that it is inflicted to gratify his own bad passions, the law will not invade the domestic forum, or go behind the curtain. It prefers to leave the parties to themselves, as the best mode of inducing them to make the matter up and live together as man and wife should.

In 1874, just 10 years later, the North Carolina court again expressed concern about excessive abuse but advised against public scrutiny of, or interference in, domestic and marital relationships. In *State v. Richard Oliver,* the court found:

> From motives of public policy and in order to preserve the sanctity of the domestic circle, the Courts will not listen to trivial complaints. . . . If no permanent injury has been inflicted, nor malice, cruelty, nor dangerous violence shown by the husband, it is better to draw the

curtain, shut out the public gaze, and leave the parties to forget and forgive.

A Change in Direction

In a landmark Alabama case in 1871, a court found that a husband did not have the right to physically abuse his wife, even "moderately" or with "restraint." In *Fulgham v. The State,* the court ruled that "a married woman is as much under the protection of the law as any other member of the community. Her sex does not degrade her below the rank of the highest in the commonwealth." The court ruled:

A rod which may be drawn through the wedding ring is not now deemed necessary to teach the wife her duty and subjection to the husband. The husband is therefore not justified or allowed by law to use such a weapon, or any other, for her moderate correction. The wife is not to be considered as the husband's slave. And the privilege, ancient though it be, to beat her with a stick, to pull her hair, choke her, spit in her face or kick her about the floor, or to inflict upon her like indignities, is not now acknowledged by our law.

The court concluded that "the rule of love has superseded the rule of force." A little more than a decade later, in 1882, Maryland enacted a law that punished wife beaters with 40 lashes with a whip or a year in jail, but this law was repealed in 1953.

In 1910 the U.S. Supreme Court ruled in *Thompson v. Thompson* that a wife had no cause for action on an assault and battery charge against her husband because it "would open the doors of the courts to accusations of all sorts of one spouse against the other and bring into public notice complaints for assaults, slander and libel."

Civil Liability

Although court decisions affirmed that a husband could no longer legally beat his wife, a battered wife still had no legal recourse against her husband. The rulings of a 1962 landmark case forever changed the legal consequences of physical abuse of a spouse.

In *Self v. Self,* the Supreme Court of California agreed with earlier rulings, stating that a spouse's right to sue would "destroy the peace and harmony of the house." Despite that finding, the court observed that this outdated assumption was based "on the bald theory that after a husband has beaten his wife there is a state of peace and harmony left to be disturbed." Therefore, "one spouse may maintain an action against the other" for physical abuse.

Despite the ruling enabling victims to seek legal recourse, by 1965 there had been little change. Jurisdictions throughout the United States ignored the complaints of battered women—in Washington, D.C., 7,400 women filed official complaints and just 200 arrest warrants were issued.

In 1973 the first battered women's shelter opened in St. Paul, Minnesota, and by 1976 there were 400 pro-

TABLE 1.1

Gender violence throughout the life cycle

Phase	Type of violence present
Prebirth	Sex-selective abortion (China, India, Republic of Korea); battering during pregnancy (emotional and physical effects on the woman; effects on birth outcome); coerced pregnancy (for example, mass rape in war)
Infancy	Female infanticide; emotional and physical abuse; differential access to food and medical care for girl infants
Girlhood	Child marriage; genital mutilation; sexual abuse by family members and strangers; differential access to food and medical care; child prostitution
Adolescence	Dating and courtship violence (for example, acid throwing in Bangladesh, date rape in the United States); economically coerced sex (African secondary school girls having to take up with "sugar daddies" to afford school fees); sexual abuse in the workplace; rape; sexual harassment; forced prostitution; trafficking in women
Reproductive age	Abuse of women by intimate male partners; marital rape; dowry abuse and murders; partner homicide; psychological abuse; sexual abuse in the workplace; sexual harassment; rape; abuse of women with disabilities
Elderly	Abuse of widows; elder abuse. (In the United States, the only country where data are now available, elder abuse affects mostly women)

SOURCE: Lori L. Heise, et al, "Box 2. Gender violence throughout the life cycle," in *Violence Against Women: The Hidden Health Burden,* The International Bank for Reconstruction and Development, The World Bank, Washington, DC, 1994

grams for battered women operating in the United States. EMERGE, the first treatment program for male offenders, opened in Boston, Massachusetts, in 1977 and the following year many states enacted laws to protect victims of domestic violence.

A decade later, in 1988, the U.S. surgeon general declared wife abuse the leading health hazard to women in the United States. By 1990 the number of battered women's programs had mushroomed to 1,200. In 1994 the U.S. Domestic Violence Act was allocated $1.6 billion for services and granted civil rights protection to battered women.

Although spouse abuse is illegal in the United States and women may now sue their abusers for damages, access to legal recourse has not put an end to battering. Many women still feel helpless and trapped in abusive relationships, unable to tell others about their problems and unsure of where to seek and obtain help.

ABUSE IN OTHER CULTURES

Abuse threatens women's health and human rights throughout the world. Global estimates suggest as many as 30 percent of the world's women are at risk for violence (beatings, coerced sexual activity, or other physical abuse) at least once in their life. It may occur in the home, the workplace, or the community and it may take different forms throughout the stages of a woman's life. (See Table 1.1.) Women of all races, ethnic backgrounds, and ages are subjected to forced abortion, rape, genital mutilation, and other acts of violence, often at the hands of their partners or persons known to them.

Data about violence against women are scarce and most researchers agree that when the data are available, reported rates of sexual abuse and domestic violence are significantly underestimated because many incidents are unreported. Still, even the official statistics which are collected by organizations such as the Statistical Commission and Economic Commission for Europe and the UN Interregional Crime and Justice Research Institute (UNICRI), are believed to be underreported. These organizations paint frightening pictures of the magnitude of the problem. For example, the UNICRI surveys estimate that from 1 to 8 percent of women are sexually assaulted in many countries in the world. Another survey finds that reported instances of domestic abuse in the Ukraine rose by 16 percent in the five years ending January 1, 2000.

This section describes selected examples of violence against women practiced in various cultures. Although these practices are among the most extreme and dramatic instances of abuse, the very fact that they have persisted into the twenty-first century is a shocking acknowledgment of a social problem of global proportions.

Bride Burning

In India, Pakistan, and Bangladesh, disputes over a bride's dowry—the money, property, or belongings given to the man by the bride's family after marriage—has created a serious domestic violence crisis. The inability of a bride's family to meet dowry demands often results in brutality and sometimes death. Authorities estimate that every year about 5,000 women are killed over dowry disputes. Many are victims of bride burning, a preplanned homicide committed by the groom and his family, and often aided by the bride's mother-in-law.

The phenomenon of torching brides who are unable to meet exorbitant dowry demands is alarming. Women's organizations estimate that 1 woman is burned every 12 hours in New Delhi alone. In the urban centers of Maharashtra state and greater Bombay, 19 percent of deaths to women aged 15 to 44 are due to "accidental burns." That rate is 1 in 4 for younger women aged 15 to 24. During an eight-month period in 1998, a special New Delhi court assigned to handle cases of bride burning tried only six defendants, and all were acquitted.

Although India has had an antidowry law since 1961, it is not enforced. Men merely need to claim that their wives died as a result of a house fire or cooking accident or committed suicide to be freed from blame or suspicion.

Female Wage Earners Also at Risk

Economic considerations, including dowry, wages, and earnings, also influence whether women are at risk for abuse in India and Pakistan. Several surveys indicate that a woman who controls some or all of her earnings may experience fewer threats and acts of violence than a woman who relinquishes her wages to her husband. Other studies find that a Pakistani woman who seeks to work or earn wages is at greater risk for beatings from her husband, and in south India a woman with higher earnings than her husband is also more likely to be beaten. The relationship between employment and violence seems to be strongest when families are in economically stressful circumstances. Since men's social position and self-esteem are linked to being successful enough that their wives do not have to work, those with working wives often suffer from low self-esteem. Feelings of low self-esteem, coupled with financial insecurity, are believed to trigger aggression toward women and instances of physical abuse.

An Accepted Form of Discipline

In Iran and much of the Middle East, wife beating is an accepted form of discipline. The Koran, the basis of Islamic law, states:

> The men are placed in charge of the women, since God has endowed them with the necessary qualities and made them breadearners. The righteous women will accept this arrangement obediently, and will honor their husbands in their absence, in accordance with God's commands. As for the women who show rebellion, you shall first enlighten them, then desert them in bed, and you may beat them as a last resort. Once they obey you, you have no excuse to transgress against them. God is high and most powerful.

This passage of the Koran has been interpreted by some as allowing an Islamic husband to physically punish his wife whenever he determines she has misbehaved.

In a 1996 study by Egypt's National Population Council, 86 percent of the 14,779 married women who responded said they believe a man is justified in beating his wife for refusing sex, talking back, talking to other men, neglecting his children, wasting money, or burning food. Agreement with a man's right to beat his wife varied according to the respondents' age, education, employment, and place of residence. The study also found that one out of every three married women had been beaten at least once by her spouse. Thirty-two percent of pregnant women received a beating from their husbands; 44 percent of those women said they were beaten as often or more often during pregnancy than they were before becoming pregnant.

Since pre-marital virginity and post-marital sexual fidelity are also required of Islamic women, it is traditionally the role of male relatives to enforce chaste sexual conduct. Often, the way to do that is through murder, known as "honor killing." In Islamic countries, men who kill a female relative because they perceive she is no longer chaste are generally given a lighter sentence than men convicted of other types of murders.

Any Iraqi man who kills his own mother, sister, daughter, aunt, niece, or female cousin for adultery may receive immunity from prosecution under a 1990 law. In Pakistan a woman who is raped can be imprisoned for adultery if her rapist is acquitted.

The Hudood ordinances, enacted in 1979, provide even harsher punishments for violators of Islamic law. Under these ordinances, a female or non-Muslim witness is not allowed to testify in a court of law. Consequently, if a male rapes a woman in the presence of several females, he cannot be convicted by their testimony. Punishment under the Hudood ordinances include death by stoning for unlawful sexual relations.

Increased conservatism in the Islamic world has forced more and more women to wear head scarves, undergo female circumcision, and avoid men in school and the workplace. The fundamentalist Taliban regime governing Afghanistan until 2002 banned women from any work outside the home, kept them from seeking and receiving needed medical care, and prevented girls from attending school. Women and girls could not appear outside the home unless they were accompanied by a male family member and wore a "burqa," a garment that covered their bodies from head to toe.

During 2002 Afghan women and girls took their first tentative steps toward a new life by returning to school and work. Still, many women and girls remain trapped by poverty and rules imposed by strict husbands. In October 2002 CNN chief international correspondent Christiane Amanpour traveled to Afghanistan and broadcast a report on the CBS newsmagazine *60 Minutes* depicting impoverished families who sold their young daughters and others who persist in the belief that girls should not be educated.

Rape

In many parts of the world, women who are raped have nowhere to turn for help. In Colombia, for example, fewer than 0.5 percent of investigated rape cases in 1995 went to trial. Most cases—95 percent, according to Colombia's Institute for Legal Medicine—are never reported because the women know no action will be taken against their rapists. In poor families where parents and children sleep in the same bed, women have no place to go to remove their children from a partner's unwanted attention.

The use of rape as a weapon of war occurs in many parts of the world. The high rates of rape in war are attributed to the idea that women are viewed as property, and men gain ownership of women by taking sexual liberties with them. Rape in the context of war is also provoked by the tendency to demonize and dehumanize the enemy and the climate of anger, hate, and immediate fear of death. During the Bosnian civil war, for example, it is estimated that Serbs, aware of how important chastity is to Muslims, raped more than 20,000 Muslim women, forcing many to bear Serbian children. In Rwanda thousands of ethnic Tutsi women were raped by the majority Hutu military during a bloody civil war in the 1990s. According to one estimate, about 35 percent of the women became pregnant as a result of those rapes. Because abortion is illegal in Rwanda, many women sought illegal abortions, abandoned their babies, or committed infanticide. For those who kept their children, survival has been precarious. Most of these women watched as their husbands and families were murdered at the same time they were raped. Now, their Tutsi neighbors shun their offspring and blame the mothers for their existence.

The UN established war crimes tribunals for Rwanda and the former Yugoslavia, although neither has had much success. In 1997 the Rwanda Tribunal filed its first indictment for rape and sexual abuse. Plans are currently underway within the international community to establish a permanent International Criminal Court (ICC) to prosecute persons accused of crimes against humanity, including sexual violence, who are not brought to justice in their own countries. The ICC was to be formally established when 60 countries had ratified the Rome Statute of the International Criminal Court. On April 11, 2002, 10 nations simultaneously ratified the statute, bringing the total to 66 and triggering its adoption. The Rome Statute entered into force on July 1, 2002.

Historically, the United States had expressed concern about putting itself under Rome Statute jurisdiction for war crimes, an issue distinct from crimes against humanity. Increasingly, however, rape is being considered as both a war crime and a crime against humanity. Although under the administration of President Bill Clinton the United States had entered the ICC, on May 6, 2002, the United States formally renounced its signature on the statute. The administration of President George W. Bush cited serious reservations about the ICC and its functions and expressed concerns that it would have unchecked prosecutorial power and might undermine the UN Security Council's efforts to preserve international peace. Despite the U.S. decision to withdraw, there is widespread optimism about the establishment of the ICC and its potential global contribution to an effective justice system free of political influence. International affairs experts and historians mark the Rome Statute adoption as a historic achievement and the ICC as the most significant advance in international law since the founding of the UN.

CONSEQUENCES OF RAPE. The immediate consequences of rape include emotional symptoms, such as shock, anger, shame, fear, and helplessness, as well as psychological problems, such as confusion, disturbing or recurring memories, and self-blame. Physical injuries, sexually transmitted diseases, fatigue, and changes in appetite and sleep patterns may also occur in response to the trauma. Long-term consequences can be serious and debilitating. Rape victims may suffer from anger, distrust, and psychiatric disorders including:

- Post-traumatic stress disorder—Recurring memories and dreams, memory impairment, anxiety, sleep disorders, and social and emotional withdrawal

- Depression—Feelings of hopelessness, helplessness, loss of focus and purpose in life, fatigue, despair, and thoughts of suicide

- Alcohol and drug abuse—Substance abuse may occur as the victim attempts to self-medicate to relieve unpleasant memories, feelings, physical pain, or other emotional distress

Female Genital Mutilation

Female genital mutilation is practiced in 28 African countries, in some parts of Asia and the Middle East, and among immigrant communities in Europe, Australia, Canada, and the United States. Each year, an estimated 2 million girls undergo genital mutilation of some type, with the total number of mutilated women estimated to be 150 million. Surveys of five African nations find that 93 percent of women in Mali and 89 percent of Sudanese women have been genitally mutilated. Slightly less than half the women of the Central African Republic and the Ivory Coast and 12 percent of Togo's women have also been circumcised.

Since different societies practice different rituals of "circumcision," young girls can undergo a variety of procedures. Some procedures remove the foreskin of the clitoris; others involve "infibulation," in which the clitoris and labia are surgically removed and the two sides of the vulva are sewn together, usually with catgut. These procedures are performed without an anesthetic and often with primitive, unsterilized tools. Immediate health risks include hemorrhage, tetanus, blood poisoning, shock, and sometimes death. Those who survive are left with terrible scarring, and their future sexual relationships are joyless and usually very painful. The too-small openings for the flow of urine and menstrual blood can cause urinary tract infections and sometimes sterility, the ultimate disaster for women whose value is based on their fertility (ability to reproduce).

Infibulated women who do give birth must be surgically reopened, only to be resewn again after childbirth. In Somalia, a study of 33 infibulated women found that their final stage of labor was 5 times longer than normal, 5 of the babies died, and 21 babies suffered oxygen deprivation from the prolonged, obstructed labor (Lori L. Heise et al., *Violence against Women: The Hidden Health Burden,* World Bank, Washington, DC, 1994).

Female circumcision stems from men's desire to control women's sexuality. Some Muslims believe the Koran

demands it; others see women's genitals as unclean and believe circumcision is a ritual purification. Men in these cultures will not marry uncircumcised women, believing them to be unclean, promiscuous, and sexually untrustworthy. Many women do not object to the procedure since they view it as a tradition and a natural part of their role in life. Some women, however, are trying to increase awareness about the procedure. They insist that female genital mutilation is not an "important African tradition" that must be maintained in the face of Western influence. Rather, they see it as violence directed against women.

In June 1996 efforts to educate the public about this practice paid off when the U.S. Immigration and Naturalization Service (INS) recognized for the first time that the fear of genital mutilation was legitimate grounds for asylum. Fauziya Kasinga, a 19-year-old Tobago woman who feared she would be circumcised if she returned home, was detained in prison for one year while the INS made its decision. The ruling quoted an INS report that said that "women have little legal recourse and may face threats to their freedom, threats or acts of physical violence or social ostracization for refusing to undergo this harmful traditional practice or attempting to protect their female children."

The U.S. Congress outlawed female genital cutting in the United States under the Federal Prohibition of Female Genital Mutilation Act of 1996. Anyone found guilty of performing this surgery faces up to five years in jail. In addition, U.S. representatives to the World Bank and other international financial institutions are required to oppose loans to the 28 African countries where the practice exists if those countries fail to conduct educational programs to prevent it.

In Egypt a 1995 government-supported study indicated that over 97 percent of the 14,770 never-married women participants had undergone circumcision. Two years later, an Egyptian court overturned Egypt's ban on female genital mutilation. The ban was later restored through a decision from the Egyptian Supreme Court. Although it remains in effect, women's rights groups continue to work to change the Muslim tradition in villages where midwives and barbers still perform circumcisions.

The Missing Women

In China, South Korea, India, Nepal, and other Asian countries where sons are favored over daughters for their economic value and their ability to carry on the family name, girls often receive less medical care, education, and food than their brothers. Human rights groups estimate that at least 10,000 cases of female infanticides occur yearly in India alone, primarily in poor rural areas. In India and China, many pregnant women undergo abortions if they learn their babies will be female. The preference for a male child is largely economic—a female child is more likely to present a financial burden to her family, while a male child is a potential breadwinner and will not require expenditures such as a dowry. As many as 97.5 percent of all abortions at one Chinese hospital were of female fetuses, one doctor told a Chinese newspaper.

Based on comparisons of male-to-female sex ratios, Princeton University demographer Ansley Coale estimates that at least 90 million women are missing, mainly from Asia and North Africa. These are females who have been aborted, given inferior care in childhood, underfed, and subjected to various forms of gender violence resulting in death. In India, the male-to-female ratio has increased to 100 males to every 92.7 females, a large demographic difference. The World Health Organization estimates China's male-to-female ratio to be 117 to 100, another huge difference. In contrast, the U.S. ratio is 96 males to every 100 females.

CHAPTER 2

SPOUSE AND PARTNER ABUSE—WHO, WHAT, AND WHEN?

Although domestic violence has occurred for centuries, the rise of the women's movement during the late 1960s and 1970s focused attention on this previously suppressed and ignored health and social problem. The first important research about domestic violence was conducted toward the end of the 1970s. The 1974 British study "Scream Quietly or the Neighbors Will Hear" was among the first examinations of the plight of battered women. In 1975 Susan Brownmiller's *Against Our Will* (Simon and Schuster, New York, 1975), a book about men, women, and the politics and sociology of rape, was published in the United States.

During 1978 congressional hearings, when the U.S. Commission on Civil Rights held a conference titled "Battered Women—Issues of Public Policy," the topic of domestic violence finally arrived at the forefront of public consciousness.

Today, the issue of spousal abuse is the subject of countless books, films, and stage plays. Of these, one of the most memorable is *The Burning Bed,* based on the true story of Francine Hughes, an East Lansing, Michigan, woman who burned her abusive husband to death in 1977 as he slept, after having suffered 17 years of abuse. Hughes was acquitted of murder based on a defense of temporary insanity caused by years of physical and psychological abuse. Her case gave rise to the "battered woman's defense," which is now widely used to defend abused women who have killed their partners. A made-for-television movie based on Hughes's case aired in 1984 to an audience of 75 million, giving momentum to the battered women's movement and significantly influencing legislative reform.

The subject resurfaced in 1995 in the media with the highly publicized murder trial of O. J. Simpson, who was accused of the brutal slaying of his ex-wife, Nicole Brown, and her friend, Ronald Goldman. Simpson, a former football star and popular sports commentator, was acquitted of murder, but not before millions of Americans heard a recording of Nicole begging police for help and saw a photo of her face, bruised and bloody from a beating, which was among the evidence presented at Simpson's trial.

Celebrities from the sports and entertainment industries who have been convicted of domestic violence attract the media spotlight. According to the Family Violence Prevention Fund, a national, nonprofit organization, when society continues to celebrate and reward actors and athletes who are violent to their partners, it not only condones their bad behavior, but also suggests that their abusive behavior is glamorous and desirable. The organization regularly updates a celebrity "Wall of Shame" on its Web site. As of October 2000 the Family Violence Prevention Fund's Wall of Shame listed more than 50 celebrities, including:

- Steven Adler. The Guns n' Roses drummer has several domestic violence convictions and charges from women he has dated. He was sentenced to jail, a year of counseling, and placed on probation.

- Rick Allen. An admitted batterer, the Def Leppard drummer pleaded guilty to spousal assault. He was sentenced to probation and counseling and was required to attend Alcoholics Anonymous meetings.

- Jim Brown. This member of the Professional Football Hall of Fame was ordered to receive counseling and pay a fine after smashing his wife's car.

- Dale Ellis. In February 2002 the former SuperSonics basketball player pleaded guilty to domestic violence charges. He had been convicted 13 years earlier of assaulting his wife and resisting arrest.

- Charlie Sheen. The actor was given a one-year suspended sentence and a two-year probation for physically abusing a former girlfriend.

TABLE 2.1

Definitions of violence against women

Behavior by the man, adopted to control his victim, which results in physical, sexual and/or psychological damage, forced isolation, or economic deprivation or behavior which leaves a woman living in fear. (Australia, 1991)

Any act involving use of force or coercion with an intent of perpetuating/promoting hierarchical gender relations. (Asia Pacific Forum on Women, Law and Development, 1990)

Any act of gender-based violence that results in, or is likely to result in, physical, sexual or psychological harm or suffering to women, including threats of such acts, coercion or arbitrary deprivations of liberty, whether occurring in public or private life. Violence against women shall be understood to encompass but not be limited to:

Physical, sexual and psychological violence occurring in the family and in the community, including battering, sexual abuse of female children, dowry-related violence, marital rape, female genital mutilation and other traditional practices harmful to women, non-spousal violence, violence related to exploitation, sexual harassment and intimidation at work, in educational institutions and elsewhere, trafficking in women, forced prostitution, and violence perpetrated or condoned by the State. (UN Declaration against Violence against Women)

Any act, omission or conduct by means of which physical sexual or mental suffering is inflicted, directly or indirectly, through deceit, seduction, threat, coercion or any other means, on any woman with the purpose or effect of intimidating, punishing or humiliating her or of maintaining her in sex-stereotyped roles or of denying her human dignity, sexual self-determination, physical, mental and moral integrity or of undermining the security of her person, her self-respect or her personality, or of diminishing her physical or mental capacities. (Draft Pan American Treaty against Violence against Women)

Any act or omission which prejudices the life, the physical or psychological integrity or the liberty of a person or which seriously harms the development of his or her personality. (Council of Europe, 1986)

SOURCE: Lori L. Heise, et al, "Appendix Box B. 1. Definitions of violence against women," in *Violence Against Women: The Hidden Health Burden,* The International Bank for Reconstruction and Development, The World Bank, Washington, DC, 1994

In July 2002 the killings of four military wives in a six-week period, allegedly by their husbands based at Fort Bragg, North Carolina, once again focused public and media attention on the issue of spousal violence. Three of the four husbands were special operations soldiers who had been deployed to Afghanistan, and some news media reports speculated that the murders may have been caused by stress. In September 2002 the U.S. Army and Congress launched a full-scale investigation of the crimes to determine their causes and prevent similar tragedies.

DEFINITIONS OF ABUSE

Early definitions of domestic abuse focused exclusively on physical assault and bodily injury. Today, a broader interpretation is accepted and abuse is understood to include sexual and psychological actions and harm, such as marital rape and forced isolation.

A definition of abuse by the Colorado Committee of the Advisory Committee to the U.S. Commission on Civil Rights in *The Silent Victims: Denver's Battered Women* (Washington, DC, 1977) describes a "battered wife" as "a woman who has received deliberate, severe and repeated physical injury from her husband, the minimal injury being severe bruising." The authors observe that since a battered woman may not be legally married to her abuser,

"battered woman is the more accurate term to employ than battered wife."

In their groundbreaking work based on the 1975 and 1985 National Family Violence Surveys (NFVS), Murray Straus and Richard Gelles define "spousal violence" in specific actions, known as the Conflict Tactics Scale (CTS). That scale is now the measure most widely used to estimate the extent of spousal abuse. According to the CTS, a spouse can be considered abusive if he or she:

• Throws something at a partner

• Pushes, grabs, or shoves

• Slaps

• Kicks, bites, or hits the partner with a fist

• Hits or tries to hit the partner with an object

• Beats up the partner

• Threatens the partner with a knife or a gun

• Uses a knife or fires a gun at the partner

A decade later, the definition of abuse was expanded to encompass issues of intent, control, and power. Table 2.1 shows definitions of violence against women developed by different organizations around the world. The National Coalition Against Domestic Violence (NCADV) defines battering as a pattern of behavior through which a person establishes power and control over another person by means of fear and intimidation. The mistakenly held belief that abusers are entitled to control their partners is a primary cause of aggression and abuse, according to the NCADV.

The NCADV also describes battering as emotional, economic, and sexual abuse, as well as using children, threats, male privilege, intimidation, isolation, and various other strategies to maintain fear, intimidation, and power. It is important to view all these behaviors as battering in order to understand how battering can escalate from verbal threats, a single slap, or an insult to a life-threatening situation.

An international examination of violence by Lori Heise et al. (*Violence against Women: The Hidden Health Burden,* World Bank, Washington, DC, 1994) defines abuse in terms broad enough to include the wide variety of abuses that occur throughout the world. Heise and colleagues observe that violence against women is tolerated partly because the victims are female. They distinguish between cultural customs and abuse intended to harm. Genital mutilation, for instance, is a ritual or tradition intended by its practitioners to guarantee marriage for the female victim, rather than abuse that is intended to harm. Still, whether it is considered custom or ritualized abuse, this practice can cause long-term physical and psychological harm, suffering, and even death.

Heise and colleagues caution against using the overly broad definitions of abuse proposed by some organizations, which encompass gender inequalities such as unequal pay or lack of access to contraception or other health care services. They term such inequalities "discrimination," rather than "abuse." Abuse against women, according to the study, is defined as verbal or physical force, coercion, or deprivation directed against a woman or girl that causes physical or psychological harm, humiliation, loss of liberty, or other female subordination.

HOW MUCH ABUSE OCCURS?

Because domestic violence is often unreported, it is impossible to be certain exactly how many domestic assaults occur each year. Varying definitions of violence and abuse, the types of questions posed by researchers, and the context in which they are asked compound the difficulty. For example, when victims are questioned in the presence of their abusers, or even other family members, they are often more reluctant to report instances of violence. Studies on the subject are sometimes contradictory, but most show that domestic violence remains a growing concern, and many researchers fear that available data represent only the tip of the iceberg of a problem of glacial proportions.

To understand why there are so many varying estimates of domestic violence, it is necessary to consider the surveys, studies, and reports themselves. The source and purpose of the research, the definition of abuse used, the population surveyed, and the survey setting, as well as the political agendas of the surveyors and researchers, may elicit different data and varying interpretations of these data.

According to the World Health Organization (WHO), in countries where large-scale studies are conducted, between 10 and 50 percent of women report physical abuse from an intimate partner (intimates usually include spouses, former spouses, boyfriends, and girlfriends). Population-based estimates suggest that from 12 to 25 percent of women experience attempted or completed forced sex with an intimate partner or former partner during their lives. The WHO also observes that prostitution and trafficking for sex, activities strongly linked to violence against women and girls, appeared to be on the rise during the late 1990s and early 2000.

The NFVS are among the most analyzed and cited data in the literature about intimate partner violence. Using data from the 1975 and 1985 NFVS, Straus and Gelles estimated that about 1.8 million women are beaten by their partners annually.

Other national data are derived from national sample surveys, such as the National Crime Victimization Surveys (NCVS), which measure violent assaults by intimate partners, including rape and sexual assault, and the Uniform Crime Reports, which supplement NCVS data with information about homicides. One advantage of these surveys is that they enable researchers to observe trends in interpersonal violence. For example, NCVS data reveal a decline in intimate partner violent victimizations during the 1990s (except for a slight increase from 1997 to 1998).

A joint effort of the U.S. Departments of Justice and Health and Human Services and the Centers for Disease Control and Prevention, the National Violence Against Women Survey (NVAWS) collected data about intimate and nonintimate partner violence during the 1990s. The only government-sponsored surveys focusing specifically on violence against women, the NVAWS and NCVS are considered the most reliable sources of data about intimate partner violence even though their differing approaches make data comparisons difficult. For example, the NCVS is a survey about crime, and since some victims do not consider instances of intimate partner violence crimes, they may be less likely to disclose them in the NCVS.

In *Extent, Nature and Consequences of Intimate Violence: Findings from the National Violence Against Women Survey* (National Institute of Justice and Centers for Disease Control and Prevention, Washington, DC, July 2000), researchers Patricia Tjaden and Nancy Thoennes find that intimate violence is pervasive in American society, with women suffering about three times as much of this violence as men.

The researchers find that an estimated 22.1 percent of women are physically assaulted by a loved one during the course of their lifetime. In addition, intimates physically assault 7.4 percent of men during their lifetimes. About 1.5 percent of the surveyed women and 0.9 percent of the men reported they had been raped and/or physically assaulted by a partner in the 12 months preceding the survey. This translates to approximately 4.8 million women and 2.9 million men assaulted every year.

The *Special Report on Intimate Partner Violence* (Washington, DC, May 2000) by the Bureau of Justice Statistics (BJS) finds that although the number of intimate violence victims decreased between 1993 and 1998, women still experienced about 900,000 violent incidents at the hands of intimates in 1998, down from 1.1 million 5 years earlier.

The NCADV contended in 2002 that more than 50 percent of all women will experience some form of violence from their spouses. The NCADV estimates that more than one-third, or approximately 18 million women, are battered repeatedly every year.

The National Violence Against Women Survey (NVAWS)

The NVAWS collected information from interviews with 8,000 men and 8,000 women to assess their experiences as victims of various types of violence, including domestic violence. The NVAWS asked survey respondents about physical assaults and rape, but excluded other sexual assaults, murders, and robberies.

TABLE 2.2

Persons victimized by an intimate partner in lifetime and in previous 12 months, by type of victimization and gender

	In lifetime			
	Percent		Number[a]	
Type of victimization	Women (n = 8,000)	Men (n = 8,000)	Women (100,697,000)	Men (92,748,000)
Rape[b***]	7.7	0.3	7,753,669	278,244
Physical assault[b***]	22.1	7.4	22,254,037	6,863,352
Rape and/or physical assault[b***]	24.8	7.6	24,972,856	7,048,848
Stalking[b***]	4.8	0.6	4,833,456	556,488
Total victimized[b***]	25.5	7.9	25,677,735	7,327,092
	In previous 12 months			
	Percent		Number[a]	
Type of violence	Women (n = 8,000)	Men (n = 8,000)	Women (100,697,000)	Men (92,748,000)
Rape	0.2	—[c]	201,394	—[c]
Physical assault[b*]	1.3	0.9	1,309,061	834,732
Rape and/or physical assault[b*]	1.5	0.9[d]	1,510,455	834,732
Stalking[b**]	0.5	0.2	503,485	185,496
Total victimized[b***]	1.8	1.1	1,812,546	1,020,228

[a]Based on estimates of women and men 18 years of age and older: Wetrogen, S.I., *Projections of the Population of States by Age, Sex, and Race: 1988 to 2010*, Current Population Reports, Washington, D.C.: U.S. Bureau of the Census, 1988: 25–1017.
[b]Differences between women and men are statistically significant: χ^2, *$p \leq .05$, **$p \leq .01$, ***$p \leq .001$.
[c]Estimates not calculated on fewer than five victims.
[d]Because only three men reported being raped by an intimate partner in the previous 12 months, the percentage of men physically assaulted and physically assaulted and/or raped is the same.

SOURCE: Patricia Tjaden and Nancy Thoennes, "Persons victimized by an intimate partner in lifetime and in previous 12 months, by type of victimization and gender," in *Extent, Nature, and Consequences of Intimate Partner Violence: Findings from the National Violence Against Women Survey*, National Institute of Justice and Centers for Disease Control and Prevention, Washington, DC, July 2000

In *Extent, Nature, and Consequences of Intimate Partner Violence,* Tjaden and Thoennes find that 22.1 percent (22 million) of all women and 7.4 percent (7 million) of all men were physically assaulted by an intimate partner in their lifetimes. (See Table 2.2.) Women were also more likely to become victims of rape, stalking, and physical assault by intimates than their male counterparts at some time during their lifetimes. Furthermore, women physically assaulted by their partners averaged nearly 7 assaults by the same person, as opposed to men, who averaged 4.4 assaults.

During the twelve months that preceded the interview, women also reported higher rates of rape, stalking, and physical assault. According to this research, more than 1.3 million (1.3 percent) women and 834,732 men (0.9 percent) had been physically assaulted by an intimate partner in the past year.

The rates of violence between intimate partners vary by race. Asian/Pacific Islanders report lower rates of violence than men and women from other minority groups, and African American and American Indian/Alaska Natives report higher rates. (See Table 2.3.)

Not surprisingly, Tjaden and Thoennes conclude that the majority of partner abuse and violence is not reported to the police. Women reported about one-fifth of rapes, one-quarter of physical assaults, and one-half of stalkings to police, while men who had been victimized reported abuse to police even less frequently. Table 2.4 shows the reasons victims did not report their abuse to the police. Many victims said they felt the police would not or could not do anything on their behalf. These expressions of helplessness and hopelessness—feeling that others in a position to assist would be unwilling or unable—is a common characteristic shared by many victims of intimate partner violence.

MORE ABUSE IS REPORTED BY SAME-SEX COUPLES. The NVAWS also finds that same-sex couples who lived together reported far more intimate violence than heterosexual cohabitants. Among women, 39.2 percent of the same-sex cohabitants and 21.7 percent of the opposite-sex cohabitants reported being raped, physically assaulted, or stalked by a partner during their lifetimes. Among men, the comparative figures were 23.1 percent and 7.4 percent, respectively.

Though survey findings indicate that members of same-sex couples experience more intimate partner violence than do heterosexual couples, the reported violence does not necessarily occur within the same-sex relationship. When comparing intimate partner victimization rates among same-sex and opposite-sex cohabitants by the gender of the perpetrator, Tjaden and Thoennes find that 30.4 percent of the same-sex women cohabitants reported being victimized by a male partner sometime in their

TABLE 2.3

Persons victimized by an intimate partner in lifetime, by victim gender, type of victimization, and victim race

Victim gender/ Type of victimization	Persons victimized in lifetime (%)				
	White	African- American	Asian Pacific Islander	American Indian/ Alaska Native	Mixed Race
Women	(n = 6,452)	(n = 780)	(n = 133)	(n = 88)	(n = 397)
Rape[1]	7.7	7.4	3.8[2]	15.9	8.1
Physical assault[3,4]	21.3	26.3	12.8	30.7	27.0
Stalking	4.7	4.2	—[5]	10.2[2]	6.3
Total victimized[3]	24.8	29.1	15.0	37.5	30.2
Men	(n = 6,424)	(n = 659)	(n = 165)	(n = 105)	(n = 406)
Rape	0.2	0.9[2]	—[5]	—[5]	—[5]
Physical assault	7.2	10.8	—[5]	11.4	8.6
Stalking	0.6	1.1[2]	—[5]	—[5]	1.2[2]
Total victimized	7.5	12.0	3.0[2]	12.4	9.1

[1]Estimates for American Indian/Alaska Native women are significantly higher than those for white and African-American women: Tukey's B, $p \leq .05$.
[2]Relative standard error exceeds 30 percent; estimates not included in statistical testing.
[3]Estimates for Asian/Pacific Islander women are significantly lower than those for African-American, American Indian/Alaska Native, and mixed-race women: Tukey's B, $p \leq .05$.
[4]Estimates for African-American women are significantly higher than those for white women: Tukey's B, $p \leq .05$.
[5]Estimates not calculated on fewer than five victims.

SOURCE: Patricia Tjaden and Nancy Thoennes, "Persons Victimized by an Intimate Partner in Lifetime by Victim Gender, Type of Victimization, and Victim Race," in *Extent, Nature, and Consequences of Intimate Partner Violence: Findings from the National Violence Against Women Survey,* National Institute of Justice and Centers for Disease Control and Prevention, Washington, DC, July 2000

TABLE 2.4

Distribution of rape, physical assault, and stalking victims who did not report their victimization to the police, by reasons for not reporting and gender[1]

Reason for not reporting[2]	Rape victims (%)	Physical assault victims (%)		Stalking victims (%)	
	Women (n = 311)	Women (n = 2,062)	Men (n = 468)	Women (n = 165)	Men (n = 30)
Police couldn't do anything	13.2	99.7	100.0	100.0	100.0
Police wouldn't believe me	7.1	61.3[3,***]	45.1	98.2	93.3
Fear of perpetrator	21.2	11.7[3]	1.9[4]	38.2[3,**]	16.7[4]
Minor, one-time incident	20.3	37.9[3,***]	58.5	33.9	36.7[4]
Ashamed, wanted to keep incident private	16.1	10.4[3,**]	7.1	61.8	76.7
Wanted to handle it myself	7.7	7.3	5.8	7.9	—[5]
Victim or attacker moved away	—[5]	2.4	—[5]	12.1	—[5]
Attacker was a police officer	—[5]	4.7	3.8	7.9	—[5]
Too young, a child	3.5	2.2	1.5[4]	—[5]	—[5]
Reported to the military or someone else	—[5]	0.8[4]	—[5]	—[5]	—[5]
Didn't want police, court involvement	5.8	32.0[3,**]	24.6	35.2	40.0
Wanted to protect attacker, relationship, or children	8.7	34.8[3,**]	29.5	45.5	43.3

[1]Estimates are based on the most recent intimate partner victimization since age 18. Estimates not calculated for male rape victims because there were fewer than five victims when stratified by variables.
[2]Estimates exceed 100 percent because some victims gave multiple responses.
[3]Differences between women and men are statistically significant: χ^2, ***$p \leq .001$, **$p \leq .05$.
[4]Relative standard error exceeds 30 percent; statistical tests not performed.
[5]Estimates not calculated for fewer than five victims.

SOURCE: Patricia Tjaden and Nancy Thoennes, "Distribution of Rape, Physical Assault, and Stalking Victims Who Did Not Report Their Victimization to the Police, by Reasons for Not Reporting and Gender," in *Extent, Nature, and Consequences of Intimate Partner Violence: Findings from the National Violence Against Women Survey*, National Institute of Justice and Centers for Disease Control and Prevention, Washington, DC, July 2000

lifetimes, whereas 11.4 percent reported being victimized by a female partner. The researchers conclude that same-sex cohabiting women were three times more likely to report being victimized by a male partner than by a female partner. In comparison, women who lived with men were nearly twice as likely to report being victimized by a male than same-sex cohabiting women were to report being victimized by a female partner. (See Figure 2.1.)

FIGURE 2.1

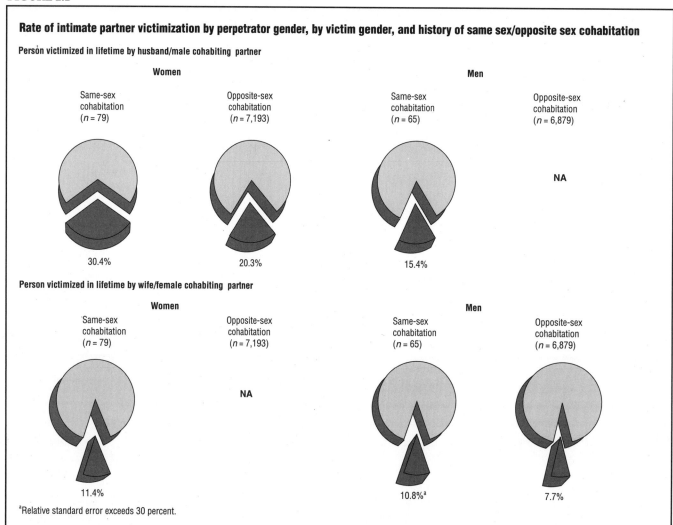

Rate of intimate partner victimization by perpetrator gender, by victim gender, and history of same sex/opposite sex cohabitation

Person victimized in lifetime by husband/male cohabiting partner

Women   Men

Same-sex cohabitation (n = 79)   Opposite-sex cohabitation (n = 7,193)   Same-sex cohabitation (n = 65)   Opposite-sex cohabitation (n = 6,879)

30.4%   20.3%   15.4%   NA

Person victimized in lifetime by wife/female cohabiting partner

Women   Men

Same-sex cohabitation (n = 79)   Opposite-sex cohabitation (n = 7,193)   Same-sex cohabitation (n = 65)   Opposite-sex cohabitation (n = 6,879)

11.4%   NA   10.8%[a]   7.7%

[a]Relative standard error exceeds 30 percent.

SOURCE: Patricia Tjaden and Nancy Thoennes, "Rate of intimate partner victimization, by perpetrator gender, by victim gender, and history of same sex/opposite sex cohabitation," in *Extent, Nature, and Consequences of Intimate Partner Violence: Findings from the National Violence Against Women Survey*, National Institute of Justice and Centers for Disease Control and Prevention, Washington, DC, July 2000

Male same-sex partners reported more partner violence than men who lived with women. About 23 percent of men who lived with men said they had been raped, sexually assaulted, or stalked by a male cohabitant, as opposed to just 7.4 percent of men who reported comparable experience with female cohabitants. This finding confirms the widely held observation that violence and abuse in intimate partner relationships is primarily inflicted by men, whether a partner is male or female.

In comparison to the research on intimate partner violence between men and women, the literature about same-sex violence is very small. This is in part because many respondents may consider disclosing same-sex relationships risky and revealing partner violence even more sensitive. Furthermore, not all persons who engage in same-sex relationships identify themselves as homosexual, leading to more questions about the quality of data gathered. The research that examines same-sex partner violence reveals that it is quite similar to heterosexual partner violence—abuse arises in the attempts of one partner to exert control over the other and it escalates throughout the course of the relationship.

The National Crime Victimization Surveys (NCVS)

The NCVS are ongoing federal surveys that interview 80,000 persons from a representative sample of households biannually to estimate the amount of crime committed against persons over age 12 in the United States. While the surveys cover all types of crime, they were extensively redesigned in 1992 to produce more accurate reports of rape, sexual assault, and other violent crimes committed by intimates or family members.

The most recent report of NCVS trends from 2000 to 2001 finds that although the rate of violent crime fell by 10 percent—from 28 to 25 violent victimizations per 1,000 persons—the reduction was largely the result of a drop in the rate of simple assaults (attacks without weapons resulting in no injury, minor injury, or undetermined injury requiring less than 2 days of hospitalization). The 10 percent decline was comparable to declines observed in the mid-1990s, but lower than the 15 percent drop from 1999 to 2000. Although the 2002 NCVS's criminal victimization estimates are the lowest since 1973, when the NCVS began, the numbers are still staggering: 5.7 million violent crimes (rape, sexual assault, robbery, aggravated assault, and simple assault). (See Figure 2.2.) The 2002 survey also finds that for the first time in nearly 20 years, males and females are victims of simple assault at similar rates.

For both genders, the rate of violent victimizations by intimate partners was 10.4 percent in 2000. Women were victimized by intimate partners at a greater rate than were men—more than 20 percent of female victims named an intimate partner as the offender, compared to less than 3 percent of men. In sexual assault cases, 18.3 percent of women and no male victims reported that the rapist was an intimate, friend, or relative. (See Table 2.5.)

In 2001 women continued to identify the offender as an intimate, friend, other relative, or acquaintance in about two-thirds of violent crimes, while more than half of male victims identified the offender as a stranger. Male victims knew the offender in about 4 out of 10 violent crimes during 2001. Almost half (46 percent) of female rapes and sexual assaults and 36 percent of aggravated assaults were not committed by intimates but by persons the victims had considered friends or acquaintances. (See Table 2.6.)

Although men continued to experience higher rates of violent victimizations than women, the rates for both genders, as well as persons in most racial, ethnic, and socio-economic groups, declined from 1993 to 2001. (See Figure 2.3, Figure 2.4, and Figure 2.5.)

The most significant annual declines in violent crime rates were observed among males, blacks, and persons living in households with annual incomes of less than $7,500. Between 1993 and 2001 people in these three groups experienced almost 5 fewer violent crimes per 1,000 people each year. (See Table 2.7.)

Almost half of all violent victimizations were reported to the police in 2001—39 percent of rape and sexual assaults, 59 percent of aggravated assaults, and 45 percent of simple assaults. Women reported the offenses more often than men did (53 percent and 46 percent, respectively).

The 1985 National Family Violence Survey (NFVS)

The NFVS, considered by many to be the most important research on family violence, was originally conducted in 1975 for the Family Research Laboratory at the University of New Hampshire, Durham. Ten years later, in a follow-up to the landmark study, Straus and Gelles find that the rate of assaults by husbands on wives had dropped only slightly during the decade, from 121

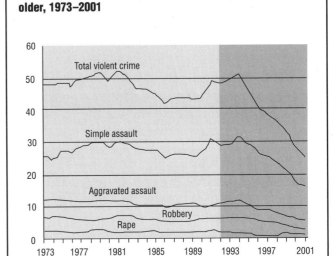

FIGURE 2.2

Violent crime victimization rate per 1000 persons age 12 or older, 1973–2001

SOURCE: Callie Rennison, "Violent crime victimization rate per 1,000 persons age 12 and older, 1973–2001," in *Criminal Victimization 2001 Changes 2000–01 with Trends 1993–2001*, U.S. Department of Justice, Bureau of Justice Statistics National Crime Victimization Survey, Washington, DC, September 18, 2002

instances per 1,000 couples in 1975 to 113 instances per 1,000 couples in 1985. The rate of severe violence, such as hitting, kicking, or using a weapon, however, had declined sharply, from 38 to 30 per 1,000 couples—a 21 percent drop.

The study's most controversial finding appears to indicate that women were initiating domestic violence at a rate equal to men. The 1985 study reports that in half of the cases, the abuse was mutual. After reassessing their data in 1990 and again in 1993, Straus and Gelles conclude that although there were similar levels of abuse between men and women, men were six times more likely to inflict serious injury.

In a paper presented to the World Congress of Sociology titled *Changes in Spouse Assault Rates from 1975 to 1992: A Comparison of Three National Surveys in the United States* (1994), Murray Straus and Glenda Kaufman Kantor compare the rates of abuse from the 1975 and 1985 NFVS and a 1992 survey conducted by Kantor. When the researchers reclassify "minor assault" to include pushing, grabbing, shoving, and slapping, and "severe assault" to include behavior likely to cause serious injury, such as kicking, punching, beating, and threatening with a weapon, they find some startling results.

The rates of reclassified minor assaults, which were considered less likely to cause injuries requiring medical treatment, decreased for husbands between the 1975 and 1985 surveys, yet remained constant for wives. The researchers find the same trend held true for severe

TABLE 2.5

Percent distribution of victimizations, by characteristics of victims, type of crime, and victim/offender relationship, 2000

Characteristic		Total victimizations	Percent of all victimizations					
			Nonstrangers				Stranger	Don't know Relationship
			Total	Intimate	Other relative	Friend or Acquaintance		
Both genders	Crimes of violence	100 %	53.4 %	10.4 %	5.4 %	37.7 %	44.8 %	1.8 %
	Rape/Sexual assault/[a]	100	62.1	17.3	1.8 *	43.0	34.2	3.7 *
	Robbery	100	27.8	5.2	2.8 *	19.8	69.3	2.9 *
	Assault	100	56.5	10.7	5.9	39.8	41.9	1.6
	Aggravated	100	42.6	5.1	5.2	32.2	55.8	1.7 *
	Simple	100	60.9	12.5	6.1	42.3	37.5	1.6
Male	Crimes of violence	100	43.9	2.7	3.0	38.2	53.9	2.3
	Rape/Sexual assault/[a]	100 *	62.7 *	0.0 *	0.0 *	62.7 *	37.3 *	0.0 *
	Robbery	100	22.9	0.0 *	0.5 *	22.5	73.9	3.1 *
	Assault	100	47.1	3.2	3.4	40.5	50.7	2.1
	Aggravated	100	35.9	2.0 *	4.0	29.9	61.7	2.3 *
	Simple	100	51.8	3.7	3.1	45.0	46.2	2.0
Female	Crimes of violence	100	66.1	20.5	8.6	37.0	32.6	1.3
	Rape/Sexual assault/[a]	100	62.1	18.3	1.9 *	41.9	34.0	3.9 *
	Robbery	100	38.0	16.0	7.7 *	14.3	59.7	2.3 *
	Assault	100	69.5	21.3	9.4	38.9	29.6	0.9 *
	Aggravated	100	58.7	12.7	8.1	37.8	41.3	0.0 *
	Simple	100	71.7	23.0	9.6	39.1	27.2	1.1 *
All Races	Crimes of violence	100	53.4	10.4	5.4	37.7	44.8	1.8
	Rape/Sexual assault/[a]	100	62.1	17.3	1.8 *	43.0	34.2	3.7 *
	Robbery	100	27.8	5.2	2.8 *	19.8	69.3	2.9 *
	Assault	100	56.5	10.7	5.9	39.8	41.9	1.6
	Aggravated	100	42.6	5.1	5.2	32.2	55.8	1.7 *
	Simple	100	60.9	12.5	6.1	42.3	37.5	1.6
White	Crimes of violence	100	53.5	10.5	5.2	37.8	44.5	2.0
	Rape/Sexual assault/[a]	100	68.0	18.4	2.2 *	47.4	27.6	4.4 *
	Robbery	100	29.9	6.5	2.3 *	21.1	66.7	3.4 *
	Assault	100	55.5	10.5	5.7	39.3	42.8	1.7
	Aggravated	100	41.2	5.3	5.1	30.8	57.8	1.0 *
	Simple	100	59.8	12.1	5.9	41.8	38.3	1.9
Black	Crimes of violence	100	54.1	9.9	6.8	37.4	44.6	1.3 *
	Rape/Sexual assault/[a]	100	44.7 *	15.8 *	0.0 *	28.9 *	55.3 *	0.0 *
	Robbery	100	23.6	1.1 *	4.6 *	17.9	74.4	2.0 *
	Assault	100	62.7	12.0	7.7	43.0	36.2	1.1 *
	Aggravated	100	51.4	4.6 *	7.1 *	39.8	44.7	3.9 *
	Simple	100	67.2	15.0	8.0	44.3	32.8	0.0 *
Other	Crimes of violence	100	47.1	10.0 *	2.3 *	34.9	51.6	1.3 *
	Rape/Sexual assault/[a]	100 *	0.0 *	0.0 *	0.0 *	0.0 *	100.0 *	0.0 *
	Robbery	100	19.7 *	10.4 *	0.0 *	9.3 *	80.3 *	0.0 *
	Assault	100	54.9	10.5 *	2.8 *	41.5	43.5	1.6 *
	Aggravated	100	32.8 *	4.2 *	0.0 *	28.6 *	61.9	5.3 *
	Simple	100	64.8	13.4 *	4.1 *	47.3	35.2	0.0 *
Ethnicity	Crimes of violence	100	53.4	10.4	5.4	37.7	44.8	1.8
	Rape/Sexual assault/[a]	100	62.1	17.3	1.8 *	43.0	34.2	3.7 *
	Robbery	100	27.8	5.2	2.8 *	19.8	69.3	2.9 *
	Assault	100	56.5	10.7	5.9	39.8	41.9	1.6
	Aggravated	100	42.6	5.1	5.2	32.2	55.8	1.7 *
	Simple	100	60.9	12.5	6.1	42.3	37.5	1.6
Hispanic	Crimes of violence	100	53.5	11.1	6.6	35.8	44.4	2.1 *
	Rape/Sexual assault/[a]	100 *	55.8 *	0.0 *	0.0 *	55.8 *	44.2 *	0.0 *
	Robbery	100	23.1	2.3 *	0.0 *	20.8 *	73.7	3.2 *
	Assault	100	60.1	13.2	8.2	38.7	38.0	1.9 *
	Aggravated	100	39.4	3.2 *	4.4 *	31.8	57.8	2.8 *
	Simple	100	66.7	16.4	9.4	40.9	31.7	1.6 *

assaults by husbands versus those by wives. While the rate of severe assaults by men against their wives declined 50 percent in the 17 years from 1975 to 1992, severe assaults by women remained fairly steady.

Straus and Kantor conclude that the reason for the decline in severe assaults by husbands was that over time men became increasingly aware that battering was a crime and grew reluctant to admit the abuse. At the same time, women have been encouraged not to tolerate abuse and to report it, accounting for an increase in the reporting of even minor instances of abuse.

When abuse is measured based on separate reports by men and women, Straus and Kantor find that minor assaults by husbands decreased from 1975 to 1985. Based

TABLE 2.5

Percent distribution of victimizations, by characteristics of victims, type of crime, and victim/offender relationship, 2000 [CONTINUED]

Characteristic		Total victimizations	Percent of all victimizations					
			Nonstrangers				Stranger	Don't know Relationship
			Total	Intimate	Other relative	Friend or Acquaintance		
Non-Hispanic	Crimes of violence	100	53.4	10.3	5.3	37.8	44.9	1.7
	Rape/Sexual assault/ᵃ	100	64.3	17.9	2.0 *	44.4	34.3	1.4 *
	Robbery	100	28.6	5.8	3.4 *	19.4	68.6	2.8 *
	Assault	100	56.0	10.4	5.7	39.9	42.4	1.6
	Aggravated	100	42.8	5.4	5.4	31.9	55.7	1.5 *
	Simple	100	60.2	12.0	5.7	42.4	38.2	1.6

Note: Detail may not add to total shown because of rounding.
*Estimate is based on about 10 or fewer sample cases.
ᵃ/Includes verbal threats of rape and threats of sexual assault.

SOURCE: "Percent distribution of victimizations, by characteristics of victims, type of crime, and victim/offender relationship," in *Criminal Victimization in the United States, 2000 Statistical Tables National Crime Victimization Survey*, U.S. Department of Justice, Bureau of Justice Statistics, Washington, DC, August 2002

on the husbands' reports, these rates continued to decline from 1985 to 1992, but wives reported an increase over the same period. Men also reported a decrease in the rate of severe abuse between 1975 and 1985, while women reported no change. In contrast, between 1985 and 1992 men reported a slight increase in the rate of severe abuse while women reported a sharp drop of 43 percent. These findings appear to contradict Straus and Kantor's hypothesis that the rate change was a result of men's reluctance to report abuse and women's greater freedom to report it.

Minor abuse perpetrated by wives against their husbands declined from 1975 to 1985, according to women, but increased substantially from 1985 to 1992. Men, however, said the rate of minor abuse by their wives increased over both periods. Women also reported that the rate of severe assaults against their husbands remained steady during the first decade but increased between 1985 and 1992. Husbands reported a steady decrease in severe assaults by their wives during both periods.

DRAWING CONCLUSIONS FROM THE DATA. Straus and Kantor observe that the large decrease in severe assaults by husbands is supported by Federal Bureau of Investigation (FBI) statistics showing an 18 percent drop in the number of women killed by their husbands during that same time period. Straus and Kantor speculate that strides made over the past several years, such as justice system interventions to punish abusive husbands, along with the greater availability of shelters and restraining orders, play a role in the decrease of severe abuse. The lack of change in minor assaults by husbands may reflect the emphasis that has been placed on severe assault, which may have allowed men to mistakenly assume that an occasional slap or shove does not constitute abusive behavior.

To explain the increase in minor assaults by women, Straus and Kantor suggest that there has been no effort to condemn assaults by wives, and with increasing gender equality, women may feel entitled to hit as often as their male partners. The decrease in severe abuse by wives as reported by their husbands, which is inconsistent with the wives' responses, may reflect men's reluctance to admit they have been victims of abuse.

WHO STRIKES THE FIRST BLOW?

The NFVS data on violence by women has triggered a firestorm of protest from feminist academicians, scholars, and activists, who claim the analysis of survey data not only ignores the context in which the violence occurred, but also fails to consider the fact that women often must resort to violence in self-defense.

In his book *Abused Men: The Hidden Side of Domestic Violence* (Greenwood, Westport, CT, 1997), Philip W. Cook supports the mutual abuse argument. Using data from the 1985 NFVS and Straus's 1993 work "Physical Assault by Wives: A Major Social Problem" (*Current Controversies on Family Violence,* Sage, Newbury Park, CA, 1993), Cook concludes that, in most cases, men and women share equally when engaging in domestic abuse. Cook also finds that women are 11 percent more likely to hit first during an argument.

Straus arrives at a similar conclusion in "Physical Assault by Wives." He observes that the number of women who hit first is about the same as the number of men, regardless of how dangerous the assault is. Straus concludes that self-defense does not account for all the attacks by women, and that 25 to 30 percent of violence is attributable to physical aggression by the wife.

Abuse by Women

Demie Kurz and Kersti Ylöö present a feminist perspective in *Physical Assaults by Husbands: A Major*

TABLE 2.6

Victim and offender relationship, 2001

Relationship with victim	Violent crime Number	Violent crime Percent	Rape or sexual assault Number	Rape or sexual assault Percent	Robbery Number	Robbery Percent	Aggravated assault Number	Aggravated assault Percent	Simple assault Number	Simple assault Percent
All victims										
Total	5,743,820	100%	248,250	100%	630,690	100%	1,222,160	100%	3,642,720	100%
Nonstranger	3,094,490	54%	162,820	66%	184,240	29%	586,370	48%	2,161,060	59%
Intimate	638,410	11	38,720	16	60,930	10	109,680	9	429,080	12
Other relative	340,070	6	5,210	2*	13,670	2*	57,490	5	263,710	7
Friend/acquaintance	2,116,010	37	118,900	48	109,640	17	419,200	34	1,468,280	40
Stranger	2,546,090	44%	75,010	30%	434,440	69%	599,110	49%	1,437,540	40%
Relationship unknown	103,240	2%	10,420	4%*	12,010	2%*	36,680	3%	44,130	1%
Male victims										
Total	3,027,400	100%	22,930	100%*	427,330	100%	721,700	100%	1,855,440	100%
Nonstranger	1,310,480	43%	15,400	67%*	90,880	21%	299,410	42%	904,790	49%
Intimate	91,400	3	0	0*	11,140	3*	38,330	5	41,930	2
Other relative	104,900	4	0	0*	0	0*	24,260	3*	80,630	4
Friend/acquaintance	1,114,180	37%	15,400	67%*	79,740	19%	236,810	33%	782,220	42%
Stranger	1,669,740	55%	7,530	33%*	331,520	78%	406,860	56%	923,830	50%
Relationship unknown	47,180	2%	0	0%*	4,930	1%*	15,440	2%*	26,820	1%*
Female victims										
Total	2,716,420	100%	225,320	100%	203,360	100%	500,460	100%	1,787,280	100%
Nonstranger	1,784,020	66%	147,420	65%	93,360	46%	286,970	57%	1,256,270	70%
Intimate	547,010	20	38,720	17	49,800	25	71,350	14	387,140	22
Other relative	235,170	9	5,210	2*	13,670	7*	33,220	7	183,070	10
Friend/acquaintance	1,001,830	37	103,490	46	29,890	15	182,390	36	686,060	38
Stranger	876,350	32%	67,480	30%	102,920	51%	192,250	38%	513,710	29%
Relationship unknown	56,050	2%	10,420	5%*	7,090	4%*	21,250	4%*	17,310	1%*

Note: Percentages may not total to 100% because of rounding.
*Based on 10 or fewer sample cases.

SOURCE: Callie Rennison, "Table 4. Victim and offender relationship, 2001," in *Criminal Victimization 2001 Changes 2000–01 with Trends 1993–2001*, U.S. Department of Justice, Bureau of Justice Statistics National Crime Victimization Survey, Washington, DC, September 18, 2002

FIGURE 2.3

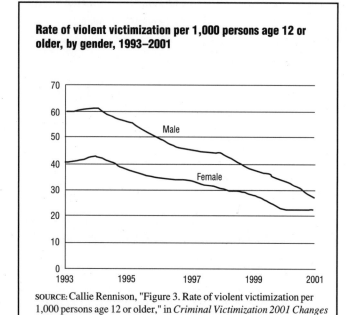

Rate of violent victimization per 1,000 persons age 12 or older, by gender, 1993–2001

SOURCE: Callie Rennison, "Figure 3. Rate of violent victimization per 1,000 persons age 12 or older," in *Criminal Victimization 2001 Changes 2000–01 with Trends 1993–2001*, U.S. Department of Justice, Bureau of Justice Statistics National Crime Victimization Survey, Washington, DC, September 18, 2002

FIGURE 2.4

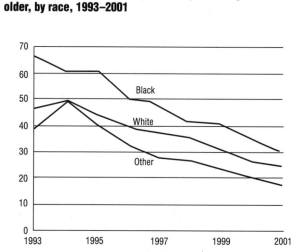

Rate of violent victimization per 1,000 persons age 12 or older, by race, 1993–2001

SOURCE: Callie Rennison, "Figure 3. Rate of violent victimization per 1,000 persons age 12 or older," in *Criminal Victimization 2001 Changes 2000–01 with Trends 1993–2001*, U.S. Department of Justice, Bureau of Justice Statistics National Crime Victimization Survey, Washington, DC, September 18, 2002

Social Problem (1987). Kurz and Yllöo observe that gender strongly influences how society functions, and they assert that feminists are critical of research that categorizes "spouse abuse" as just one of several types of abuse that include elder and child abuse. They contend that this categorization reduces women to simply one victimized group among many. Instead, feminists believe, wife abuse should be grouped with other criminal acts of male dominance, such as marital and other types of rape, sexual harassment, and incest.

For these and many other feminists, violence is an issue of power, and in both society and marriage, power is held almost exclusively by men. They caution that approaching the issue of spousal abuse using a family violence model may have negative repercussions for women because this model reinforces the notion that women become victims of abuse by provoking their partners. They also argue that research and analyses based on the family violence model often lead to policy decisions that are harmful to women, such as reduced funding for women's shelters or testimony against battered women in court. Furthermore, they argue that the family violence model encourages mental health workers and counselors to propose interventions and actions that focus on a client's personal problems without identifying the social, political, and economic inequalities between men and women that feminists contend form the basis for battering.

FIGURE 2.5

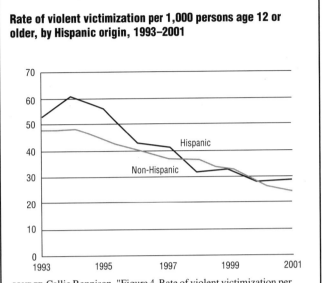

Rate of violent victimization per 1,000 persons age 12 or older, by Hispanic origin, 1993–2001

SOURCE: Callie Rennison, "Figure 4. Rate of violent victimization per 1,000 persons age 12 or older," in *Criminal Victimization 2001 Changes 2000–01 with Trends 1993–2001*, Bureau of Justice Statistics National Crime Victimization Survey, Washington, DC, September 18, 2002

TABLE 2.7

Violent victimization rates of selected demographic categories, 1993–2001

Demographic categories	Number of violent crimes per 1,000 persons age 12 or older									Change in the rate each year per 1,000, 1993-2001	Percent change, 1993-2001
	1993	1994	1995	1996	1997	1998	1999	2000	2001		
Gender											
Male	59.8	61.1	55.7	49.9	45.8	43.1	37.0	32.9	27.3	-4.7[1]	-54.3[1]
Female	40.7	43.0	38.1	34.6	33.0	30.4	28.8	23.2	23.0	-2.7[1]	-43.5[1]
Race											
White	47.9	50.5	44.7	40.9	38.3	36.3	31.9	27.1	24.5	-3.5[1]	-48.9[1]
Black	67.4	61.3	61.1	52.3	49.0	41.7	41.6	35.3	31.2	-4.5[1]	-53.7[1]
Other	39.8	49.9	41.9	33.2	28.0	27.6	24.5	20.7	18.2	-3.5	-54.3[1]
Hispanic origin											
Hispanic	55.2	61.6	57.3	44.0	43.1	32.8	33.8	28.4	29.5	-4.0	-46.6[1]
Non-Hispanic	49.5	50.7	45.2	41.6	38.3	36.8	32.4	27.7	24.5	-3.5[1]	-50.5[1]
Annual household income											
Less than $7,500	84.7	86.0	77.8	65.3	71.0	63.8	57.5	60.3	46.6	-4.9[1]	-45.0[1]
$7,500-$14,999	56.4	60.7	49.8	52.1	51.2	49.3	44.5	37.8	36.9	-2.8[1]	-34.6[1]
$15,000-$24,999	49.0	50.7	48.9	44.1	40.1	39.4	35.3	31.8	31.8	-2.8[1]	-35.1[1]
$25,000-$34,999	51.0	47.3	47.1	43.0	40.2	42.0	37.9	29.8	29.1	-2.5[1]	-42.9[1]
$35,000-$49,999	45.6	47.0	45.8	43.0	38.7	31.7	30.3	28.5	26.3	-3.8[1]	-42.3[1]
$50,000-$74,999	44.0	48.0	44.6	37.5	33.9	32.0	33.3	23.7	21.0	-3.3[1]	-52.3[1]
$75,000 or more	41.3	39.5	37.3	30.5	30.7	33.1	22.9	22.3	18.5	-1.7[1]	-55.2[1]

Note: These rates are based on the collection year. Thus, the 1993, 1994, and 1995 rates differ from rates published in *Changes in Criminal Victimization, 1994-95* (March 1997, NCJ 162032), which are based on data years. Values for the "change in the rate each year" are measured with the regression coefficient (b), 1993-2001, based on a linear trend test which takes into account rate fluctuations during the period

[1]1993-2001 difference is significant at the 95%-confidence level.

SOURCE: Callie Rennison, "Appendix Table 1. Violent victimization rates of selected demographic categories, 1993–2001," in *Criminal Victimization 2001 Changes 2000–01 with Trends 1993–2001*, U.S. Department of Justice, Bureau of Justice Statistics National Crime Victimization Survey, Washington, DC, September 18, 2002

A CRITIQUE OF THE CONFLICT TACTICS SCALE (CTS).
Kurz and Yllöo also criticize the CTS, a measure that is widely used in surveys of domestic violence. They argue that the CTS is an invalid measurement because the continuum of violence in the scale is so broad that it does not adequately discriminate between different kinds of violence. Kurz and Yllöo contend that a woman's bite should not be compared to a kick from a man. They also discredit the CTS's focus on individual violent acts because it serves to deflect attention from destructive ongoing patterns, including verbal, psychological, and sexual abuse, that occur in relationships. (Verbal abuse is, in fact, often included in the CTS.)

Kurz and Yllöo question whether violence can or should be measured as a conflict tactic. Instead, they believe, it is better to view it as a strategy to reinforce the husband's power and control. They argue that the CTS excludes information on economic deprivation, sexual abuse, intimidation, isolation, stalking, and terrorizing, which are common features of wife battering and are infrequently inflicted on men by women.

Kurz and Yllöo observe that when women are asked about their use of violence, most report that they used violence in self-defense. Other feminist scholars contend that researchers exclude the context of the situation when they ask who initiated the violence, and fail to take into account that violence is often preceded by name-calling and other psychological abuse. Women's advocates argue that women, viewing these behaviors as early warning signs of future violence, may hit first in the hope of preventing physical abuse. Even when women initiate violence, they conclude, it may very well be an act of self-defense. Research revealing that wives often report their use of violence as self-defense or retaliation supports this theory. Violent men, on the other hand, attribute their aggression to external causes to coercion and control.

Russell P. Dobash and colleagues also question the findings that result from use of the CTS. In "Separate and Intersecting Realities: A Comparison of Men's and Women's Accounts of Violence Against Women" (*Violence Against Women,* vol. 4, no. 4, August 1998), the researchers dispute the assumption that the CTS accounts of violence, whether from men or women, are unbiased and reliable. Comparing men's accounts of their violence with accounts given by women, Dobash et al. find an overall pattern of inconsistency between the reports of men and women. An even greater discrepancy is seen in the reported frequency of violent acts.

CAUSES AND PREVENTION OF ABUSE BY WOMEN. The difficulty with these feminist viewpoints, Straus and Gelles contend, is that they explain wife abuse in terms of patriarchy, which focuses on the power and control men exert over women and overlooks other important vari-

ables. Furthermore, patriarchy does not explain many other types of domestic violence, such as child abuse, sibling abuse, elder abuse, and violence by women.

Straus and Gelles claim that in some cases data on assaults by women have intentionally been suppressed. The *Survey of Spousal Violence Against Women in Kentucky* (Washington, DC, 1979) was one of the first issue-defining studies, yet it did not publish the data gathered on violence committed by women. When other researchers obtained the survey data set, they reported that among violent couples, 38 percent of attacks were committed by women who had not been attacked first by their male partners.

Straus and Gelles confirm that the greater size, strength, and aggressiveness of men means that the same action taken by a man is likely to inflict more pain or injury than a comparable act committed by a woman. They also allow that some violence inflicted by women against men is in retaliation or self-defense.

Still, violence by women cannot be ignored. Straus and Gelles maintain that efforts to prevent it are needed for several reasons. A fundamental reason is the intrinsic moral incorrectness of attacking a spouse, whether woman or man. Other reasons to prevent female-initiated or -instigated abuse include the danger of escalation, the model of violence as perceived by children, and the validation of any type of violence between spouses. When women hit, they legitimize the abuse they receive from men. If a woman slaps her partner, she gives him justification to hit her when he does not like her behavior.

In "Conceptualization and Measurement of Battering Implications for Public Policy" (*Women Battering: Policy Responses,* Anderson, Cincinnati, OH, 1991), Straus offers three reasons why injury should not be used as a criterion for defining abuse. First, the effect on legislation would be detrimental to women who must rely on police ability and authority to make arrests without visible evidence of injury. Second, injury-based rates would eliminate from the data 97 percent of assaults by men that did not result in injury but are still serious and harmful. Finally, focusing exclusively on injury rates would make it easier to ignore the abuse by women because physical violence inflicted by women frequently does not result in significant injury.

Violence Reexamined

The National Youth Survey (NYS), a self-reported longitudinal study following selected participants over time, measures problem behavior in a national sample of young people. It began in 1976 when the respondents were 11 to 17 years old and followed the participants for 16 years into adulthood in 1992, when they were 27 to 33 years old. Analyzing data from the 1983, 1986, 1989, and 1992 surveys, researcher Barbara Morse determines the level of violence between married or cohabiting partners and describes her conclusions in "Beyond the Conflict Tactics Scale: Assessing Gender Differences in Partner Violence" (*Violence and Victims,* vol. 10, no. 4, Winter 1995).

The surveys found high levels of violence in many relationships—54.5 percent of partners reported some violence in 1983, declining to 32.4 percent by 1992. About one-quarter reported severe violence in the first survey, compared to 15.8 percent in 1992. These high rates, three to four times the rate reported by Straus, were attributed to the youth of the NYS respondents.

About 10 percent of the couples reported at least one incidence of severe male-to-female violence in the year that preceded both the 1983 and 1989 surveys; however, the rate dropped to 5.7 percent in 1992. The NYS rates of female-to-male violence were remarkably high. About 48 percent of NYS respondents reported one or more female-to-male assaults in their relationships in 1983. The rate declined sharply to 27.9 percent in 1992, but was still higher than rates reported by other researchers.

Who Was Responsible?

Morse concedes that the NYS rates are higher than those of most other studies and contradict common beliefs as well as police and hospital records. One explanation of the contradictory findings may be that men tend to underreport violence while women are more likely to be accurate reporters. Morse, however, finds that both genders underreported violence when their accounts were compared to their partners' reports.

Morse finds that women were significantly more likely than men to slap or throw something at their partners, as well as to kick, bite, or hit their partners with a fist or an object. On the other hand, males were much more likely than females to "beat up" their partners. Among men who beat their partners, the reported frequency of battering averaged three to four times per year. That was at least three times as often as women who engaged in similar behavior.

Morse also finds that the violence was mutual in about half the cases and in the remaining half, women accounted for about two-thirds of the nonreciprocal violence. This finding was supported by reports from both men and women. When asked who started the fight that led to the violence, men claimed that both parties were responsible 44 percent of the time, that 26 percent of the time they started it, and that 30 percent of the time their partners initiated it. In comparison, women blamed their partners 46 percent of the time, took equal responsibility 36 percent of the time, and took full blame 18 percent of the time.

Women were also more likely to receive medical treatment for their injuries. About 20 percent of the

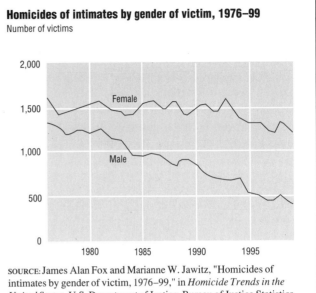

SOURCE: James Alan Fox and Marianne W. Jawitz, "Homicides of intimates by gender of victim, 1976–99," in *Homicide Trends in the United States,* U.S. Department of Justice, Bureau of Justice Statistics National Crime Victimization Survey, Washington, DC, January 4, 2001

female respondents in each survey reported that the violence led to personal injury. In contrast, 10 percent of the men reported injuries in 1989 and 14 percent in 1992.

According to the BJS, spouses are responsible for slightly more than half of all intimate assaults and former spouses account for about 5 percent. Three-quarters of the victims of assault are 20 to 39 years old, and 80 percent of abuse occurs in the victim's home. Alcohol consumption plays a role in one-quarter of all incidents. Female victims of intimate partner violence are likely to be younger, separated or divorced, of lower socioeconomic status, and unemployed.

ABUSED TO DEATH

In 1999, the latest year for which statistics are available, 11 percent of all murders of men and women were by an intimate partner, according to the FBI. Only 26 percent of the 1,642 victims were men.

Although these statistics sound alarming, they reflect a positive trend in domestic homicides. Since 1976, when the FBI first began keeping statistics on intimate murders, the number of men and women killed by an intimate partner has dropped significantly. The number of men killed by an intimate declined by 69 percent between 1976 and 1999 and the number of women killed was stable until 1993 when it began to decline. (See Figure 2.6.) The peak for intimate murders occurred in 1976, when 2,957 men and women were killed.

Although the number of white females killed by an intimate increased during the 1980s, it declined after 1983 and reached its lowest point in the past two decades in 1997. Nevertheless, in 1999 the percentage of all female homicide victims killed by an intimate was comparable with rates reported nearly 20 years earlier. (See Figure 2.7.)

The number of intimate homicides for all other race and gender groups declined over the same period, with a drop of 78 percent for black males killed by an intimate and a 53 percent decrease for black females. The number of white males killed by an intimate declined 55 percent during the same span of time. (See Figure 2.7.)

Women of every age are still substantially more likely to be killed by an intimate partner than men. Every year, about one-third of all females murdered in the United States are killed by an intimate. In comparison, only 4 percent of all male murder victims are killed by an intimate. Most female victims are between the ages of 30 and 49, with 4 out of 10 women murder victims in this age group. (See Table 2.8.)

Women are also more likely to be killed by their spouses, although this rate has declined substantially in the years since the survey was first conducted. The intimate homicide rate declined for blacks of both genders and every relationship category but was actually higher for white girlfriends in 1999 than it had been in 1976.

FIGURE 2.7

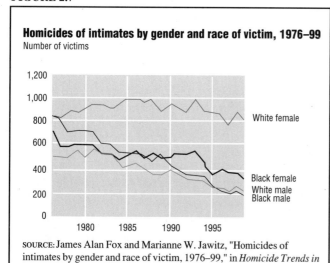

Homicides of intimates by gender and race of victim, 1976–99
Number of victims

SOURCE: James Alan Fox and Marianne W. Jawitz, "Homicides of intimates by gender and race of victim, 1976–99," in *Homicide Trends in the United States,* U.S. Department of Justice, Bureau of Justice Statistics, National Crime Victimization Survey, Washington, DC, January 4, 2001

TABLE 2.8

Percent of all murders by intimates, 1976–99

	Male victims	Female victims
Under 18	1%	6%
18–24	2	29
25–29	5	36
30–34	7	41
35–39	9	43
40–44	10	41
45–49	11	40
50–59	10	32
60+	7	20

SOURCE: James Alan Fox and Marianne W. Jawitz, "Percent of all murders by intimates, 1976–99," in *Homicide Trends in the United States,* U.S. Department of Justice, Bureau of Justice Statistics, National Crime Victimization Survey, Washington, DC, January 4, 2001

FIGURE 2.8

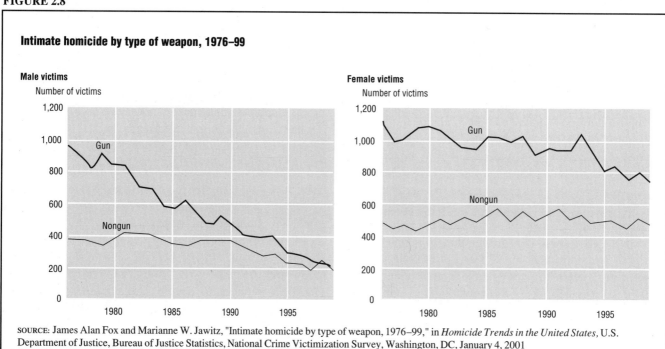

Intimate homicide by type of weapon, 1976–99

SOURCE: James Alan Fox and Marianne W. Jawitz, "Intimate homicide by type of weapon, 1976–99," in *Homicide Trends in the United States,* U.S. Department of Justice, Bureau of Justice Statistics, National Crime Victimization Survey, Washington, DC, January 4, 2001

Of all intimate homicides committed during this period, guns were used in a majority of the murders, although other weapons, such as knives, were also used. In the period between 1990 and 1999, two-thirds of all spouses and former spouses were killed by guns. However, almost half of the boyfriends murdered by their partners were killed with knives. Intimate homicides were more likely to involve knives than murders by nonintimates. (See Figure 2.8 and Table 2.9.)

DOMESTIC ABUSE AMONG SAME-SEX COUPLES

One aspect of domestic abuse that has often been overlooked is violence between lesbians—women in same-sex relationships. There are few published studies about this subject, but investigator Vernon R. Wiehe (*Understanding Family Violence,* Sage, Thousand Oaks, CA, 1998) finds that comparable forms of physical, emotional, and sexual abuse occur between partners in same-sex relationships as heterosexual partners with one difference: emotional abuse may also include threats to disclose a partner's homosexuality.

In "Addressing Culture in Batterers' Intervention: The Asian Indian Community as an Illustrative Example" (*Violence Against Women,* vol. 5, no. 6, 1999), researchers Rhea V. Almeida and Ken Dolan-Delvecchio use a "power and control" wheel in a study of perceptions of ethnicity and homosexuality. (See Figure 2.9.) The illustration is a good example of how various personal, environmental, economic, cultural, and political influences interact to generate intimate violence among same-sex partners.

Researchers have difficulty comparing the prevalence of partner abuse in same-sex relationships to abuse rates in heterosexual relationships because they must rely on nonrandom, self-selected samples. These studies consider persons who identify themselves as homosexuals and agree to participate in a research study as opposed to randomly selected persons representative of the population to be studied. As with other forms of abuse, same-sex partners may underreport violence in their relationships. Most of the published studies examining same-sex domestic violence indicate that abuse rates are about the same for male and female same-sex couples.

How Abusive Are Women in Same-Sex Relationships?

There is some survey data about female same-sex relationships that indicate considerable levels of physical and sexual violence. Linda A. Bernhard, in "Physical and Sexual Violence Experienced by Lesbian and Heterosexual Women" (*Violence Against Women,* vol. 6, no. 1, 2000), observes that while lesbians, like other women, are at risk of abuse from past and present male partners, they also risk being victimized by their female partners. In addition, since lesbians are also at greater risk for hate crimes than

TABLE 2.9

Homicides by relationship and weapon type, 1990–99

Relationship of victim to offender	Total	Gun	Knife	Blunt object	Force	Other weapon
Intimate						
Husband/ex-husband	100 %	66 %	27 %	2 %	1 %	4 %
Boyfriend	100	43	49	2	2	4
Wife/ex-wife	100	67	14	5	7	8
Girlfriend	100	58	19	5	10	9
Nonintimate	100	68	13	5	6	8

SOURCE: James Alan Fox and Marianne W. Jawitz, "Homicides by relationship and weapon type, 1990–1999," in *Homicide Trends in the United States,* U.S. Department of Justice, Bureau of Justice Statistics, Washington, DC, 2001

their heterosexual counterparts, they may experience more violence than heterosexual women.

In a study to determine the differences in violence between these two groups, Bernhard questioned 136 lesbians and 79 heterosexual women about physical and sexual violence in their relationships and the actions they took after being abused. The results of this survey show that significantly more lesbians experienced nonsexual physical violence than did heterosexual women. Bernhard finds that lesbians were also more likely to report nonsexual violence. The only difference observed between the two groups is that heterosexual women were more likely to report threatening incidents when a weapon was not used.

The most frequent response to the violence by both groups was to tell someone about the occurrence. The only difference between the two groups in their responses to violence is that lesbians were more likely than heterosexual women to take no action.

When questioned about sexual violence, 54 percent of lesbian women and 44 percent of heterosexual women reported experiencing at least one incidence of sexual violence. Many women reported sexual violence at several ages, with the highest frequency occurring during the teens and twenties for both groups. (See Table 2.10.) In addition, 44 percent of all women who reported being forced into sex said they experienced this before the age of 14. There is also great similarity between the two groups when it comes to the actions they took in response to sexual violence. The most frequent actions both groups took were to avoid the perpetrator, do nothing, or confide in someone they trusted.

Bernhard also finds that there are no significant differences between the two groups with regard to the perpetrators of violence, with family members and intimate partners being the most frequent offenders. (See Table 2.11.) Lesbians identified fathers, followed by both parents, then brothers as the family members who were the perpetrators in violent incidents. Heterosexual women

FIGURE 2.9

Public context: the misuse and abuse of power toward lesbians and gays

Sexual abuse
Lesbians raped to make them "straight." Physical violence based on what gays and lesbians do sexually, lesbians eroticized and objectified by men, verbal harassment usually of sexual nature.

Emotional abuse
Name calling. Negative words associated with homosexuality. Exclusion and rejection by heterosexuals. Institutionalized oppression. Coming out is seen as hostile, "flaunting it." Blamed for AIDS epidemic.

Using children
Child custody battles, accusation of pedophilia, gays and lesbians thought to be incompetent parents.

Intimidation
Destroying property, gay establishments, abusive graffiti, police raids, glorification of violence toward gays, stalking.

Spiritual/religious abuse
Most churches and organized religions view homosexuals as sinners. Gays and lesbians are forced to give up religious traditions and not permitted as clergy.

POWER & CONTROL

"Gay Bashing" "Lesbian Bashing"

Physical abuse
Slapping, shoving, entrapment, punching, beating, killing.

Economic abuse
Job discrimination and no protection under the law. "Passing" of hiding identity necessary for access to jobs. (Gay male couples have more economic power than lesbian couples.)

Isolation
Lack of positive lesbian and gay role models or representation through media, isolation and separation from peers and colleagues, lack of accessibility to gay affirming institutions, many heterosexual services not offered to gays and lesbians.

Using heterosexual privilege
No legal protection from violence, no legal marriage or benefits (tax deduction, insurance coverage, hospital visitation, medical decision making, funeral leave, etc.) adoption difficulties, exclusion from military.

Threats
Verbal threats to gay bash, threat to be "outed" to employer, landlord, family, etc., threat of homelessness for adolescents, threats to be disowned, arrested or deported as undocumented immigrants.

Racism Colonization/ Imperialism

Gender Oppression

Homophobia/ Heterosexism

Domestic Violence

SOURCE: Rhea V. Almeida and Ken Dolan-Delveccio, "Addressing Culture in Batterers Intervention: The Asian Indian Community as an Illustrative Example," in *Violence Against Women,* vol. 5, no. 6, copyright © 1999 by Sage Publications. Reprinted by permission of Sage Publications, Inc.

identified husbands and fathers. In almost all instances, perpetrators were men. Only five heterosexual women reported a violent incident with another woman. Of the lesbian study participants, 35 percent reported violence perpetrated against them by a woman, primarily "spouses," other intimate partners, or mothers.

Bernhard cautions that there are limitations to these study findings, but concludes that they reveal an alarming rate of violence against women perpetrated by people they know. Bernhard also speculates that had the study included a measure of hate crimes, the prevalence of violence might have been even higher.

Based on the limited research done on lesbian violence, it appears the risk factors for abuse are similar to those of heterosexual wives. Dependency and jealousy, both of which may precipitate abuse in heterosexual relationships, have been identified as the main contributors of lesbian battering. The literature about this subject also contains clinical case studies and anecdotal reports indicating that lesbian batterers may also abuse alcohol or drugs, feel powerless, and suffer from low self-esteem.

Battered lesbians are among the most underserved population of battered women, often facing denial from other lesbians and homophobia from health and social service providers. Complicating the issue are the myths that same-sex violence is mutual and the abuse is not as dangerous or destructive as heterosexual abuse. In fact, according to health care providers, the abuse is rarely mutual and may be just as harmful as abuse in heterosexual relationships.

Gender Issues in Same-Sex Relationships

In a study of gender issues in male and female same-sex relationships, Linda M. Waldner-Haugrud and colleagues interviewed 165 gays and 118 lesbians, all of them white and highly educated. In "Victimization and Perpetration Rates of Violence in Gay and Lesbian Relationships: Gender Issues Explored" (*Violence and Victims,* vol. 12, no. 2, 1997), Waldner-Haugrud et al. find that 47.5 percent of lesbians and 29.7 percent of gays reported being involved in violent relationships at some point in their lives. Pushing and threatening were the most frequent methods of abuse, while use of a weapon ranked lowest.

Thirty-eight percent of lesbian respondents reported perpetrating the violence, primarily by pushing, slapping, or threatening. Victimization and perpetration rates were higher for lesbians than for gays, with the exception of violence inflicted with a weapon. One tactic that showed a significant difference between the two groups was that lesbians were far more likely to report pushing or being pushed than gays.

Waldner-Haugrud et al. conclude that several factors may increase the likelihood of violence in lesbian couples. Among these factors are "prejudice-encouraged" social isolation, overdependency of one partner on the other, the tendency of lesbians to create "closed" relationships, and sexual-orientation identity issues. The researchers also acknowledge the probability of underreporting of partner abuse by gays as well as the limitations of the findings from this exclusive nonrepresentative sample. Still, the implications of the findings seem to indicate a need to move beyond theories that use gender to define victim and perpetrator.

EMOTIONAL AND VERBAL ABUSE

Most definitions of abuse focus on situations where physical violence was either threatened or used. Official definitions used by the courts and police, however, do not include emotional or psychological abuse that can, in many instances, cause more long-term damage than acts of physical violence. One woman with an abusive, alcoholic father remembers, "Those cuts and bruises healed but, to this day, I can still hear my father yelling at me. That's what really hurts; it was the yelling that really hurt."

Emotional and psychological abuse is usually harder to define than physical abuse, where bruises and scars are clearly evident. Almost all couples scream and shout at one another at some point, but abuse is distinguished from the heated arguments that may ensue in the course of otherwise healthy relationships because the abuser uses words to project power over a mate in a demeaning way, producing serious and often debilitating emotional or psychological consequences.

Some domestic violence researchers and counselors equate emotional abuse with the Amnesty International

TABLE 2.10

Ages at which sexual violence was experienced

Age (in years)	Lesbians (*n* = 73)		Heterosexual women (*n* = 35)	
	n	%	*n*	%
Younger than 5	18	25	6	17
5–9	27	23	10	29
10–14	22	30	12	34
15–19	30	41	11	31
20–29	32	44	17	49
30–39	14	19	7	20
40–49	0	0	2	6
50–59	2	3	4	11

SOURCE: Linda A. Bernhard, "Physical and Sexual Violence Experienced by Lesbian and Heterosexual Women," in *Violence Against Women,* vol. 6, no. 1, copyright © 2000 by Sage Publications. Reprinted by permission of Sage Publications, Inc.

TABLE 2.11

Perpetrators of violence against women

	Physical violence				Sexual violence			
	Lesbians (*n* = 68)		Heterosexual women (*n* = 26)		Lesbians (*n* = 71)		Heterosexual women (*n* = 35)	
	n	%	*n*	%	*n*	%	*n*	%
Family member	36	53	18	69	48	68	22	63
Sex partner	27	40	8	31	17	24	8	23
Stranger	9	13	3	12	10	14	2	6
Friend	8	12	3	12				
Date					19	27	13	37

SOURCE: Linda A. Bernhard, "Physical and Sexual Violence Experienced by Lesbian and Heterosexual Women," in *Violence Against Women,* vol. 6, no. 1, copyright © 2000 by Sage Publications. Reprinted by permission of Sage Publications, Inc.

TABLE 2.12

Abusive relationship checklist

Look over the following questions. Think about how you are being treated and how you treat your partner. Remember, when one person scares, hurts or continually puts down the other person, it's abuse.

Does your partner...

____ Embarrass or make fun of you in front of your friends or family?
____ Put down your accomplishments or goals?
____ Make you feel like you are unable to make decisions?
____ Use intimidation or threats to gain compliance?
____ Tell you that you are nothing without him/her .
____ Treat you roughly - grab, push, pinch, shove, or hit you?
____ Call you several times a night or show up to make sure you are where you said you would be?
____ Use drugs or alcohol as an excuse for saying hurtful things or abusing you?
____ Blame you for how s/he feels or acts?
____ Pressure you sexually for things you aren't ready for?
____ Make you feel like there "is no way out" of the relationship?
____ Prevent you from doing things you want - like spending time with your friends or family?
____ Try to keep you from leaving after a fight or leave you somewhere after a fight to "teach you a lesson"?

Do You...

____ Sometimes feel scared of how your partner will act?
____ Constantly make excuses to other people for your partner's behavior?
____ Believe that you can help your partner change if only you changed something about yourself?
____ Try not to do anything that would cause conflict or make your partner angry?
____ Feel like no matter what you do, your partner is never happy with you?
____ Always do what your partner wants you to do instead of what you want?
____ Stay with your partner because you are afraid of what your partner would do if you broke up?

If any of these are happening in your relationship, talk to someone. Without some help, the abuse will continue.

SOURCE: "Checklist," *The Problem,* National Coalition Against Domestic Violence, Denver, CO [Online] http://www.ncadv.org/problem/checklist.htm [accessed October 2, 2002]

TABLE 2.13

Predictors of domestic violence

The following signs often occur before actual abuse and may serve as clues to potential abuse:

1. Did he grow up in a violent family? People who grow up in families where they have been abused as children, or where one parent beats the other, have grown up learning that violence is normal behavior.
2. Does he tend to use force or violence to "solve" his problems? A young man who has a criminal record for violence, who gets into fights, or who likes to act tough is likely to act the same way with his wife and children. Does he have a quick temper? Does he over-react to little problems and frustration? Is he cruel to animals? Does he punch walls or throw things when he's upset? Any of these behaviors may be a sign of a person who will work out bad feelings with violence.
3. Does he abuse alcohol or other drugs? There is a strong link between violence and problems with drugs and alcohol. Be alert to his possible drinking/drug problems, particulary if he refuses to admit that he has a problem, or refuses to get help. Do not think that you can change him.
4. Does he have strong traditional ideas about what a man should be and what a woman should be? Does he think a woman should stay at home, take care of her husband, and follow his wishes and orders?
5. Is he jealous of your other relationships—not just with other men that you may know—but also with your women friends and your family? Does he keep tabs on you? Does he want to know where you are at all times? Does he want you with him all of the time?
6. Does he have access to guns, knives, or other lethal instruments? Does he talk of using them against people, or threaten to use them to get even?
7. Does he expect you to follow his orders or advice? Does he become angry if you do not fulfill his wishes or if you cannot anticipate what he wants?
8. Does he go through extreme highs and lows, almost as though he is two different people? Is he extremely kind one time, and extremely cruel at another time?
9. When he gets angry, do you fear him? Do you find that not making him angry has become a major part of your life? Do you do what he wants you to do, rather than what you want to do?
10. Does he treat you roughly? Does he physically force you to do what you do not want to do?

SOURCE: "Predictors of Domestic Violence," *The Problem,* National Coalition Against Domestic Violence, Denver, CO [Online] http://www.ncadv.org/problem/predictors.htm [accessed October 2, 2002]

definition of psychological torture, which includes verbal degradation, denial of power, isolation, monopolizing perceptions, and threats to kill. Health and social service workers who counsel victims cite emotional violence as one of several factors that may paralyze women, preventing them from fleeing dangerous and abusive relationships.

Table 2.12 is a checklist prepared by the NCADV to help identify characteristics and patterns of emotional abuse. The NCADV and many researchers believe that early identification of and effective intervention to end emotional abuse may prevent this form of violence from escalating to physical abuse. Table 2.13 is a list of characteristics, attitudes, and actions, presented by the NCADV in the form of 10 questions, that may predict whether a partner will become violent.

A Landmark Study of Verbal Aggression

Renowned researchers Murray Straus and Stephen Sweet return to the 1985 NFVS data to examine verbal aggression in their study "Verbal/Symbolic Aggression in Couples: Incidence Rates and Relationships to Personal Characteristics" (*Journal of Marriage and the Family,* vol.

54, 1992). Straus and Sweet find no significant differences between man-to-woman and woman-to-man verbal aggression. They also find that when one partner engaged in verbal aggression, the other responded in similar fashion. Women reported more abuse regardless of who initiated the aggression, but the researchers are unable to determine whether men minimized the incidence of verbal abuse or women exaggerated it.

Straus and Sweet's study finds no correlation between race or socioeconomic status and verbal aggression, although other studies report increased frequency of verbal aggression among black couples. There is, however, a link between age and levels of abuse, indicating that verbal aggression declines with age regardless of how much conflict there is in a relationship. Straus and Sweet also reveal a direct relationship between alcohol consumption and verbal aggression—the more often men get drunk, the more likely they are to be verbally abusive. Similarly, the more women use drugs, the greater the probability of verbal abuse. For men, however, drug use does not significantly affect the use of verbal abuse. Straus and Sweet caution that their research reveals a correlation between these two variables and not causation—in other words, it demonstrates a relationship between alcohol consumption and abuse, but does not show whether men and women drink to provide themselves with excuses for abusive behavior or whether drinking causes their aggression.

ABUSE OF IMMIGRANT WOMEN

In March 2001 the U.S. Census Bureau reported the total foreign-born population to be 28.4 million, slightly more than 10 percent of the U.S. population. Abuse of immigrant women remains a problem in the United States. Immigrant women may be at increased risk for various reasons, including a cultural background that teaches them to defer to their husbands. Many foreign-born women cannot speak English and do not know their rights in the United States. Others fear they will be deported or have no resources or support systems to turn to for help.

According to a special report issued by the U.S. Census Bureau in March 2001, Asian Americans account for 4.25 percent of the total U.S. population and along with other immigrant groups, have become increasingly aware of abuse in their communities. Some Asian women are sent to this country as the result of arranged marriages to live with men they barely know. In some cases, the husband takes his immigrant bride's money, jewelry, and passport, leaving her completely dependent on him. The abusive husband often tells his immigrant wife that if she leaves him, she will be deported. For some abused immigrant women, it would be worse to return home and bring shame on their family than to stay with the abusive partner. In some cultures, divorced women are outcasts with no place in society.

U.S. immigration laws have unintentionally contributed to the problem of abuse among immigrant women. The Immigration Marriage Fraud Amendments, passed in 1986 in an attempt to prevent immigrants from illegally obtaining resident status through a sham marriage to a U.S. citizen, require that spouses, usually husbands, petition for conditional resident status for an undocumented mate. Conditional status lasts a minimum of two years during which time the couple must remain married. If the marriage dissolves, the immigrant loses conditional status and may be deported. As a result, some wives become prisoners of abusive husbands for as long as they control their conditional resident status.

The law was amended under the Immigration Act of 1990 to permit a waiver of conditional status if the immigrant could prove battery or extreme cruelty. While the new law attempts to provide relief for battered brides, the initial filing for conditional status is still in the hands of the husband and if the abuse begins before he chooses to file the petition, the woman has no legal recourse.

The Diversity of Different Cultures

Many immigrants come from cultures that are radically different than the predominant American society. Among the Asian American community, including Chinese, Vietnamese, Indians, Koreans, Thai, and Cambodians, there is widespread acceptance of male dominance and a belief that the community and the family take priority over the individual. Asian women are generally raised to accept their husbands' dominance and are more reluctant to complain or leave than their American counterparts. Complicating the problem of domestic abuse in this community are strong family ties, economic dependency, the stigma of divorce, and fear of bringing shame to the family. There is also a lack of awareness, among women and men, that wife beating is wrong.

There is documented evidence of abuse in practically every immigrant community in the United States. For example, research conducted during the 1990s by the Immigrant Woman's Task Force of the Northern California Coalition for Immigrant Rights found that 34 percent of Latinas and 25 percent of Filipinas surveyed had experienced domestic violence in their country of origin, the United States, or both.

Language barriers compound the problem, often making it difficult for women to seek and obtain help. Women who do not speak English generally do not know how to find help, have difficulties in availing themselves of the help that does exist, and do not know their rights in the United States. Social workers report that interpreters, often male, do not always translate correctly, preferring to maintain community values rather than support the battered wife. In addition, many Asian women do not know the law and are misinformed by their husbands that they will be deported or lose their children if they report the abuse.

Figure 2.10 is an adaptation of the power and control wheel that shows some of the unique ways that battered immigrant women are abused. Threatening to report a woman to the Immigration and Naturalization Service, have her deported, or to withdraw her petition to legalize her immigration status are among the actions an abusive husband may take to control his immigrant wife.

In September 1994 President Bill Clinton signed the Violence Against Women Act (VAWA) as part of the Violent Crime Control and Law Enforcement Act of 1994. The VAWA permitted undocumented battered women to obtain lawful permanent resident status by petitioning for that status or through the suspension of deportation. In order to take advantage of this law, however, immigrant women must hire a lawyer and enter a system many of them misunderstand and mistrust.

New policies and programs for recent immigrant victims have been implemented across the country,

FIGURE 2.10

Power and control wheel indicating how battered immigrant women are abused

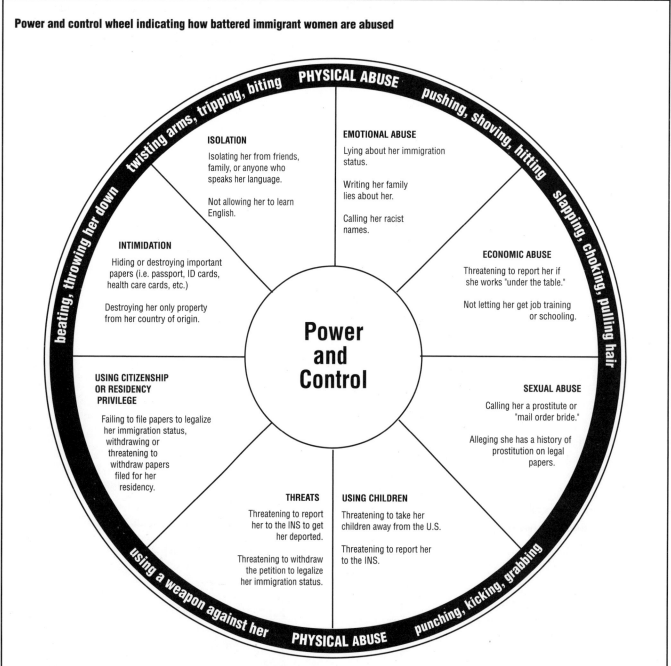

SOURCE: "Power and Control Tactics Used Against Immigrant Women," *Working with Battered Immigrant Women: A Handbook to Make Services Available,* Family Violence Prevention Fund, San Francisco, CA, 1995. Adapted from the Domestic Abuse Intervention Project in Duluth, MN. [Online] http://endabuse.org/programs/display.php3?DocID=111 [accessed November 9, 2002]

especially in cities with large immigrant populations. To improve the communication between immigrants and the criminal justice system, authorities have made special efforts to reach immigrant victims by hiring multicultural criminal justice staffs and providing informational materials in a variety of languages. Police representatives also attend meetings of immigrant groups, and members of the immigrant community are encouraged to serve as representatives on citizen police committees.

The most effective programs to assist immigrant women acknowledge the multiple pressures these women face during their efforts to become oriented and to assimilate themselves into American culture and society. Along with cultural shock and language barriers, many immigrant women confront racism, classism, and sexism. Fear of authority and the absence of social networks and support services compound the problem. Finally, recognizing that many women are brought to the United States in circumstances that increase the likelihood of victimization—

as mail-order brides, child care workers, or prostitutes—is an important step in stemming the crisis and addressing the crime of domestic violence.

Expanding and Protecting the Rights of Immigrant Women

During 2000 the National Organization for Women (NOW) Legal Defense Fund started an Immigrant Women Program (IWP) to increase and protect the legal rights and economic security of this underserved group. According to NOW, the program:

> pursues policies on a broad scale to protect immigrant women who, as victims of domestic violence, 'fall between the cracks' of both our legal safeguards and our welfare support systems. The initial focus of IWP is the creation of a legal, institutional, and policy framework that allows battered immigrant women to end the destructive role that domestic violence plays in their lives and allows all immigrant women to achieve economic self-sufficiency.

CHAPTER 3
THE CAUSES OF WIFE ABUSE

Although wife abuse has been studied for about 30 years, researchers often differ on its origins and the actions that should be taken to prevent and address the problem. Sociologists and anthropologists interpret data differently from economists and political scientists. Psychologists and other therapists perceive different facets of the problem, as do social service and shelter workers; abused women have their own perspectives on the problem.

WHO IS ABUSED?

In the past, domestic violence was viewed as a phenomenon exclusively affecting the lower classes. But when researchers began investigating the causes of family violence in the 1970s, they noticed that although lower-class women appeared to make up the majority of victims, domestic violence, in reality, spans all social and economic groups.

Middle- and upper-class women were also abused, the researchers found, but they often did not turn to hospital emergency rooms and shelters for help. Instead, they utilized private facilities and remained largely unknown, unreported, and uncounted by the public agencies that attempt to measure the rates of domestic violence and aid victims.

While women of any social class may be victims of abuse, general population studies find that women with lower incomes and less education, as well as minority women, are more likely to be the primary victims of domestic violence. Still, researchers note, classification is not exclusive. Just about anyone, rich or poor, male or female, may be a victim of domestic violence.

The Bureau of Justice Statistics (BJS) defines an intimate partner as a spouse, former spouse, or a current or former boyfriend or girlfriend, either of the same sex or the opposite sex. (See Table 3.1.) The National Crime Victimization Surveys (NCVS) find that in 1999 an estimated 671,110 million violent crimes—rape, sexual assault,

TABLE 3.1

Definitions of an intimate partner

Intimate partner relationships involve current spouses, former spouses, current boy/girlfriends, or former boy/girlfriends. Individuals involved in an intimate partner relationship may be of the same gender. The FBI does not report former boy/girlfriends in categories separate from current boy/girlfriends. Rather, they are included in the boy/girlfriend category during the data collection process.

The FBI, through the Supplementary Homicide Reports (SHR), and BJS, using the NCVS, gather information about the victim's and offender's relationship, using different relationship categories. In this report responses to the victim-offender question from both datasets are collapsed into four relationship groups: intimate, friend/acquaintance, other family, and stranger. These groups are created from the following original response categories:

	NCVS categories	SHR categories
Intimate	Spouse	Husband/wife
	Ex-spouse	Common-law husband or wife
	Boyfriend/girlfriend	Ex-husband/ex-wife
	Ex-girlfriend/ex-boyfriend	Boyfriend/girlfriend
		Homosexual relationship
Friend/ acquaintance	Friend/ex-friend	Acquaintance
	Roommate/boarder	Friend
	Schoolmate	Neighbor
	Neighbor	Employee
	Someone at work/customer	Employer
	Other non-relative	Other known
Other family	Parent or step parent	Mother/father
	Own child or stepchild	Son/daughter
	Brother/sister	Brother/sister
	Other relative	In-law
		Stepfather/stepmother
		Stepson/stepdaughter
		Other family
Stranger	Stranger	Stranger
	Known by sight only	

SOURCE: *Intimate Partner Violence*, U.S. Department of Justice, Bureau of Justice Statistics, Washington, DC, May 2000

aggravated assault, and simple assault victimizations—were committed against women by their intimate partners. (See Table 3.2.) About 85 percent of all intimate partner violent crimes were committed against women.

The NCVS data reveal that women remained far more likely to be murdered, raped, robbed, or assaulted by an

TABLE 3.2

Violence against women by intimate partners, 1999

Type of victimization	Violence against women by intimate partners		
	Number	Rate per 1,000 females	Percent
Total violent crime	671,110	5.8	100%
Rape/sexual assault	91,470	0.8	14
Robbery	65,970	0.6	10
Aggravated assault	68,810	0.6	10
Simple assault	444,860	3.8	66

Note: The population of females in 1999 used to calculate the rates was 116,243,710.

SOURCE: Callie Marie Rennison, "Table 1. Violence against females by intimate partners, 1999," in *Intimate Partner Violence and Age of Victim, 1993–99*, U.S. Department of Justice, Bureau of Justice Statistics, Washington, DC, October 2001

TABLE 3.3

Overall violence against women by intimate partners, by age, 1999

Victim's age	Number	Rate per 1,000	Percent
Total	671,110	5.8	100%
12-15	9,900	1.3*	1
16-19	119,630	15.4	18
20-24	144,100	15.7	21
25-34	182,070	9.4	27
35-49	194,380	6.0	29
50 or older	21,030	0.5*	3

Note: Rates between 16-19 and 20-24 age groups as well as rates between 12-15 and 50 or older age groups do not differ significantly. All other pairs of rates differ at the 95%-level of confidence.
*Based on 10 or fewer sample cases.

SOURCE: Callie Marie Rennison, "Table 2. Overall violence against females by intimate partners, by age, 1999," in *Intimate Partner Violence and Age of Victim, 1993–99*, U.S. Department of Justice, Bureau of Justice Statistics, National Crime Victimization Survey, Washington, DC, October 2001

intimate partner than were men. Women between the ages of 16 to 19 and 20 to 24 experienced the highest rate of domestic violence, with nearly 16 out of 1,000 women in both age groups reporting violence from an intimate partner. (See Table 3.3.)

WHO ARE THE OFFENDERS?

Like victims of domestic abuse, batterers come from all socioeconomic groups and all ethnic backgrounds. They may be male or female, young or old. They share a common characteristic—they all have personal relationships with their victims.

In the BJS report *Criminal Victimization 2001: Changes 2000–01 with Trends 1993–2001,* Bureau of Justice Statistics, Washington, DC, 2002), statistician Callie Rennison analyzes general crime trends and confirms that most female violent crime victims in 2001 knew their offenders, while most men were victimized by strangers. Rape and sexual assault victims were the most likely victims to know their assailants. Of the 5.7 million violent crimes that took place in 2001, Rennison finds that intimates were offenders in 20 percent of the violent assaults on females; intimates were involved in only 3 percent of violent assaults on males. (See Table 2.6 in Chapter 2.)

Marital status was a factor in much of the violence. According to Rennison, never married, divorced, and separated men and women experienced higher rates of victimization than persons who were married or widowed. (See Table 3.4.)

The Effects of Poverty

Murray Straus, a highly regarded researcher and co-director of the Family Research Laboratory at the University of New Hampshire, finds that serious physical acts of wife abuse are more likely to occur in poorer homes. His research shows that for lower levels of violence, such as shoving or slapping, the differences in socioeconomic sta-

tus are small. For more serious types of violence, the rates increase dramatically as the socioeconomic status drops.

University of Massachusetts researchers Gerald T. Hotaling and David B. Sugarman find that in 8 of 11 studies of socioeconomic status, low socioeconomic status was consistently related to wife assault. Hotaling and Sugarman propose two interpretations for this finding. First, men of lower socioeconomic status are exposed to greater stress and possess fewer resources to cope with it, such as economic security or education. Second, the relationship between lower socioeconomic status and wife abuse is a response to a subculture of violence that makes these individuals more likely to hold values permitting the abuse of women.

The 1985 National Family Violence Survey (NFVS), based on 6,002 households, provides researchers with the primary data to test their observations against a database large enough to produce statistically significant, valid findings. In the NFVS, families living at or below the poverty level had a rate of marital violence 500 percent greater than more affluent families.

Recent research funded by the National Institutes of Health offers additional support for the relationship between socioeconomic status and abuse. Deborah Pearlman et al. presented the findings of an analysis of police-reported domestic violence in relation to variables including socioeconomic conditions, age, race, and ethnicity (*Neighborhood Environment, Racial Position and Domestic Violence Risk: Contextual Analysis,* Academy for Health Service Research and Health Policy, Annual Meeting, June 24, 2002). Pearlman et al. find a complex, but strong relationship between poverty and domestic violence. They speculate that one explanation for the increased risk of domestic violence in poorer neighborhoods might be

TABLE 3.4

Rates of violent crime and personal theft, by household income, marital status, region, and location of residence of victims, 2001

		Victimizations per 1,000 persons age 12 or older						
		Violent crimes						
					Assault			
Characteristic of victim	Population	All	Rape/ sexual assault	Robbery	Total	Aggra- vated	Simple	Per- sonal theft
Household income								
Less than $7,500	9,178,150	46.6	3.7	4.7	38.2	16.1	22.1	1.0*
$7,500 - $14,999	16,276,910	36.9	1.6*	4.4	31.0	8.9	22.1	0.8*
$15,000 - $24,999	24,993,740	31.8	2.0	4.3	25.5	7.8	17.6	0.9*
$25,000 - $34,999	25,901,020	29.1	1.3	2.2	25.6	4.5	21.0	1.0*
$35,000 - $49,999	31,998,650	26.3	1.1	2.4	22.9	6.0	16.8	0.6*
$50,000 - $74,999	34,786,680	21.0	0.8	2.3	17.9	3.7	14.1	0.6*
$75,000 or more	40,799,640	18.5	0.6*	1.6	16.3	3.1	13.1	0.6
Marital status								
Never married	72,594,400	44.7	2.1	5.0	37.6	9.6	28.1	1.8
Married	116,743,830	11.4	0.3	1.1	10.0	2.5	7.5	0.2*
Divorced/separated	24,631,090	42.0	2.0	4.8	35.2	9.0	26.2	0.8*
Widowed	13,713,590	7.7	0.4*	1.8*	5.5	1.1	4.5	0.8*
Region								
Northeast	43,544,930	20.2	0.7	2.7	16.7	3.7	13.1	1.1
Midwest	54,661,340	24.4	1.2	2.1	21.2	5.1	16.0	1.1
South	81,955,920	23.8	1.1	3.0	19.6	5.5	14.2	0.4
West	49,053,110	32.3	1.2	3.1	27.9	6.8	21.1	1.0
Residence								
Urban	63,821,430	33.2	1.9	4.9	26.5	7.5	19.0	1.7
Suburban	109,473,240	22.3	0.9	2.2	19.2	4.3	14.9	0.5
Rural	55,920,620	21.1	0.5*	1.4	19.2	5.0	14.2	0.4

Note: The National Crime Victimization Survey includes as violent crime rape, sexual assault, robbery, and assault. Because the NCVS interviews persons about their victimizations, murder and manslaughter cannot be included.
*Based on 10 or fewer sample cases.

SOURCE: Callie Rennison, "Table 3. Rates of violent crime and personal theft, by household income, marital status, region, and location of residence of victims, 2001," in *Criminal Victimization 2001, Changes 2000–01 with Trends 1993–2001*, U.S. Justice Department, Bureau of Justice Statistics National Crime Victimization Survey, Washington, DC, September 2002

differences in law enforcement availability and practices—economically deprived communities might have less police notification, attention, and documentation.

A QUESTION OF POWER

The control of power in a relationship appears to play a significant role in battering. Some researchers suggest that the need to exert control over one's partner begins long before marriage.

In a study by Diane R. Follingstad et al., titled "Risk Factors and Correlates of Dating Violence: The Relevance of Examining Frequency and Severity Levels in a College Sample" (*Violence and Victims*, vol. 14, no. 4, Winter 1999), 290 male and 327 female college students were questioned about violence in their dating relationships. Follingstad et al. find that students who used physical force in dating relationships often did so to exercise greater control over their dating partners. Jealousy also played a significant role.

In their analysis, Follingstad et al. find that, compared to students who did not use violence in their dating relationships, respondents who reported using force were more likely to express anger, experience higher levels of jealousy, have poorer communication skills, report more daily stressors, display more irrational behavior and beliefs, and have more difficulty controlling their anger. These same respondents also reported more problems with alcohol, more verbal aggressiveness, and more efforts to control their dating partners than the students who never used force. The only characteristics that did not differ between the two groups were self-esteem, fear of negative evaluation, and problem-solving skills.

Follingstad et al. conclude that intervention in the area of dating violence should focus specifically on an individual's need to control his or her dating partner and the motivations for the need to control.

The Balance of Power

The desire to dominate one's partner may be manifested in other ways, such as through attempts at financial, social, and decision-making control. Some researchers theorize that because men of lower socioeconomic status are more likely to batter, they do it to assert the power that they lack economically. Violence becomes the tactic that compensates for the control, power, independence, and self-sufficiency these men lack in other areas.

In "Marital Power, Conflict, and Violence in a Nationally Representative Sample of American Couples" (*Violence and Victims,* vol. 1, no. 2, 1986), Diane Coleman and Murray Straus analyze data from the 1975 NFVS to determine the characteristics of families most prone to violence. They asked respondents to indicate "who has the financial say" when it comes to buying a car, having children, choosing a house or apartment, the type of job either partner should take, whether a partner should work, and how much money to spend each week for food. The response options were divided into "husband only," "husband more than wife," "husband and wife exactly the same," "wife more than husband," and "wife only."

Coleman and Straus arranged the responses to create four categories: male-dominant, female-dominant, equalitarian, and divided power. The difference between the equalitarian and divided-power types was that in the former the wife and husband made most decisions jointly, while in the latter they divided responsibility for decisions, with each having the final say for different decisions.

The highest likelihood of violence occurred in relationships where one partner was dominant. Equalitarian and divided-power relationships, in contrast, had the lowest likelihood of violence. Coleman and Straus also find that equalitarian relationships could tolerate more conflict before violence erupted than other power relationships.

Coleman and Straus attribute most of the difference in violence to higher rates of marital conflict among unequal relationships than among equal and divided ones. The more conflict, the greater the likelihood of violence. Inequality, they posit, inevitably leads to attempts to even out the relationship, which in turn causes conflicts and perhaps violence. Couples in female-dominant relationships also have to contend with an "unusual" relationship in a traditionally male-dominated society, thus adding to the tension. The researchers observe that male- or female-dominant relationships in which the partners accepted their status in the relationship were likely to experience lower levels of conflict and violence.

Further elaboration of the balance of power was provided by J. E. Prince and I. Arias in "The Role of Perceived Control and the Desirability of Control Among Abusive and Non-abusive Husbands" (*American Journal of Family Therapy,* vol. 22, no. 2, 1994). Assessing the relationship between control and self-esteem, Prince and Arias find two patterns. In one, men with high self-esteem but a poor sense of control over their lives, such as men who were unemployed, used violence in an attempt to gain control. In the second pattern, men who had low self-esteem and felt powerless became violent in response to frustration. Prince and Arias conclude that the lack of control over life events is a more significant predictor of battering than self-esteem.

Learned Gender Roles

Pointing to history, some researchers see wife abuse as a natural consequence of a woman's second-class status in society. Among the first to express this viewpoint were Emerson Dobash and Russell Dobash in *Violence Against Wives,* Free Press, New York, 1979). Dobash and Dobash believe that men who assaulted their wives were actually living up to roles and qualities expected and cherished in Western society—aggressiveness, male dominance, and female subordination—and that they used physical force as a means to enforce these roles. Many sociologists and anthropologists believe that men are socialized to exert power and control over women. Some men may use both physical and emotional abuse to attain the position of dominance in the spousal relationship.

Kersti Yllöo agrees, and in "Through a Feminist Lens: Gender, Power, and Violence" (*Current Controversies on Family Violence,* Sage, Newbury Park, CA, 1994), she states that violence often grows out of inequality within an intimate relationship and reinforces male dominance and female subordination. Violence against women in all of its forms, including sexual harassment and date rape, is a tactic of male control. For Yllöo, domestic violence is not just a conflict of interests, it is domination by men. Other researchers find that higher levels of dominance are associated with higher levels of violence.

Murray Straus compares data on wife battering with indices to measure gender equality, income, and social disorganization variables as part of his research work "State-to-State Differences in Social Inequality and Social Bonds in Relation to Assaults on Wives in the United States" (*Journal of Comparative Family Studies,* vol. 25, no. 1, Spring 1994). Gender equality is evaluated by measuring 24 indicators to determine the extent to which women have parity with men in economic, political, and legal arenas. Income inequality is assessed using census data on family income. Social disorganization measures the level of societal instability, such as geographic mobility, divorce, lack of religious affiliation, female- or male-headed households, and the ratio of tourists to residents in each state.

In all 50 states studied, Straus finds that gender equality is the variable most closely related to the rate of wife assault—states where the status of women is higher are less likely to report high rates of wife abuse. Social disorganization is also related to abuse in that the higher degree of social disorganization, the greater the probability that the state will have a high rate of wife assault. Surprisingly, Straus finds that economic inequality does not appear to be related to wife abuse rates.

Attitudes Toward Violence

Some researchers believe attitudes about violence are shaped early in life, long before the first punch is thrown in a relationship. In "The Attitudes Towards Violence

Scale: A Measure for Adolescents" (*Journal of Interpersonal Violence,* vol. 14, no. 11, November 1999), Susan B. Funk et al. asked junior high and high school students attending an inner-city public school in a Midwestern city about their attitudes toward violence. Some students identified themselves as victims of violence and others completed the survey before and after participating in a violence awareness program.

Using the responses of 638 students who took the survey prior to the violence awareness program, the researchers examine the correlation of violence with gender, grade, and ethnicity. They find that males endorsed more proviolence attitudes independent of age, grade, and ethnicity as did those students who identified themselves as victims of violence. African American teenagers endorsed "reactive violence," or violence used in response to actual or perceived threats, at higher levels than other groups. Endorsement of reactive violence was linked to having violent behaviors in one's repertoire, willingness to act in a violent manner, and supporting the actual choice of a violent response. Hispanic Americans endorsed "culture of violence" measures, reflecting a pervasive identification with violence as a valued activity, at slightly higher levels. Culture of violence measures included the conviction that the world is a dangerous place where the best way to ensure survival is to be vigilant and prepared to take the offensive. European Americans scored lower on measures of "reactive violence" as well as "total proviolence attitudes."

The study finds that gender, ethnicity, and self-identification as a victim of violence were all related to proviolence attitudes. Males, regardless of cultural background, were determined to be more likely than females to endorse proviolence attitudes. Funk et al. conclude that a combination of biological, environmental, and social influences are responsible for these findings.

Does a Patriarchal Society Breed Violence?

Donald Dutton, a professor of psychology and director of a treatment program for batterers, questions the role of male domination, pointing out that there are alternative explanations for violence in "Patriarchy and Wife Assault: The Ecological Fallacy" (*Violence and Victims,* vol. 9, no. 2, 1994). According to the patriarchal model, societies that place a high value on male dominance should have high rates of abuse. But Dutton and other investigators cite studies that contradict this premise. For example, Coleman and Straus find that in marriages where spouses agreed that the husband should be dominant, violence levels were low.

Other research discounts the weight of the patriarchal theory of abuse. David B. Sugarman and Susan Frankel, in "Patriarchal Ideology and Wife-Assault: A Meta-analytical Review" (*Journal of Family Violence,* vol. 11, no. 1, 1996), examine studies for evidence of a relationship between patriarchy and violence. They measured

whether violent husbands had a higher acceptance of violence than nonviolent men and whether they believed that women should exhibit traditional gender roles of obedience, loyalty, and deference. The researchers also measured whether assaultive men were more likely to possess a traditional "gender schema," an internal perception of an individual's own levels of masculinity, femininity, or androgyny. They also considered whether assaulted wives held more traditional gender attitudes than wives who were not battered and whether battered wives held more traditional feminine gender schemas.

Overall, their analysis finds support for only two of the five hypotheses. Predictably, assaultive husbands found marital violence more acceptable than nonviolent husbands, and battered wives were more likely to be classified as having "traditional" feminine gender schemas than wives who were not assaulted. At best, Sugarman and Frankel conclude, the findings offer only partial support for the patriarchy theory.

PSYCHOLOGICAL EXPLANATIONS OF ABUSE

K. Daniel O'Leary, in "Through a Psychological Lens: Personality Traits, Personality Disorders, and Levels of Violence" (*Current Controversies on Family Violence,* Sage, Newbury Park, CA, 1994), approaches the causes of violence by considering the factors in a relationship that are likely to predict violence. Not surprisingly, aggression is the major factor along with acceptance of aggression, past use of aggression, and relationship conflict.

Most sociologists and psychologists agree that lower levels of aggression, such as slapping and shoving, are likely to escalate over time into more severe forms of abuse, such as battering and weapon use. Furthermore, while most relationships characterized by severe violence begin with milder forms of abuse, many partners limit their aggressive physical behavior to pushing and slapping. These aggressive behaviors occur in so many marriages that they are essentially normal. O'Leary believes that the different levels of aggression—verbal, mild physical aggression, and severe physical violence—are three distinct but related behaviors. Though they exist along a continuum, he contends that men who engage in the milder forms of aggression are not motivated by the same impulses as men who commit severe abuse.

As further evidence of the differences in levels of abuse, O'Leary observes that in marriages with low levels of physical violence, the abuse is often mutual, and that women do not describe their use of force as self-defense. In severely violent relationships, however, women claim to use violence, sometimes to the point of murder, in self-defense. O'Leary maintains that this difference is important because while marital therapy may be appropriate and effective treatment for low-level violence, it is neither appropriate nor effective for relationships characterized by severe abuse.

O'Leary finds that mildly abusive men score high on personality tests for impulsiveness, a readiness to defend oneself, aggression, suspicion of others, and a tendency to take offense easily. Men in treatment programs for abuse—generally extremely abusive men—have been diagnosed with serious psychological disorders, including schizoid/borderline, narcissistic/antisocial, and possessive/dependent/compulsive personality traits. These men are also significantly different from men who are in bad marriages but are not abusive. O'Leary contends that these findings are evidence of a strong psychological component to abuse rather than a social system that promotes the domination of women.

Some feminist researchers disagree with the concept of distinguishing between types of abuse and theories that link the causes of abuse to the severity of the violence. They consider all violence against women unacceptable, and they reject the idea that the pathological personality characteristics of the perpetrators (serious mental health diagnoses) explain or excuse all of their violent behaviors. Feminist researchers and academics question psychological interpretations of violence that portray batterers as psychologically different from the rest of society because many believe that any man has the capability to become a batterer simply by virtue of living in a patriarchal society.

SOCIOLOGICAL EXPLANATIONS OF ABUSE

Richard Gelles, the chair of Child Welfare and Family Violence and interim dean of the University of Pennsylvania School of Social Work, thinks it is risky to place too much emphasis on a psychological explanation of abuse. He contends that the picture of a mentally deranged, violent abuser focuses attention on only the most extreme cases of abuse stereotyped by a psychotic offender and an innocent victim. According to Gelles, only about 10 percent of abusive incidents are caused by mental illness. The rest, he asserts, cannot be explained by a psychological model. Gelles believes a more complete understanding of the causes of abuse may be gained from an examination of sociological models, which are based on four primary theories.

General Systems Theory

The general systems theory views violence as a system rather than as a result of individual mental disturbance. It describes the factors that promote violence in families and explains how violence is managed.

Straus develops eight concepts to illustrate the general systems theory:

1. Violence between family members has many causes and roots, and personality, stress, and conflicts are only some of the causes of domestic violence

2. More family violence occurs than is reported

3. Most family violence is either denied or ignored

4. Stereotyped family-violence imagery is learned in early childhood from other family members

5. The family-violence stereotypes are continually reaffirmed through ordinary social interactions and the mass media

6. Violent acts by violent persons may generate positive feedback; that is, these acts may produce desired results

7. Use of violence, when contrary to family norms, creates additional conflict

8. Persons who are labeled violent may be encouraged to play out a violent role, either to live up to the expectations of others or to fulfill their own self-concepts of being violent or dangerous

The Resource Theory

The second theory in sociological models is known as the resource theory. According to this theory, the more resources—social, personal, and economic—a person can command, the more force he or she can potentially call on. The individual who is rich in terms of these resources has less need to use force in an open manner. In contrast, a person with little education, low job prestige and income, or poor interpersonal skills may use violence to compensate for a real or perceived lack of resources and to maintain dominance.

The Exchange/Social Control Theory

The exchange/social control theory argues that violence can be explained by the principle of costs and rewards. The private nature of the family, the reluctance of social institutions to intervene, and the low risk of other interventions reduce the risk of negative consequences from abuse. This theory maintains that cultural sanction and approval of violence increase the potential rewards for violence.

The Subculture of Violence Theory

The fourth theory posits that there is a subculture of violence in which some groups within society hold values that permit, and even encourage, the use of violence. This theory is offered as an explanation of why some segments of society and some cultures are more violent than others. This theory is perhaps the most widely accepted theory of violence.

SUBSTANCE ABUSE AND VIOLENCE

The role of alcohol and drug abuse in family violence has been examined in many studies and is considered by some researchers to be a factor in violent confrontations. Although alcohol and drug use is generally not considered the cause of the violence, researchers find that it can contribute to, accelerate, or increase aggression. A variety of data sources establish correlation (a complementary or parallel relationship) between substance abuse and violence, but correlation does not establish causation. In theory, and possibly even in practice, substance abuse may promote or provoke domestic violence, but both may also be influenced by other factors, such as environmental, biological, and situational stressors. To date, based on available research, it remains unclear whether substance abuse is a key factor in most domestic violence incidents.

Analyzing 1999 NCVS data, the BJS report *Drugs and Crime Facts* (Bureau of Justice Statistics, Washington, DC, 2002) finds that about 28 percent of victims of violent assaults believed their offenders had been using drugs alone or in combination with alcohol. Based on victim reports, about one out of four violent victimizations involved the combination of alcohol and drugs. (See Figure 3.1.) Data from the 2000 NCVS reveal that in 70 percent of cases in which the victim formed an opinion, 31 percent believed the offender was under the influence of drugs or alcohol.

While anecdotal evidence suggests that alcohol and drugs appear to be linked to violence and abuse, in controlled studies the connection is not as clear. For example, some research finds that heavy, binge drinking is more predictive of abuse than daily consumption of alcohol. Other research reveals little evidence that drug use directly causes people to become aggressive or violent, and some investigators believe that the substance abuse–violence link varies across individuals, over time within an individual's life, and even in response to environmental influences, such as epidemics of drug use and changing law enforcement policies.

In "Alcohol and Other Drugs Are Key Causal Agents of Violence" (*Current Controversies on Family Violence,* Sage, Newbury Park, CA, 1994), Jerry Flanzer suggests that while not all alcoholics are violent, alcoholism does cause family violence. He observes that personality characteristics of alcoholics and abusers are remarkably similar, marked by behaviors such as blaming others, jealousy and possessiveness, depression, low self-esteem, and "blacking out" critical incidents.

Given the strong similarities between these two groups, Flanzer proposes that perhaps they are the same group of families who have been approached from two different directions through studies of physical abuse and studies of alcohol abuse. Not all alcoholic families are violent and not all violent families are alcohol abusers, but Flanzer speculates that a careful examination of family histories would reveal overlap between violence and alcohol abuse. Research shows that the link between alcohol and family violence does not apply only to the offender. Abused children are more likely to become alcoholics, and children from alcoholic homes are more likely to become abusers.

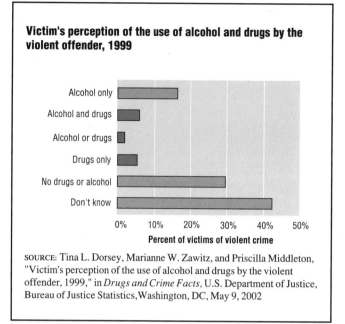

FIGURE 3.1

Victim's perception of the use of alcohol and drugs by the violent offender, 1999

SOURCE: Tina L. Dorsey, Marianne W. Zawitz, and Priscilla Middleton, "Victim's perception of the use of alcohol and drugs by the violent offender, 1999," in *Drugs and Crime Facts,* U.S. Department of Justice, Bureau of Justice Statistics, Washington, DC, May 9, 2002

Alcohol acts as a disinhibitor, allowing an individual to act out emotions, including anger, that were previously held in check. It also impairs an individual's understanding of a situation, which may lead a drinker to respond inappropriately with anger. Alcohol is also frequently used to rationalize erratic behavior and violence, allowing an abuser to avoid responsibility for violent behavior by blaming it on the effects of alcohol. Finally, alcoholism distorts the family system by constantly forcing the family to accommodate the short-term demands of the alcoholic to maintain some measure of family stability. This restructuring of family life establishes an atmosphere that tolerates and accommodates violence.

An Excuse, Not a Cause

Gelles disagrees with Flanzer and others who present substance abuse as a cause of family violence in "Alcohol and Other Drugs Are Not the Cause of Violence" (*Current Controversies on Family Violence,* Sage, Newbury Park, CA, 1994). Although substantial evidence links alcohol and drug use to violence, there is little scientific evidence that alcohol or other drugs, such as cocaine, have pharmacological properties that produce violent and abusive behavior. Although amphetamines have been proven to generate increased aggression, there is no evidence that such aggression is routinely expressed as family or intimate partner violence. Gelles maintains that although alcoholism may be associated with intimate violence, it is not a primary cause of the violence.

If alcohol had the pharmacological property of inducing violence, it would do so in all cultures, Gelles argues. Cross-cultural studies of alcohol consumption and violence, however, do not support this correlation between alcohol and violence. In some cultures individuals who drink become passive; in others they become aggressive. In our culture, Gelles notes, drinking disinhibits, permitting violent behavior without responsibility. Social expectations about drinking and drinking behavior exacerbate the problem, teaching people that if they want to avoid accountability or responsibility for their violence, one socially acceptable justification is to attribute their behavior to alcohol consumption.

Experiments using college students as subjects find that when the students thought they were consuming alcohol, they acted more aggressively than if they were told they had been given nonalcoholic drinks. According to Gelles, it is the expectation of the effects of alcohol that influences behavior, not the actual liquor consumed. He also observes that although abusive families may also abuse alcohol, an analysis of the drinking behavior at the time of the abuse finds that alcohol was not used immediately prior to the abuse in a majority of cases.

The "Drunken Bum" Theory of Wife Beating

Glenda Kaufman Kantor and Murray Straus test three commonly held beliefs: that alcohol and wife abuse are related, that wife abuse is more common in blue-collar than white-collar families, and that the acceptance of violence contributes to spousal abuse.

In "The 'Drunken Bum' Theory of Wife Beating" (*Physical Violence in American Families,* Transaction, Piscataway, NJ, 1990), Kantor and Straus find that the combination of blue-collar work status, drinking, and approval of violence was associated with the highest likelihood of wife abuse. Men with these characteristics had a rate of abuse that was 7.8 times greater than the rate of white-collar men who drank little and disapproved of violence.

Kantor and Straus emphasize that in three-quarters of the cases (76 percent), alcohol was not consumed immediately prior to the instance of wife abuse. In about 14 percent of the instances, only the male was drinking, in 2 percent only the female was drinking, and in 8 percent both the male and female were drinking. The researchers find a definite correlation between the amount of alcohol consumed and violence. Approximately 6.8 percent of those who abstained from alcohol abused their wives, while almost three times as many binge drinkers, or 19.2 percent, used violence. Kantor and Straus, however, underscore the importance of not overlooking the considerable amount of wife abuse perpetrated by nondrinkers and moderate drinkers.

The researchers also find that the major factor determining wife abuse was whether the individual approved of the use of violence against women. Not surprisingly, those who approved of a man hitting his wife were far more likely to have hit their wives than those who disapproved.

In another survey of abusers, Dutton finds that assaultive men, in general, have very high alcohol use scores (*The Batterer: A Psychological Profile,* Basic, New York, 1995). According to Dutton, abusers were depressed and anxious and, in response, used alcohol and anger to suppress these uncomfortable feelings. The outcome of this "self-medication" was a dangerous combination of unhappy, angry men with few or no inhibitions who were at high risk for violence.

Dutton warns, however, that alcohol use and violence do not cause each other but are both symptoms of an abusive personality. He concludes that this type of personality is formed much earlier than behaviors such as learning to use alcohol or physical aggression.

The Relationship Is Complex

In "Refining the Brushstrokes in Portraits of Alcohol and Wife Assaults" (*Alcohol and Interpersonal Violence: Fostering Multidisciplinary Perspectives,* National Institute on Alcohol Abuse and Alcoholism Research, Rockville, MD, 1993), Glenda Kaufman Kantor warns that considering alcohol as simply a disinhibitor of violence understates the complexity of the problem. Finding that heavy drinking by wives can increase their risk of abuse, she proposes that this may be because intoxicated women violate what is considered to be the normal gender role. Furthermore, if women become verbally or physically aggressive under the influence of alcohol, they risk being beaten. Alcoholic women are also more likely to initiate violence from their partners than nonalcoholic women. However, this finding does not imply that the wife has brought on the abuse by her drinking. Kantor confirms that violence is initiated by the aggressor, not the victim.

In their study "When Women Are Under the Influence: Does Drinking or Drug Use by Women Provoke Beatings by Men?" (*Recent Developments in Alcoholism,* Plenum, New York, 1997), Glenda Kaufman Kantor and Nancy Asdigian find little evidence that women's drinking provokes or precedes aggression by husbands. The authors theorize that women drink or use drugs as a means of coping with violent partners. In households where the husband is a substance abuser and abuses his wife, the wife is also more likely to be a substance abuser. The authors propose that both excessive drinking and spousal abuse have common roots in childhood experiences of physical and/or sexual abuse.

Does Treatment Help?

Timothy O'Farrell and Christopher Murphy, in "Marital Violence Before and After Alcoholism Treatment" (*Journal of Consulting and Clinical Psychology,* vol. 63, no. 2, 1995), examine whether behavioral marital therapy was helpful in reducing violence in abusive relationships. The researchers find the percentage of couples who experienced violent acts decreased from about 65 percent before treatment to about 25 percent after treatment. Severe violence dropped from between 30 and 35 percent before to about 10 percent after treatment.

Following treatment, recovering alcoholics no longer had elevated violence levels but alcoholics who relapsed did. Based on women's reports of their partners' violence, 2.5 percent of nondrinking alcoholics, compared to 12.8 percent of the nonalcoholic sample, were violent. In contrast, 34.7 percent of the relapsed alcoholics were violent. O'Farrell and Murphy warn that the data do not permit drawing the conclusion that drinking caused the continued violence since other factors may have influenced behavior. They do conclude, however, that their findings support the premise that recovery from alcoholism can reduce the risk of marital violence.

ABUSE OF PREGNANT WOMEN

Research about intimate partner violence reveals that violence does not stop when women become pregnant, instead pregnancy appears to be a period during which the risk for violence increases. The Centers for Disease Control and Prevention's (CDC) Division of Reproductive Health gathers data about the health of expectant mothers using its Pregnancy Risk Assessment Monitoring System (PRAMS). An analysis of PRAMS data reveals that between about 4 and 7 percent of women report being physically hurt by their husbands or partners in the year before they gave birth.

Studies estimating even higher rates of abuse of pregnant women—as many as 324,000 women per year and rates as high as 20 percent of pregnant women—have been reported (Julie Gazmararian et al., "Prevalence of Violence Against Pregnant Women," *Journal of the American Medical Association,* vol. 275, no. 24, 1996; and Julie Gazmararian et al., "Violence and Reproductive Health: Current Knowledge and Future Research Directions," *Maternal and Child Health Journal,* vol. 4, no. 2, 2000). Higher abuse rates were reported later in pregnancy, with 7.4 to 20 percent of that violence occurring in the third trimester. The lowest rates were reported in a study of women with higher socioeconomic status who were treated in a private clinic. The assailants were mainly intimate or former intimate partners, parents, or other family members. Two studies that also examined violence in the period after birth found that violence was more prevalent after birth than during pregnancy.

Research has not yet confirmed whether violence occurring during pregnancy is specific to the pregnancy or a part of an ongoing pattern of violence. Nor has research suggested the reasons that pregnant women appear to be at high risk for violence. Gazmararian et al., in an earlier study, find that women with unwanted pregnancies had 4.1 times the risk of experiencing physical violence by a husband or boyfriend during the months prior to delivery than did women with desired pregnancies. Researchers find higher rates of violence during pregnancy for women who are young, have less than 12 years of education, are unmarried, are of low socioeconomic status, have postponed or foregone prenatal care, or have an unintended pregnancy. Other studies find more reported violence when the partner is unhappy about the pregnancy.

Many researchers, including Gazmararian et al., warn that violence during pregnancy may be more common than the actual physical complications associated with pregnancy, such as pregnancy-induced diabetes or preeclampsia (dangerously high blood pressure caused by pregnancy). Some research links violence during pregnancy to poor health outcomes, including low birth weight, preterm labor, spontaneous abortion, and other medical complications. Others speculate that the connection between violence and poor health outcomes of pregnancy may result not only from direct trauma to the unborn child, but also from the stress of living in a relationship characterized by physical and emotional abuse.

INTERGENERATIONAL ABUSE

Research demonstrates a relationship between having been a victim of violence and becoming violent in future relationships. In fact, a 1996 report prepared by the American Psychological Association Task Force on Violence and the Family concludes that children's exposure to their father abusing their mother is the single strongest risk factor for passing violence down from one generation to the next. Straus, however, cautions against jumping to the conclusion that once violence occurs in a family, it will inevitably or automatically be transmitted to the next generation. Not all men who grow up in violent families end up abusing their spouses, and not all abused children or abused wives will abuse others. Conversely, some violent individuals grow up in nonviolent families.

Gelles and Straus, in *Intimate Violence* (Simon and Schuster, New York, 1989), report that the learning experience of children seeing their parents strike one another is more significant than being hit. Experiencing and, more importantly, observing violence as a child teaches three lessons:

- Those who love you are also those who hit you and those you love are people you can hit

- Seeing and experiencing violence in your home establishes the moral rightness of hitting those you love

- If other means of getting your way, dealing with stress, or expressing yourself do not work, violence is permissible

Hotaling and Sugarman, in "An Analysis of Risk Markers in Husband to Wife Violence: The Current State of Knowledge" (*Violence and Victims,* vol. 2, no. 2, 1989), consider 52 studies of domestic violence for 97 potential risk markers, defined as attributes or characteristics associated with an increased risk of either the use of husband-to-wife violence or of being victimized by husband-to-wife violence.

They find only one consistent risk for the victims in the relevant literature: women who have experienced physical spousal abuse are more likely to have witnessed violence between parents or caregivers during their childhoods. Experiencing violence is a weaker predictor of severe husband-to-wife violence than is witnessing violence. Hotaling and Sugarman hypothesize that physical punishment may be so common during childhood that it is no longer useful as a predictor of future abuse.

Shame

Dutton et al., in "The Role of Shame and Guilt in the Intergenerational Transmission of Abusiveness" (*Violence and Victims,* vol. 10, no. 2, Summer 1995), test the theory that being shamed in childhood leads to an assaultive adulthood. The distinction between shame and guilt is that shame produces disturbances in self-identity, while guilt produces bad feelings and remorse about the condemned behavior but not the self.

Using a series of psychological tests with 130 battering men, Dutton et al. conclude that shaming experiences in childhood contribute to the formation of a borderline personality disorder, including identity disturbances, temporary psychotic experiences, and the use of defenses such as projecting blame on someone else or the "splitting" of an individual's personality. According to Dutton et al., shaming experiences result in personality disturbances, while parental abuse contributes the model behavior for expressing anger. The researchers also identify shame as driving the contrition phase of the abuse cycle, leading the batterer to atone for his bad behavior.

Beaten Child, Beaten Wife

Ronald Simons et al., in "Explaining Women's Double Jeopardy: Factors that Mediate the Association Between Harsh Treatment as a Child and Violence by a Husband" (*Journal of Marriage and the Family,* vol. 55, 1993), examine the link between women who received harsh treatment in childhood and later married abusive husbands. Simons et al. assert that women who were abused in childhood marry abusive husbands—not because they have learned that violence is permissible but because they are apt to marry men from similar backgrounds.

Children raised in violent environments are often noncompliant, defiant, aggressive, and perform poorly in school. Simons et al. find that the abusive behavior by adults who were abused in childhood is part of a long-standing pattern of interpersonal difficulties and antisocial behavior. Persons who have these behavior patterns tend to affiliate with similar individuals.

Simons et al. study single mothers, many of whom have a much higher likelihood of having been in an abusive marriage than women who remained married, and find that harsh treatment by a mother rather than a father was more likely to be associated with entering an abusive marriage. Simons et al. do not find a connection between abuse and traditional gender beliefs that men are supposed to be dominant. Nor do they find a connection between the level of control the women felt they had in their lives and the incidence of abuse. On the contrary, the women in abusive marriages were not submissive; they tended to have a history of aggressive, deviant behavior. Simons et al. theorize that rebellious girls are more likely to date and marry equally antisocial, rebellious young men and end up in abusive relationships.

STRESS AND SPOUSE ABUSE

Straus and Gelles find that selected variables, including employment status, income, and number of children, are often associated with domestic violence in a given family. Families with the lowest incomes, the most children, and the lowest level of employment of the husband tend to be at greater risk for spouse abuse.

In *Behind Closed Doors: Violence in the American Family* (Anchor Books, Garden City, NY, 1980), Murray Straus, Richard Gelles, and Suzanne Steinmetz constructed a scale to measure overall family stress and applied it to NFVS data. In addition to income, number of children, and employment, they included other stressors: illness or death in the family, arrest or conviction of a family member, relocation, sexual difficulties, and problems with in-laws. They find a strong correlation between the number of stressful events experienced during the past year and the rates of family violence and abuse. The greater the stress, the greater the likelihood of abuse.

Women were even more influenced by stress than men. Families with 10 or more stressful events had a wife abuse rate of 25 percent and a husband abuse rate of 50 percent. Straus, Gelles, and Steinmetz also speculate that differences in family stress might be a major factor in the racial differences they find in family violence. Since minority families are more likely to have lower incomes, more unemployment, more children, and more experience with social discrimination and frustration in daily life, it is not surprising that they suffer more from domestic violence.

The study "Frequency and Correlates of Intimate Partner Violence by Type: Physical, Sexual, and Psychological Battering" (*American Journal of Public Health,* 2000) reveals that stressors, such as a male partner's unemployment and alcohol and/or drug use, are associated with an increased risk for physical, sexual, and emotional abuse.

INTIMATE PARTNER VIOLENCE DECLINES WITH INCREASING AGE

Jill Suitor, Karl Pillemer, and Murray Straus in "Marital Violence in a Life Course Perspective" (*Physical Violence in American Families,* Transaction, Piscataway, NJ, 1990), find that both marital conflict and verbal aggression consistently decline with age over every 10-year period. Analysis of the NFVS data from 1975 and 1985 reveals that the rate of violence in the 18- to 29-year-old group dropped when its members entered the 30- to 39-year-old group. The rate dropped even further when the older group became the 40- to 49-year-old group. The consistent decline applied to both men and women in all age groups between 18 and 65.

Suitor, Pillemer, and Straus conclude that marital conflict and verbal aggression decrease with age. They consider several different possible explanations for this observation, including greater pressure to conform (perhaps because of a greater stake in society), the greater cost of deviating from accepted patterns—having "more to lose"—and greater expectations. They observe, however, that there is not adequate data available for a conclusive link between age and marital violence.

Subsequent studies confirm declining intimate partner violence with advancing age. Analyzing NCVS data, Rennison finds married women age 20 to 24 had 8 victimizations per 1,000 women, compared to just 1 per 1,000 among married women age 50 or older (*Intimate Partner Violence and Age of Victim, 1993–99,* Bureau of Justice Statistics, Washington, DC, 2001).

Spousal Abuse Among Older Adults

Spouse abuse is a known form of elder abuse, but there is little known about its precise causes or frequency. The rate of spouse abuse among older adults is estimated to be less than 20 percent of all elder abuse reported by the *National Elder Abuse Incidence Study* (National Center on Elder Abuse, Washington, DC, 1998). Researchers speculate that an abusive relationship between older adults may simply be a continuation of abuse that began earlier in a marriage or may begin in response to age-related stresses, such as retirement, failing health, caregiver burdens, or increased dependency. Historically, social and support services for abused older adults have been largely health related and there is scant help available for elders trapped in abusive intimate partner relationships.

Sarah Harris, in "For Better or for Worse: Spouse Abuse Grown Old" (*Journal of Elder Abuse and Neglect,* vol. 8, no. 1, 1996), uses the 1985 NFVS data to compare respondents under 60 years old to those over age 60. Although the incidence of spouse abuse in older couples was significantly less than that of younger couples, many of the risk factors for violence were the same. Not surpris-

ingly, abuse occurred most often in situations where there was a high degree of conflict.

The factors associated with older partner violence included lower education levels, lower family income, verbal aggression, drug abuse, depression, perceived stress, low use of reasoning tactics, and marital conflict. Racial/ethnic group affiliation also played a part: blacks and Hispanics in the younger group and blacks in the over 60 group were more likely to experience couple violence. When violence was reported for more than the 12 months preceding the survey, intergenerational violence and poor physical health were also found to be significant.

Harris finds that the different contributing factors support different theories of abuse. Low income, poor health, verbal aggression, and low marital aggression are linked to perceived stress, supporting the theory that stress causes domestic violence.

High use of verbal aggression in the elders' relationships may be interpreted as support for the dynamic model of abuse. According to this model, the batterer blames his or her abuse on his or her partner's behavior. Verbal abuse, such as nagging or name-calling, can provoke abusive behavior from a person who has learned violence from his or her family.

Low income and racial/ethnic group factors support the theory that a subculture of violence causes or promotes abuse. That is, violence is considered more normal in some cultures and is therefore more prevalent in certain ethnic and socioeconomic groups.

SIGNS OF POTENTIAL VIOLENCE

Predictive Characteristics and Risk Markers

Can a woman expect to see certain signs of potential violence in a man she is dating or living with before she becomes a victim of abuse? The National Coalition Against Domestic Violence, believing she can, published a checklist of predictive behaviors in men that signal violence. (See Table 2.13 in Chapter 2.) Along with the predictors described in the checklist, there are other indicators, known as risk markers, that may indicate an increased propensity for violence. These include:

- An unemployed male

- A male who uses illegal drugs

- Males and females with different religious backgrounds

- A male who saw his father hit his mother

- Male and female unmarried cohabitants

- Males with blue-collar occupations

- Males who did not graduate from high school

- Males between 18 and 30 years of age

- Males or females who use severe violence toward children in the home

- Total family income is below the poverty level

A 1994 analysis by Richard Gelles, Regina Lackner, and Glen Wolfner ("Men Who Batter: The Risk Markers," *Violence Update*) of abusive men finds that in families where two risk markers were present, there was twice as much violence as those with none. In homes with seven or more of those factors, the violence rate was a staggering 40 times higher.

A separate analysis by Hotaling and Sugarman looks at risk markers in more than 400 studies. In "A Risk Marker Analysis of Assaulted Wives" (*Journal of Family Violence,* vol. 5, no. 1, 1990) and in "Prevention of Wife Assault" (*Treatment of Family Violence,* Wiley, New York, 1990), Hotaling and Sugarman find that abused women do not differ in specific personality traits from women who are not abused in terms of age, educational level, race, occupational status, length of time in the relationship, and number of children. Furthermore, a woman's poor self-esteem does not appear to be a risk factor but rather a consequence of abuse.

Contrary to other researchers, Hotaling and Sugarman find that being an abused child or seeing a parent being abused does not necessarily mean a woman has a greater chance of becoming a battered wife. Instead, severe male batterers can be distinguished from nonassaultive and verbally abusive men, as well as men who commit minor abuse, by the greater likelihood of having witnessed violence between their parents. In addition, men who engage in minor physical aggression are more likely to have experienced violence in the past than are men who were verbally abusive.

After carefully analyzing the data, Hotaling and Sugarman conclude that the only factor that differentiates abused wives from wives who are not abused is the level of marital conflict. Obviously, if a marriage has very little or no conflict, there is no reason or provocation for violence. The researchers maintain that while there is some level of conflict in every relationship, it does not necessarily result in violence. Individuals in adequately functioning relationships negotiate their way through disagreements, while individuals in violent relationships lack these skills and resort to violence.

Four factors are most often associated with abuse: marital conflict, the frequency of the husband's drinking, expectations about the division of labor in the relationship, and a measure of educational incompatibility. Hotaling and Sugarman conclude that to understand wife abuse, researchers are better served by consideration of the perpetrators' behavior rather than the characteristics of the victims.

RISK MARKERS AND A CONTINUUM OF AGGRESSION. Sugarman et al. use the analysis of risk markers to test the theory that there is a continuum of aggression in husband-to-wife violence that is linked to some of the risk markers. The risk markers considered are marital conflict, depressive symptoms, alcohol use, attitude toward interpersonal violence, violence in the family where the individuals grew up, nonfamily violence level, and socioeconomic status.

Sugarman et al. find that an increase in the severity of husband-to-wife violence is associated with an increase in depressive symptoms in the husband, along with his greater acceptance of marital violence and a higher likelihood that he experienced and witnessed violence in his family as a child. In addition, greater alcohol use and higher levels of nonfamily violence by the couple are linked to more severe violence. The data for women are very similar to the men's—the same risk factors increase severity of violence for both genders.

Three risk markers are unique, in that they can be either causes or effects of marital violence. Research does not reveal whether depressive symptoms precede the violence or are the result of the violence. Similarly, Sugarman et al. are unable to determine if marital discord causes violence or if it simply increases in response to violence. Finally, alcohol may be used by men as an excuse for violence or by women as an escape from violence. In either case, alcohol consumption may add to the conflict, which increases the violence.

Consistent with other research, Sugarman et al. conclude that persons who engage in minor violence do not necessarily progress to severe violence, but those who use severe violence almost always also began with minor violence. The most important implication of this finding is that early intervention may prevent more severe abuse. Most treatment programs are only initiated after a woman has suffered severe battering. Prevention programs that emphasize the importance of seeking treatment for low-level abuse before it escalates to serious violence might encourage women to escape abuse before it claims their health or their lives.

CHAPTER 4
THE EFFECTS OF ABUSE—WHY DOES SHE STAY?

One of the most frequently asked questions about abused women is: Why do they stay? Not all women do. Many leave abusive relationships and situations without turning to the police or support organizations. While their number is unknown, most who leave without asking for help usually have strong personal support systems of friends and family or employment and earnings that enable them to live economically independent of their abusive partners. Yet, there can be little question that a large percentage of women remain with their abusers. There are as many reasons why women stay as there are consequences and outcomes of abusive relationships.

REASONS TO STAY

Women stay in abusive relationships for a variety of reasons. Some are strictly economic. Many women feel they are better off with a violent husband than facing the challenge of raising children on their own. Some truly harbor deep feelings for their abusive partners and believe that over time they can change their partners' behavior. Others mistakenly interpret their abusers' efforts to control their life as expressions of love. Other frequently reported considerations include:

- Most women have at least one dependent child who must be cared for.

- Many are unemployed.

- Their parents are either distant, unable, or unwilling to help.

- The women may fear losing mutual friends and the support of family, especially in-laws.

- Many have no property that is solely their own.

- Some lack access to cash, credit, or any financial resources.

- If the woman leaves, then she risks being charged with desertion and losing her children and other joint assets.

- She may face a decline in living standards for both herself and her children, and her children, especially older ones, might resent this decrease in living standard.

- The woman and/or children may be in poor health.

Some battered women hold values and beliefs that experts term a "traditional ideology." This ideology may include:

- The belief that divorce is not a viable alternative and that marriage is a permanent commitment.

- A belief that having both a mother and father is crucial for children.

- An emotional dependence on her husband, who has replaced the father who "took care of her."

- A feeling of isolation from friends and family that may have been forced on her by a jealous and possessive husband who did not allow her any freedom. Some social isolation may be self-imposed by a woman who is ashamed and neither wishes to admit that the person she loves is an abuser, nor wants visible signs of wife beating to be seen by friends or family.

- Feelings of helplessness and a belief that she is dependent on a man and unable to take the initiative to escape her situation.

- A belief that a "successful marriage" depends on her, leading her to assume responsibility or to blame herself for the abuse.

- Feelings of low self-esteem and self-worth.

- The rationalization that her situation is caused by heavy stress, alcohol, problems at work, or unemployment.

- A cycle of abuse that includes periods when her husband is exceedingly romantic, leading her to believe that she still loves him or that he is basically good.

The National Resource Center on Domestic Violence assembled an information packet that explains why many women stay in abusive relationships. According to the center's information, battered women reported the following reasons for staying with their abusers:

- Hope for change—Many abusive men become contrite after beating their wives and vow that the abuse will not recur. "When the batterer acknowledges the error of his ways, when he breaks down and cries out in despair and concedes the need for dramatic change, hope is often born anew for battered women."

- Isolation—Men who batter are often highly possessive and extremely jealous. They believe they own their partners and are entitled to their exclusive attention and absolute obedience. Batterers isolate their spouses from family, friends, or institutions out of fear that this support will threaten their control.

- Societal denial—Abused women discover that many institutions trivialize their complaints. Physicians, for example, may prescribe tranquilizers, priests may recommend prayer, or the police may not remove an abusive husband from the home. Furthermore, many violent husbands hide their behavior behind closed doors and appear pleasant in public, leaving the woman to fear that no one will believe her if she discloses the abuse or leaves.

- Prevention by the batterer—Batterers may make it difficult for a woman to leave the home by threatening to commit suicide, withhold financial support, take her children, or escalate the violence. In fact, many women killed by batterers are murdered after they have left the abusive relationship.

- Belief in batterer treatment—Many battered women are reluctant to leave their partners while the men are in treatment programs. They mistakenly assume the program will help their partners make immediate and profound changes necessary to stop the violence. It is crucial that battered women receive full information about the relative success of treatment programs.

Whether a separated woman will permanently leave her battering spouse largely depends on whether she has the economic resources to survive without him. It is important, therefore, that all women learn about child-support awards, job training, and other economic opportunities.

Leaving an abusive partner is a process some therapists and counselors have termed an "evolution of separation," because many victimized women have to make several attempts before they depart from and remain parted from their abusive husbands.

The Top Reasons Women Stay in Abusive Relationships

A 1999 research project in Maricopa County, Arizona, considered intimate partner violence and asked women who participated why they remained in emotionally and physically abusive situations. Although nearly half of the study participants said they fought weekly, or even daily, with their abusive partners, 62 percent felt they would be unlikely to leave their current partners. The reasons they offered for remaining in dangerous and destructive relationships included:

- Income—60 percent of participants said they earned less than $20,000 per year and 32 percent said they had no money of their own.

- Hope—55 percent felt they would be able to repair the relationship.

- Fear—45 percent worried that they could not take their children with them if they left their abusers.

- Opportunity—44 percent could not see any way they could earn enough money to support themselves and their children.

- Education—40 percent reported no education beyond high school.

- Lack of information—36 percent of respondents said they did not know where to go to escape an abusive relationship.

More than 30 percent of the participants said they had been abused as children and more than half had grown up watching their parents in abusive relationships. Analyzing these data, Jude Miller-Burke concludes that along with the stated economic reasons and practical logistical considerations involved in exiting abusive relationships, many women remain because they mistakenly believe they either cause or deserve the abuse.

Miller-Burke also cautions about the value of strong, highly judgmental reactions to women who disclose abuse. The natural response to a woman's revelation of abuse may be a statement such as, "That type of behavior is unacceptable and any woman who puts up with it must be crazy." Women in abusive relationships may not, however, view such a statement as a condemnation of violence and abuse; instead, they may view it as yet another criticism of their own behavior. As a result of feeling blamed and shamed, they may feel even more powerless to leave their harmful relationships.

How Will Abusive Men Respond When Women Want to Leave?

A battered woman's fear of reprisal is very real and well founded. Lenore Walker, the author of several well-regarded books about intimate partner violence, explains in *Terrifying Love: Why Battered Women Kill and How Society Responds* (Harper and Row, New York, 1989) that batterers often panic when they think women are going to end the relationship. In the personal stories women told

Walker, they repeatedly related that after calling the police or asking for a divorce, their partners' violence escalated.

Walker observes that in an abusive relationship it is often the man who is desperately dependent on the relationship. Battered women are likely to feel that the batterers' sanity and emotional stability is their responsibility—that they are their men's only link to the normal world. Walker alleges that almost 10 percent of abandoned batterers committed suicide when their women left them.

It appears, however, that more batterers become homicidal, rather than suicidal. Angela Browne, the author of When Battered Women Kill, and Kirk Williams, of the Family Research Laboratory, in "Resource Availability for Women at Risk and Partner Homicide" (both published in Law and Society, University of New Hampshire, Durham, 1989), find that more than 50 percent of all female homicide victims were murdered by former abusive male partners.

LEARNED HELPLESSNESS?

Do women learn to be helpless from their life experiences?

Martin Seligman, in Helplessness: On Depression, Development and Death (1975), reports his renowned experiment in which animals randomly shocked in their cages seemed to become totally passive, even when they were shown how to escape. On closer inspection, Seligman discovered that the animals had developed coping skills, such as by lying in their own excrement in areas of their cages with the least electrical stimulation, where they were able to insulate themselves against the electrical impulses.

Observing comparable behavior in her clients, Walker concludes that victimized people tend to stop trusting their instinctive responses that protect them after they have experienced inescapable pain in apparently random and variable circumstances. When a person no longer controls his or her own life and does not know what to expect, the individual becomes helpless and develops coping skills to try to minimize the pain. Walker contends that battered women have learned helplessness. Although outsiders may not understand why they do not leave their abusers, battered women become conditioned to believe that they can not predict their safety and that nothing can be done to change their situations.

Based on her research, much of which focused on severely abused women who killed their husbands, Walker identifies five factors in childhood and seven factors in adulthood that she believes contribute to learned helplessness. The childhood factors include physical or sexual abuse, traditional sex roles, health problems, and periods during childhood when a child loses control of events, such as in frequent moves or the death of a family member. Adult factors include patterns of physical and sexual abuse, jealousy and threats of death from the batterer, psychological torture, seeing other abuse committed by the batterer, and drug or alcohol abuse by either partner.

Women Are Not Helpless

Lee Bowker, in "A Battered Woman's Problems Are Social, Not Psychological" (Current Controversies on Family Violence, Sage, Thousand Oaks, CA, 1994), believes that women remain trapped in violent marriages because of conditions in the social system rather than because they suffer from psychological problems. According to Bowker, battered women are not as passive as they are portrayed in abuse literature and routinely take steps to make their lives safer or free themselves of the abuse. He sees the duration of time it took them to escape from abuse as reflecting their husbands' unwillingness to stop being dominant as well as a lack of support from traditional social institutions.

Bowker analyzes survey questionnaires completed by 1,000 women and finds that women used several major strategies to end abuse. They tried to extract promises from their partners that the battering would stop, threatened to call police or file for divorce, avoided their partners or certain topics of conversations, hid or ran away, tried to talk the men out of violent behavior, covered their bodies to deflect the blows, and, in some cases, tried to hit back. Of these, the promise to change, with a 54 percent positive reaction, was judged the most effective strategy, while self-defense was the least effective.

Because the effectiveness of these strategies was limited, most women turned to outside sources for help. First, they contacted family or friends. However, for most this proved ineffective. Generally, these women then turned to organized or institutional sources of aid, such as police, physicians, clergy, lawyers, counselors, women's groups, and shelters. Calling a lawyer or prosecutor was deemed the most effective way to end the battering, followed by seeking assistance from women's groups and social service agencies offering referral to shelters or counselors.

Bowker does not believe that loss of self-esteem inevitably paralyzes women into remaining in abusive relationships. While battered women do lose self-esteem for a time, many still escape from their abusers. This suggests that when all seems hopeless, an innate need to save themselves emerges and propels them to escape from their situations. Bowker theorizes that the reason women's groups and shelters are effective is because they counter the effects of abuse by supporting personal growth and nurturing the women's strength.

Bowker also asked the women who remained in violent relationships why they chose to stay with their abusers. They responded that there were situations they perceived to be worse than their own abusive relationships. Some of the situations the women feared included spousal threats leveled against other family members and pets, fear of homelessness, loss of financial resources, the shame of having a failed marriage, and the loss of social identity and their current lifestyle.

Bowker concludes that because women recover from their feelings of helplessness as they gain strength, battered woman syndrome (BWS) symptoms are fundamentally different from the long-lasting symptoms that characterize most psychiatric disorders. In Bowker's interpretation, BWS refers to the social, economic, psychological, and physical circumstances that keep women in abusive relationships for long periods. The abusive relationship engenders feelings of learned helplessness that are difficult to escape. Conditioned by their batterers to feel helpless, such women have not yet learned how to resist this type of brainwashing and how to compel their abusers to retreat without having to leave or kill them.

Battered Woman Syndrome

The term "battered woman syndrome" (BWS) first came into common use in 1977 during the murder trial of Francine Hughes, an East Lansing, Michigan, mother of three who was accused of killing her abusive spouse. At the trial, Hughes's lawyer argued that the defendant suffered temporary insanity, caused by years of physical and mental abuse at the hands of her husband, before she killed him by setting his bed on fire as he slept. Her acquittal spurred legislative changes and resulted in clemency for other abused spouse killers.

In "The Battered Woman Syndrome Is a Psychological Consequence of Abuse" (*Current Controversies on Family Violence,* Sage, Thousand Oaks, CA, 1994), Walker claims that BWS is common among severely abused women and that it is part of the recognized pattern of psychological symptoms called posttraumatic stress disorder (PTSD). Women suffering from BWS learn that they cannot predict the outcomes of their actions because they cannot reliably determine if a particular response will bring them safety. Walker emphasizes that although they do not respond with total helplessness, they narrow their choices, choosing the ones that seem to have the greatest likelihood of success.

Normally, fear and the responses to fear abate once the feared object or circumstance is removed. People who have suffered a traumatic event often continue to respond to the fear with flashbacks and violent thoughts long after the event has passed. Symptoms of PTSD can afflict individuals regardless of whether they suffer from other psychological problems. Otherwise normal, mentally healthy, and emotionally stable people can develop these symptoms as an adaptive mechanism—a coping strategy to survive abnormal or unusually frightening experiences.

Symptoms of PTSD involve cognitive, psychological, and emotional changes that occur in response to severe trauma. Symptoms may include difficulty in thinking clearly and a pessimistic outlook. The abused woman's outlook often improves, however, when she regains some degree of power and control in her life.

PTSD can produce two distinct forms of memory distortions:

- Unwanted, intrusive memories of the trauma may magnify the terror.

- Partial amnesia may cause an affected individual to suppress and forget many of the painful experiences.

Abused women frequently turn to drugs or alcohol to block out intrusive memories. Other symptoms of PTSD include sleep and eating disorders and medical problems associated with persistent high levels of stress. Symptoms described under the PTSD diagnosis cover nearly every possible—and seemingly contradictory—response to battering, including chronic alertness, flashbacks, floods of emotion, detached calm, anger, inability to concentrate, sleep disturbances, indifference, profound passivity, and depression. Over time, the more aggressive symptoms decrease and are replaced by the more passive, constrictive symptoms, making the affected women appear helpless.

A LARGER CONTEXT

Evan Stark and Anne Flitcraft, best known for their research about battered women who seek help in medical emergency rooms, explore the question of traumatization in a larger context in their book *Women at Risk* (Sage, Thousand Oaks, CA, 1996). Stark and Flitcraft question whether the severe psychological symptoms caused by PTSD are a result of the violence. They believe that the damage is done by the coercive control exercised by the abuser and that the damage may be compounded when law enforcement, health, and social service institutions ignore a woman's attempts to get help. Traditional mental health treatment contributes to the coercion by assigning mutual responsibility or defining the issue in terms of the victim's behavioral problems, including her apparent helplessness. Stark and Flitcraft charge that it is easier to undervalue a woman's attempts to leave rather than to support her choices. It is simpler to accept an abused woman as a dependent victim than as an aggressive individual with a history of persistent attempts to seek help. They describe the difficulty of helping women who simultaneously act dependent in order to survive—yet fear this dependency because it places them at risk—while desperately requiring interdependence for self-esteem. Further complicating these unstable situations, attempts to help such women exacerbate their sense of not being able to help themselves. The failure to change their situations may frustrate their therapists or other would-be benefactors or sources of support. In turn, some therapists, behaving like rejected lovers, may actually start identifying with the abuser's anger.

In "Affect, Verbal Content and Psychophysiology in the Arguments of Couples with a Violent Husband" (*Journal of Consulting and Clinical Psychology,* vol. 62, no. 5, 1994), Neil S. Jacobson, a pioneering researcher in the area of marital violence, theorizes that the woman's intense anger, combined with fear and sadness, may be a part of her apparent helplessness. These women are hostile to their husbands and are by no means beaten into submission, but because of the physical abuse they are also afraid. Jacobson serves not only as a scientist, but also as a powerful champion for services and public policies to meet the needs of battered women, a population he has come to understand during the course of his research.

Characteristics of Battered Women

In her work "Battered Wives: The Home as a Total Institution" (*Victims and Violence,* vol. 6, no. 2, 1991), Noga Avni, with the Department of Criminology of Bar-Ilan University in Israel, interviewed 35 women ages 19 to 53 who sought safety from their abusers at a shelter. Of those women, only two had completed high school; the rest completed just four to eight years of elementary school. In half the families, neither spouse worked and the family depended on welfare. In 25 percent of the cases, the wife was the sole provider, while in the remaining 25 percent there was an employed husband with an average income. In all cases, the women had been severely abused throughout their marriage. For 87 percent of these women, the first violent incident took place within the first month of marriage. Only four of the women had been battered during their courtships.

Avni believes that severely battered women undergo a process in their marriages similar to the experiences of inmates in institutions where resistance is met by punishment. The women who were beaten in the first month of marriage, Avni explains, were undergoing an obedience test, and when they failed to resist, they confirmed their husbands' roles as "bosses."

As "master," the husband establishes the rules of the house. Women must fulfill the role of housekeeper, but the men are not obliged to be the providers. Women are not permitted to express their ideas or to disagree with their spouses, while men are permitted to say whatever they please. Finally, women are not permitted to bring people into the house or go where they please, although their husbands are free to do both. Avni compares these oppressed, socially isolated women to citizens in totalitarian regimes who are isolated from outside influences or ideas.

The Husband's Control

The women in this study married their husbands when they were very young; half were not yet 17 and had never been independent or taken responsibility for themselves. This lack of experience led them to depend on their husbands for support. By restricting the woman's movements, the husband curtailed her access to information, which helped him to control his jealousy and suspiciousness, emotions that frequently plague highly abusive men.

Avni describes the men's constant surveillance of their wives as psychological torture. These women reported being frequently accused of looking at other men, which became justification for a beating. Any suspicion of an actual relationship with another man would surely result in death. The women were constantly on guard and became so insecure that they further isolated themselves, afraid to leave their homes. Since the accusations were false, the women's behavior could never be sufficiently modified to appease their husbands. The women began to believe their husbands' accusations because they could not deal with the conflict between what they knew and what they were told—a process that Avni terms "brainwashing."

For the battered woman, the home is the place of maximum exposure. Intimacy and constant contact allow endless opportunities for control. The home is also a place of privacy where the husband can do as he pleases behind closed doors, and the woman maintains the privacy because she is too ashamed to tell anyone what is happening. Avni concludes that it is very difficult for a woman who is imprisoned in her home with no individual freedom to seek help, because she has been physically and psychologically locked into her situation.

DIFFERENT PERCEPTIONS OF REALITY

Self-Blame

Researchers find that women who return to abusive relationships have higher levels of self-blame than women who leave their abusers. Women who blame themselves believe that if they cause the abuse, they should be able to prevent it by changing their own behavior. In "The Relationship Between Violence, Social Support and Self-Blame in Battered Women" (*Journal of Interpersonal Violence,* vol. 11, no. 2, June 1996), Ola Barnett et al. find that battered women have higher levels of self-blame and perceive less availability of social support than women who are not battered.

Escalating levels of violence in a relationship often lead to greater use of violence by the woman as a means of self-defense or retaliation. This can result in still more self-blame, since the woman feels she is at fault for the violence. It also may deter her from seeking help and prompt her to believe no help is available. External sources of support may be less inclined to help the woman who presents the problem as her fault, and as a result the self-blaming woman may receive less assistance from health and social service agencies and organizations. To break this vicious cycle requires counselors or advisors who can help the woman shift the blame to her abusive mate. In fact, some researchers suggest that while women may blame themselves when the abuse begins, as the frequency and severity of violence increases, they eventually begin to assign the blame to the perpetrators.

The Role of Alcohol

The links between alcohol and abusive relationships have been well documented. Many batterers abuse alcohol and exhibit personality traits similar to alcoholics. One similarity is that both alcoholics and batterers tend to increase the severity and frequency of their destructive behavior over time while minimizing the consequences of their behavior. When a woman excuses her partner's violent behavior because she attributes it to alcohol, she may be less likely to leave the relationship.

In "Excuses, Excuses: Accounting for the Effects of Partner Violence on Marital Satisfaction and Stability" (*Violence and Victims,* vol. 10, no. 4, Winter 1995), Jennifer Katz et al. find that women who hold a spouse responsible for his negative behavior are less satisfied with their marriages than women who attribute the behavior to an inherent characteristic in their spouse that was unlikely to change. Alcohol abuse was seen as part of the abuser's personality, and the wife was therefore more tolerant of his negative behavior.

It's Not That Bad

In "Coping with an Abusive Relationship: How and Why Do Women Stay?" (*Journal of Marriage and the Family,* vol. 53, 1991), Tracy Herbert et al. compare the perceptual differences of women who leave abusive relationships and those who stay. They theorize that all relationships are a mixture of good and bad elements, but as long as a partner perceives that the good outweighs the bad, he or she will maintain the relationship.

Herbert et al. interviewed 130 women to find out how they viewed their relationships. They suspected that the women who stayed would stress the positive aspects of their marriages and minimize the negative, because as long as they could maintain positive images, they would remain. Studies find that women are often finally convinced to go to shelters when their husbands' abuse suddenly becomes more severe or when kindness after beatings diminishes, thereby forcing a change in the women's perceived reality.

The women reported that the frequency of abuse was, on average, once a month or less, and 78 percent reported verbal and physical abuse. Of these, 77 percent felt the verbal abuse was as difficult, or more difficult, to deal with than the physical abuse. The more frequently the woman was verbally abused, the less capable she was of seeing her relationship as positive. One woman wrote, "Bruises, cuts, etc., heal within a short time. When you

listen to someone tell you how rotten you are and how nobody wants you day after day, you begin to believe it. Verbal abuse takes years to heal but before that happens, it can ruin every part of your life."

Herbert et al. do not find evidence that the women were trapped by low self-esteem or the length of the relationship. The three variables they find most closely linked to the women who stayed were that the women:

1. Perceived more positive aspects to their relationship.

2. Saw little or no change in the frequency or intensity of the battering or love that their husbands expressed.

3. Felt their relationship was not as bad as it could be.

WHAT CAN A WOMAN DO?

Richard Gelles and Murray Straus find that only 13 percent of the severely abused women in the 1985 National Family Violence Survey felt their situations were completely hopeless and out of their control. In *Intimate Violence: The Definitive Study of the Causes and Consequences of Abuse in the American Family* (Simon and Schuster, New York, 1988), Gelles and Straus find that women who experienced more severe violence and grew up in more violent homes were more likely to stay. Predictably, women who were less educated, had fewer job skills, and were more likely to be unemployed were also more likely to stay, as were women with young children.

Avoidance

Gelles and Straus interviewed 192 women who suffered minor violence and 140 who suffered severe violence, and asked which long-range strategies they used to avoid violence. Fifty-three percent of the minor-violence victims and 69 percent of the severe-violence victims learned to avoid issues they thought would anger their partners.

Many women reported that a change in their partners' facial expressions was one of the first signs of impending abuse. "I have learned what gets him mad. I also know just by looking at him, when he gets that kind of weird, screwed-up expression on his face, that he is getting ready to be mad. Most of the time I figure I just have to walk on eggshells," one woman said.

Avoidance worked for about 68 percent of those women who suffered minor abuse, but for less than one-third of the more severely abused victims. It is an exhausting strategy. The woman can never let down her guard, and the tension becomes so great that sometimes being hit is actually a relief. One woman explained, "When he hit me, I was relieved. At least I didn't have to be so tense anymore."

Leaving

Some battered women do leave their husbands. Straus and Gelles find that 70 percent had left their spouses in the year preceding the interview. Only about half of those who left, however, reported that this was a "very effective" method of ending the abuse. In fact, for one out of eight women it only made things worse. Batterers put incredible pressure on their partners to return. Often, when the women returned they were abused more severely than before—as revenge or because the men learned that, once again, they could get away with this behavior. Women who returned also risked losing the aid of personal and public support systems, because these agencies perceived that their help or advice was useless or ignored.

Just Say "No"

The most effective means of stopping violence is to not allow it to start. Many believe that there is real truth to the statement that men abuse because they can. A wife who will not permit herself to be beaten from the very first act of minor abuse, like a slap or push, is the most successful in stopping it.

Straus and Gelles find that eliciting a promise to stop, as simplistic as that sounds, was by far the most effective strategy women could undertake—especially in cases of minor violence. Threatening to divorce or leave the home worked in about 40 percent of the minor-abuse cases, but in less than 5 percent of the severe-abuse situations. Physically fighting back was the most unsuccessful method. It worked in fewer than 2 percent of the minor-abuse cases and in less than 1 percent of the severe-abuse cases. One woman explained, "He hit me when I was nice and tried to reason. I shouldn't have been too surprised that he hit me when I hit him back."

Coping Strategies

Many battered women remain in abusive relationships out of fear, but it is not always fear of their husbands that causes them to stay. Some women fear they may lose custody of their children if they walk out on an abusive partner. Others fear they will lose their homes or their social status. For other women, religious or cultural pressures to hold the family together at all costs trap them in bad marriages, even as the abuse worsens.

Maria Eugenia Fernandez-Esquer and Laura Ann McCloskey studied a group of Mexican American and Anglo women to learn about the ethnic and social influences that pressured them to remain in or leave abusive relationships. In "Coping with Partner Abuse Among Mexican American and Anglo Women: Ethnic and Socioeconomic Influences" (*Violence and Victims,* vol. 14, no. 3, Fall 1999), they recount their interviews with 51 Mexican American and 41 Anglo women, all of whom had violent confrontations with their spouses in the year prior to the interview.

All the women had been victims of verbal abuse, but the percentages of women reporting more severe vio-

lence declined progressively as the violence level increased. Despite the decline, about half the women reported being beaten for several minutes, choked, raped, or threatened with murder if they left. About 25 percent were threatened with a gun or knife or forced to engage in sex against their will.

Although many of the ethnic differences observed were not significant, one distinct pattern emerged in the ethnic group comparison: Anglo women reported more frequent abuse in 21 of the 28 categories.

At least 25 percent of respondents in both ethnic groups reported coping tactics that included verbally aggressive intervention, "thinking through" the situation, other orientation, and physical separation. In addition, more than 25 percent of the Anglo women reported physically aggressive intervention and avoidance tactics. Only one difference reached statistical significance in the area of ethnic coping strategies: Mexican American women reported nonaggressive fantasies more often than Anglo women.

Fernandez-Esquer and McCloskey find that the socioeconomic status of battered women, as defined by education and employment, affected the way they coped internally. As socioeconomic levels rose, abuse victims tended to report more types of internal focus-coping tactics to deal with partner abuse.

Women who "think through" the situation, Fernandez-Esquer and McCloskey report, might feel more self-reliant and capable of handling the violence without police intervention. However, internal coping also involves crying spells, angry outbursts, suicidal feelings, and self-blame. Surprisingly, women of higher socioeconomic status tend to turn inward in the face of spousal aggression.

Although Fernandez-Esquer and McCloskey do not find support for their hypothesis that ethnicity influences coping, they conclude that the study illustrates similarities between ethnic groups, especially when faced with an abusive partner.

Injuries and Medical Care

There are often urgent and long-term physical and health consequences of domestic violence. Short-term physical consequences include mild to moderate injuries, such as broken bones, bruises, and cuts. More serious medical problems include sexually transmitted diseases, miscarriages, premature labor, and injury to unborn children, as well as damage to the central nervous system sustained as a result of blows to the head, such as traumatic brain injuries, chronic headaches, and loss of vision and hearing. The medical consequences of abuse are often unreported or underreported because women are reluctant to disclose abuse as the cause of their injuries and health professionals are uncomfortable inquiring about it.

A report from the Jacobs Institute of Women's Health and the Henry J. Kaiser Family Foundation (*Violence Against Women,* Washington, DC, 2001) finds that while more than half of abused women are physically injured by their abusers, only 4 out of 10 seek professional medical care. Hospital emergency department data reveal that 84 percent of women treated for injuries had received their injuries from intimate partners.

In "Intimate Partner Violence and Physical Health Consequences" (*Archives of Internal Medicine,* vol. 162, no. 10, May 2002), investigators from several medical centers and schools of public health compare the physical health problems of abused women to a control group of women who had never suffered abuse.

The investigators find that abused women suffered from 50 to 70 percent more gynecological, central nervous system, and stress-related problems. Examples of stress-related problems included chronic fear, headaches, back pain, gastrointestinal disorders, and appetite loss, as well as increased viral infections, such as colds, and cardiac problems, such as hypertension and chest pain. Although women who most recently suffered physical abuse reported the most health problems, the researchers find evidence that abused women remain less healthy over time.

SCREENING FOR DOMESTIC VIOLENCE. Although women have about a 30 to 44 percent chance of experiencing intimate partner violence at some point during their lives, health professionals detect as few as 1 out of 20 victims of physical abuse. Lorrie Elliot et al. conducted a national survey of physicians to identify factors associated with the documented low screening rates for domestic violence. In "Barriers to Screening for Domestic Violence" (*Journal of General Internal Medicine,* vol. 17, no. 2, February 2002), Elliot et al. report the responses of physicians in four medical specialties—internal medicine, family practice, obstetrics-gynecology, and emergency medicine—likely to encounter abused women.

The majority of physician respondents (88 percent) said they knew patients in their practices who had experienced domestic violence, but physicians in all specialties except emergency medicine underestimated the prevalence of the problem in their states. The physicians were questioned about the percentage of their patients they screened—specifically asked about their experience with domestic violence. Overall, just 10 percent of respondents screened their female patients for domestic violence and in this group, just 6 percent screened all female patients. Of the specialties, obstetrician-gynecologists screened the highest proportion of their patients.

Although most respondents felt they should be screening for domestic violence in their practices, most did not fulfill this responsibility. Along with unrealistically low estimates of the prevalence of the problems in their

communities, physicians also cited lack of training, lack of confidence in their abilities, fear of offending patients, and the mistaken belief that women will volunteer a history of abuse. Elliot et al. conclude that mandatory training on intimate partner violence, reminders in patients' medical charts, and physician interaction and involvement with victim service providers might all serve to increase physicians' confidence and competence to screen patients for intimate partner violence and abuse.

Hospitalization of Battered Women

The National Crime Victimization Surveys estimate that of the more than 50 percent of women battered by an intimate partner who are injured, 30 to 40 percent of these injuries require medical treatment and 15 percent require hospitalization. The hospital emergency department is often the first contact the health care system has with battered women and offers the first opportunity to identify victims, refer them to support services and safe shelters, and otherwise intervene to improve their situations.

Researchers at the University of Washington report on hospitals and battered women in "Rates and Relative Risk of Hospital Admission Among Women in Violent Intimate Partner Relationships" (*American Journal of Public Health,* vol. 90, no. 9, September 2000). They find that women who had filed for protection orders against male intimate partners had an overall increased risk for earlier hospitalization than women who had not been abused. Abused women had a 50 percent increase in hospitalization rates for any diagnosis, compared to nonabused women, and the risk of hospitalization was highest in the younger age groups of abused women.

Abused women were hospitalized much more frequently for injuries resulting from assaults, suicide attempts, poisonings, and digestive system disorders than the nonabused women and were almost four times as likely to be hospitalized with a psychiatric diagnosis. The researchers reaffirm the observation that intimate partner violence has a significant impact on women's health and their utilization of health care services.

Improving Health Professionals' Responses to Victims of Domestic Violence

In 2001 the National Academy of Sciences Institute of Medicine (IOM) released the report *Confronting Chronic Neglect: The Education and Training of Health Professionals on Family Violence* (National Academy Press, Washington, DC, 2001), which was mandated by the Health Professions Education Partnerships Act of 1998 (PL 105-392) and sponsored by the Centers for Disease Control and Prevention (CDC). Fifteen professionals from a variety of disciplines, including health sciences, mental health, law, child maltreatment, domestic violence, and elder abuse, reviewed available research about: the training of health professionals and others who come into contact with victims; the effectiveness of training and programs to screen, identify, and refer family violence in health care settings; and the outcomes of available interventions.

The report describes family violence as a serious public health problem and societal tragedy, cites inadequate training of health professionals as a serious problem, and calls for vigorous efforts to improve health professionals' abilities to screen, diagnose, treat, and refer victims of abuse. The IOM report recommends:

1. Creation of family violence centers to conduct research on the impact of family violence on the health care system and evaluate and test training and education programs for health professionals. The centers should be established by the Department of Health and Human Services and modeled after similar multidisciplinary centers in fields such as injury control research, Alzheimer's disease, and geriatric education. To lay the foundation for the centers' coordinating role, the report suggests that the U.S. General Accounting Office analyze the level and adequacy of existing investments in family violence research and training.

2. Health professional organizations and educators—including academic health center faculty—should address core competency areas for health professional curricula on family violence; effective teaching strategies; approaches to overcoming barriers to training; and approaches to promoting and sustaining behavior changes by health professionals in dealing with family violence.

3. Health care delivery systems and training settings, particularly academic health care centers and federally qualified health clinics and community health centers, should assume greater responsibility for developing, testing, and evaluating innovative training models or programs.

4. Federal agencies and other funders of education programs should create expectations and provide support and incentives for evaluating curricula on family violence for health professionals. Evaluations should focus on the impact of training on the practices of health professionals and the effects on family violence victims.

Empowerment of Battered Women

One of the most effective ways to deal with partner violence is by giving the victim the power, encouragement, and support to stop it.

In "Estrangement, Interventions and Male Violence Toward Female Partners" (*Violence and Victims,* vol. 12, no. 1, Spring 1997), Desmond Ellis and Lori Wight assert

that abused women want the violence to stop and most, if not all, attempt to do something to stop it. They find evidence showing that empowerment of the abused female is related to a decrease in the likelihood of further violence. The interventions Ellis and Wight recommend to promote gender equality include:

• Social service agencies such as counselors or shelters, which provide information and support.

• Mediation to facilitate a woman's control over the process.

• Prosecution with an option to drop the charges, which also facilitates control by female victims.

• Separation, which indicates the woman's strength in decision making.

Ellis and Wight find that separation or divorce is one of the most effective strategies for ending abuse. Postseparation violence, according to these researchers, varies with the type of legal separation or divorce proceedings. Those who participate in mediation prior to their separation are less likely to be harmed, either physically or emotionally, than those whose separation is negotiated by lawyers. Legal initiatives, such as restraining orders and protection orders, are found to be relatively ineffective in protecting female abuse victims.

Interventions to Help Battered Women

Throughout the United States, voluntary health and social service agencies and institutions, such as hospitals, mental health centers, clinics, and shelters, have developed programs that aim to help abused women break free physically, economically, and emotionally from their violent partners. Still, many abused women do not seek help from these specialized programs and services as a result of fear, shame, or lack of knowledge about how to gain access to available services. Instead, many injured women seek medical care from physicians, nurses, and other health professionals. For this reason, medical professional organizations, such as the American Medical Association and the American College of Obstetricians and Gynecologists, have guidelines to help professionals detect and intervene in cases of domestic violence and to exhort physicians to advocate on behalf of abused women.

Despite the ambitious objectives of professional societies and the widespread distribution of guidelines, many health professionals most likely to encounter victims of abuse remain untrained, fearful, and unable to even question patients about domestic violence. Barbara Gerbert et al. interviewed physicians to determine how they have overcome these and other barriers to help patients who are victims of domestic violence. Their findings were published in "Interventions that Help Victims of Domestic Violence: A Quantitative Analysis of Physicians' Experiences" (*Journal of Family Practice,* vol. 49, no. 10, October 2000).

Though physician respondents reported feeling overwhelmed, frustrated, and often ill prepared to tackle these problems, they nonetheless felt it was their responsibility to help battered women improve their situations. The technique they deemed most effective was validation—expressing concern by compassionately communicating to the woman that the abuse was undeserved. Other strategies they considered effective were:

- Overcome denial and plant seeds of change—Physicians helped the women to appreciate the seriousness of their situations and to understand that the abusers' actions were wrong and criminal. Some physicians used photographs of injuries to remind patients who denied the extent of their abuse about the severity of the injuries they had sustained.

- Nonjudgmental listening—To build trust, physicians listened without rushing to judgment or criticizing women for not fleeing their abusers.

- Document, refer, and help prepare a plan—Physicians documented abuse with photographs and detailed descriptions in the patients' medical records for use in medical and mental health treatment as well as in court proceedings. They offered ongoing, confidential referrals to hot lines, shelters, and other community resources; advised patients about when to call police; and assisted them to develop escape plans.

- Use a team approach—Physicians felt it was valuable to be able to immediately refer abused women to on-site professionals, such as counselors, nurses, social workers, or psychologists, who were able to take advantage of the medical visit as a "window of opportunity," that is, an occasion to detect and intervene to stop abuse.

- Make domestic violence a priority—Given time constraints of busy medical practices, many physicians advocated forgoing all but the most urgent medical treatment and instead used the appointment time to address the issue of abuse. They also encouraged colleagues and personnel in their practices to obtain continuing education about domestic violence, child, and elder abuse.

AN INNOVATIVE PROGRAM TO HELP BATTERED WOMEN. Collaboration between law enforcement and hospital emergency department personnel produced a novel program to prevent and intervene in domestic violence. This program was developed in Richmond, Virginia, in response to a challenge issued by Mark Rosenberg, the director of the National Center for Injury Prevention and Control at the CDC. The program, called "Cops and Docs," involves participation of emergency and trauma nurses working "handcuff in glove" with law enforcement personnel. The program was described and lauded in the *Journal of Emergency Nursing* (vol. 27, no. 6, December 2001).

Program personnel are trained together in a variety of techniques, including interviewing victims, collecting and preserving forensic evidence, as well as gathering and documenting information. In addition to helping to safeguard victims and apprehend and prosecute offenders, the program offers other health benefits to the community it serves. For example, shared emergency department data about substance abuse gives law enforcement personnel additional information to use in efforts to combat drug-related violence and crime.

CHAPTER 5

RAPE AND SEXUAL HARASSMENT AROUND THE WORLD

It went on for hours. I don't know how many policemen came through the room. It could have been 50. I will never forget their laughter, their shouting. I cried, I prayed, I asked God why me, a respectable woman, a grandmother, who had never known any man's body except my husband's.

—Ahmedi Begum, a Pakistani woman

Historically, women have been viewed as the property of men, and sexual abuse of a woman was more a violation of a man's property than a violation of a woman's "bodily integrity." Rape laws originated as a means of protecting a man's or family's property. However, primarily through the efforts of women's advocacy groups worldwide, rape is no longer viewed as a violation of family honor but as an abuse and violation of women. In most countries, rape is now considered a crime.

The United Nations (UN) Declaration of the Eradication of Violence Against Women (UN Resolution 49/104, December 1993) specifically names marital rape, sexual abuse of female children, selling women into slavery or prostitution, and other acts of violence against women in its admonishment against "any act of gender-based violence that results in or is likely to result in, physical, sexual, or psychological harm or suffering to women, including threats of such acts, coercion, or arbitrary deprivation of liberty, whether occurring in public or private life."

In many countries, only women of "good character" deserve protection from rape. In some Latin American countries, the law only recognizes rape of chaste women. These attitudes are generally based on the definition of rape as the defilement of a virgin. In the past, the traditional legal recourse required the offender to compensate the girl's father for her lost value in the marriage market.

Pakistan has perhaps the harshest attitudes toward rape in the world. Any sex outside of marriage, known as *zina,* is against the law, resulting in the arrest of the raped woman rather than the rapist. In a Karachi court, about 15

percent of the rape trials result in women facing charges and imprisonment. In one case, a patient and his two friends raped a staff nurse in a Karachi prison. Although she did not go to police, the men reported her for engaging in sex outside marriage. The judge found that if she were a "decent" woman she would not work at night and sentenced her to five years in prison, five lashes, and a fine equivalent to a year's salary.

The Pakistani court uses a "finger test" to assess a woman's virtue: if two fingers can fit in the woman's vagina, she must be habitually sexually active and her testimony is discounted. According to the Women's Action Forum, a women's rights organization, an estimated 75 percent of all women in Pakistani jails are there on charges of *zina,* many because they were raped. Once in police custody, about 72 percent are raped again, this time by the police. Human Rights Watch, an independent, nongovernmental organization dedicated to investigating and exposing human rights violations worldwide, estimates that at least 1,500 Pakistani women are in prison on charges of *zina.*

On June 22, 2002, during a tribal council in Punjab, Pakistan, Salma Bibi, a 30-year-old woman, was gang raped by four men in front of local villagers as punishment for her brother's misconduct. Bibi claimed that her brother was also raped and that police demanded a bribe to release him from custody.

In a letter to Pakistani president Pervez Musharraf urging closer scrutiny of the role of tribal councils in the abuse of women, LaShawn R. Jefferson, the executive director of the Women's Rights Division of Human Rights Watch, wrote: "We also remain concerned about the broader role of tribal councils in Pakistan and the authority they effectively enjoy to mete out punishments properly reserved to the state. Human Rights Watch believes that it is imperative that government authorities ensure that tribal councils act in accordance with the law and in a manner that respects women's rights, and do not usurp the proper judicial authority of the state. We request that you identify mechanisms by which local administrations in Pakistan can monitor the conduct of tribal councils, and intervene in instances where they have exercised jurisdiction belonging to the state."

THE PURPOSE OF RAPE

Punitive rape is sometimes practiced in countries where men resent women taking initiative or assuming positions of authority or power. In Latin America, feminists contend that women are raped as a way to force them back into the traditional sphere of home and children. In India, a leader of the Women's Development Program, an organization that helps women start businesses, was gang-raped in front of her husband by men who disapproved of her campaign against child marriages.

In most wars throughout history, rape has been practiced as a tool of war or an inherent right of victorious forces. Combatants and their sympathizers have raped women as a weapon of war with near complete impunity. In 1993, for the first time, the UN passed a resolution identifying rape as a war crime. Documented cases of wartime rape have occurred in Sierra Leone, Kosovo, the Democratic Republic of the Congo, Afghanistan, Liberia, Rwanda, El Salvador, Guatemala, Kuwait, Bangladesh, and the former Yugoslavia.

There is little accurate or comparable information on the rates of rape and sexual assault, especially in developing countries. The challenge of defining rape across cultures makes data collection difficult and underreporting raises suspicion about the actual number of incidents. For example, a 1999 UN Children's Fund study found that from 1989 to 1997 reported rapes declined in all but 3 of the 12 countries for which data were available. This decline seems unlikely since during the same years there were sharp increases in all other crime statistics.

Mary Koss, Lori Heise, and Nancy Russo, in "The Global Health Burden of Rape" (*Psychology of Women Quarterly,* vol. 19, 1994), present statistics on sexual assault and rape for different countries. At least 60 percent of the victims in each country reportedly knew their victimizers, and nearly two-thirds were girls under 15 years old. Koss, Heise, and Russo detail the many ways rape can adversely affect societies around the world.

Rape and gender-based sexual assault are closely linked to suicide, prostitution, trafficking for sex, substance abuse, murder, high-risk and unintended pregnancy, HIV/AIDS, other sexually transmitted diseases (STDs), and disability. Rape and sexual assault also increase utilization of health care services. One U.S. study finds a history of rape or sexual assault to be a stronger predictor of health care utilization than any other factor— rape victims used 2.5 times more services than women who had not been raped.

MARITAL RAPE

It was very clear to me. He raped me. He ripped off my pajamas, he beat me up. I mean, some scumbag down the street would do that to me. So to me, it wasn't any different because I was married to him, it was rape— real clear what it was. It emotionally hurt worse. I mean you can compartmentalize it as stranger rape—you were at the wrong place at the wrong time. You can manage to get over it differently. But here, you're at home with your husband and you don't expect that. I was under constant terror even if he didn't do it.

—A victim of marital rape

Rape has little to do with the sexual relations associated with love and marriage. Rape is an act of violence by one person against another. It is an act of power that aims to hurt at the most intimate level. Rape is a violation, whether it occurs at the hands of a stranger or within the home at the hands of an abusive husband.

An analysis of data from the National Violence Against Women Survey (NVAWS), sponsored jointly by the U.S. Departments of Justice and Health and Human Services and the Centers for Disease Control and Prevention (CDC), estimates that 1.5 million women and 834,700 men are raped and/or physically assaulted by an intimate partner each year. Of all surveyed women age 18 and older, 1.5 percent said they were raped and/or physically assaulted by a current or former spouse, cohabiting partner, or date in the year preceding the interview, compared to 0.9 percent of all surveyed men. Although these estimates were developed in 1998, most researchers agree that these statistics will likely remain unchanged until improved methods to collect and track data as well as to prevent and respond to violence against women are instituted.

As previous reports have consistently shown, the NVAWS reconfirms that violence against women is primarily intimate partner violence. More than three-quarters of women who were raped and/or physically assaulted since the age of 18 were assaulted by a current or former husband, cohabiting partner, or date, 9 percent were assaulted by a relative other than a husband, and 17 percent were assaulted by an acquaintance, such as a friend, neighbor, or coworker. Rape or assault by a stranger accounted for 14 percent of the incidents. By comparison, men were primarily raped and physically assaulted by strangers and acquaintances rather than by intimate partners.

Some researchers estimate that nearly 2 million incidents of marital rape occur each year and that this form of rape is more common than both stranger and acquaintance rape. Although the legal definition varies from state to state, marital rape is generally defined as any sexual activity coerced from a wife unwilling to perform it. Research on marital rape seems to indicate that 10 to 14 percent of married women have been raped by their partners and that marital rape accounts for about 25 percent of all rapes.

It is vitally important to recognize the limitations of available data about marital rape and intimate partner violence in general. In *Intimate Partner Violence and Age of Victim, 1993–99* (Bureau of Justice Statistics, Washington, DC, October 2001), Callie Rennison cautions that marital status may relate directly to a survey respondent's willingness to reveal violence at the hands of an intimate partner or spouse. For example, a married woman may be afraid to report her husband as the offender or she may be in a state of denial—unable to admit to herself or others that her husband has victimized her.

In her landmark study *Rape and Marriage* (Indiana University Press, Bloomington, 1990), Diana Russell reports on interviews with a random sample of 930 women in the San Francisco area. Of all the women who had been married, 14 percent had been raped by their spouses at least once. Of this number, one-third reported being raped once; one-third reported between 2 and 20 incidents; and one-third said they had been raped by their spouses more than 20 times.

According to Russell, the first incident of rape usually occurred in the first year of marriage. Although marital rape occurred more frequently in spousal relationships where emotional and physical abuse were present, it could also happen in marriages where there was little other violence.

M. A. Whatley, in "For Better or Worse: The Case of Marital Rape" (*Violence and Victims,* vol. 8, no. 1, 1993), reviews the research on marital rape and determines that it is most likely to occur in violent marriages and in those with alcoholic husbands. Couples that married because the woman was pregnant also have higher rates of marital rape, perhaps because the husband felt "trapped," thus he takes his revenge by raping his wife. High levels of exposure to pornography are linked to increased sexual aggression in marriage. Women who have several children, were never employed before marriage, and have less education are more likely to be victims of marital rape.

State laws on marital rape vary. On July 5, 1993, marital rape became a crime in all 50 states. In 33 states, however, there are exemptions from prosecution if, for example, the husband did not use force or if the woman is legally unable to consent because of a severe disability. There is still a tendency in the legal system to consider marital rape far less serious than either stranger or acquaintance rape.

Marital Rape Categories

Louis J. Shiro and Kersti Yllöo, in the *Maine State Bar Association Bar Bulletin* (vol. 19, no. 5, September 1985), observe that there is no single accurate depiction of marital rape—it is no more accurate to assume that marital rape is always a savage attack than to assume it is just a sexual tiff. Both scenarios are part of a spectrum.

Shiro and Yllöo interviewed 50 assault victims and, based on their findings, divided the rapes into three categories: battering rapes, force-only rapes, and obsessive rapes. About 45 percent of the women suffered battering rapes. In these rapes, the batterer used sexual assault as another brutal form of abuse against his wife. Because of the particularly demeaning and degrading nature of some of the acts, this violent behavior appeared more brutal than the other violence the abuser may have perpetrated on his wife. The battering rapist was characterized as often angry and suffering from an alcohol or other substance abuse problem.

Nonbattering, force-only rape, which involved about 45 percent of the cases, generally occurred in middle-class marriages where there was much less history of violence and abuse. The immediate reason for the rape was often a specifically sexual reason—for example, how often to have sex and the kind of sex the husband desired. The force used was much more restrained; it was enough to force intercourse but not enough to cause severe injury. This type of rape, Shiro and Yllöo observe, was not so much an instrument of anger as a tool to establish power or control or to teach a lesson.

The final category, obsessive marital rape, involved about 10 percent of those interviewed. In these instances, the husband had very unusual, often deviant sexual demands that sometimes involved other men or violence that the wife was refusing to fulfill. This type of rapist was frequently found to be heavily involved in pornography.

Raquel Kennedy Bergen (*Wife Rape,* Sage, Thousand Oaks, CA, 1996) conducted detailed interviews with 40 wife-rape victims. Fifty-five percent had been raped 20 times or more during their marriages, while 17 percent had experienced this abuse only once.

Most of the women in this sample reported that their husbands felt a sense of ownership that granted them sexual rights to their wives' bodies. Because of their perceived entitlement, the men did not interpret their behavior as rape. Several women also believed that the abuse was an attempt to punish them and that the rape was an attempt to control and assert power.

How Is Aggression Related to Marital Rape?

Since marital rape frequently occurs in relationships plagued by other types of abusive behavior, some researchers view it as just another expression of intimate partner violence. Support for this idea comes from research documenting high rates of forced sex, from 34 to 57 percent, reported by married women in battered women's shelters. Still, research has not conclusively demonstrated whether husbands who engage in physical and psychological violence will be more likely to use threatened or forced sex.

Amy Marshall and Amy Holtzworth-Munroe investigate the relationship between two forms of sexual aggression—coerecd and threatened/forced sex—and husbands' physical and psychological aggressiveness and report their findings in "Varying Forms of Husband Sexual Aggression: Predictors and Subgroup Differences" (*Journal of Family Psychology,* vol. 16, no. 3, September 2002). The researchers interviewed 164 couples and evaluated husbands using their own self-reports and their wives' reports on three measures: the revised Conflict Tactics Scale, a questionnaire called the Sexual Experiences Survey, and the Psychological Maltreatment of Women Inventory, a 58-item measure of psychological abuse.

Only physical aggression was predictive of threatened/forced sex, however, the measures distinguished between subtypes of violent behaviors. The most severely physically violent subtype was linked to sexual coercion, while physical aggression was most predictive of threatened/forced sex. Husbands who were rated as generally violent/antisocial engaged in the most threatened/forced sex. Interestingly, even the subtype of physically nonviolent men was found to have engaged in some sexual coercion in the year preceding the study.

Marshall and Holtzworth-Munroe conclude that their findings underscore the need to consider sexual aggression as a form of intimate partner abuse. They also call for research to determine the extent to which sexual coercion precedes and predicts threatened/forced sex and whether this association holds true for all relationships or only those in which there are other forms of marital violence.

The Effects of Marital Rape

Contrary to the traditional belief that victims of marital rape suffer few or no consequences, research reveals that women may suffer serious long-term medical and psychological consequences. In her review of the relevant research *Marital Rape* (Applied Research Forum, National Electronic Network on Violence Against Women, March 1999), Kennedy Bergen reports rape-related genital injuries, such as lacerations (tears), soreness, bruising, torn muscles, fatigue, vomiting, unintended pregnancy, and infection with STDs. Victims who had been battered before, during, or after the rape suffered broken bones, black eyes, bloody noses, and knife wounds, as well as injuries sustained when they were kicked, punched, or burned.

The short-term psychological effects are similar to those experienced by other victims of sexual assault and include anxiety, shock, intense fear, suicidal thinking, depression, and posttraumatic stress disorder. But marital rape victims reportedly suffer higher rates of anger and

depression than women raped by strangers, perhaps because the violence was perpetrated by a person they had loved and trusted not to harm them. Long-term consequences include serious depression, sexual problems, and emotional pain that lasts years after the abuse.

Along with other violent acts, marital rape prompts some women to leave their rapist husbands. Kennedy Bergen reports that women from selected ethnic groups, such as Latinas, appeared less likely to characterize forced sex as rape and consequently less likely to accuse or flee their spouses. The fact that married women do leave their abusers was confirmed by an analysis of National Crime Victimization Surveys (NCVS) data that compared marital status of survey respondents from one survey to the next. Table 5.1 shows that 30 percent of the female victims of intimate partner violence who were married during the previous NCVS interview when they had reported being victimized had separated by the next year, and an additional 8 percent had divorced their husbands.

Changing Attitudes About Wife Rape

Historically, the relationship between husband and wife has been considered private and the occurrence of wife rape was discounted. Researcher Kathleen Basile of Georgia State University in Atlanta sought to examine variables that might predict specific attitudes about wife rape: beliefs about the occurrence and frequency of forced sex by a husband on his wife and whether respondents would classify various scenarios as constituting rape.

Nearly all previous attitudinal research had focused on limited populations, such as college students, and could not be generalized to the public at large. Basile chose to analyze data from a nationally representative telephone survey of 1,108 adults to produce more widely applicable findings. The design, methods, and findings of this first national study to look at public opinions about wife rape are described in "Attitudes Toward Wife Rape: Effects of Social Background and Victim Status" (*Violence and Victims,* vol. 17, no. 3, June 2002).

She hypothesized that social background variables and victim status would predict how survey respondents felt about marital rape. Based on earlier research, she believed that males, blacks, and other racial minorities would express opinions more supportive of wife rape. Similarly, Basile expected that supportive attitudes would increase with age. She felt that victims and persons with higher educational attainment would hold less supportive views of wife rape.

Survey respondents were asked whether they "think husbands ever use force, like hitting, holding down, or using a weapon, to make their wives have sex when the wife doesn't want to" to find out if they thought wife rape occurs. Respondents who answered "yes" to this question were asked how often they thought this occurs to gauge their perceptions of the frequency of wife rape. They also listened to descriptions of three scenarios of forced sex: two scenarios involved forced sex between husband and wife and the other was a woman forced to have sex with someone with whom she was previously intimate. The respondents were asked whether they considered each scenario to be an instance of rape.

Basile finds that nearly three-quarters (73 percent) of respondents believed that wife rape occurs, 18 percent thought it does not occur, and 5 percent were unsure. Among those who thought it occurs, 38 percent said it happens often, and an additional 40 percent felt it happens somewhat often. Fifteen percent felt wife rape is infrequent and 4 percent said it is a rare occurrence.

Basile finds support for nearly all her of hypotheses. The older the respondents, the less likely they were to believe that wife rape occurs, and white respondents were 2.5 times more likely to believe that wife rape occurs than blacks and other minorities. Women thought wife rape occurs more frequently than did men and, predictably, victims were more than twice as likely as nonvictims to feel that wife rape occurs.

The most surprising finding was that more education was associated with the belief that wife rape is less frequent. Basile observes that this finding might simply indicate that even persons with higher educational attainment remain woefully ignorant about the frequency of wife rape.

Although Basile finds that overall national attitudes about wife rape are less supportive than she would have predicted prior to her study, the variations in attitudes toward the two marital rape scenarios prompted her to observe that many Americans still feel victims play some part in their own victimization.

ACQUAINTANCE RAPE

According to a number of widely publicized studies, young women are at high risk of sexual assault by acquaintances or boyfriends. Studies find rates ranging from a low of 15 percent for rape to 78 percent for unwanted sexual aggression. Researchers surmise that acquaintance rape is especially underreported because the victims believe that nothing can or will be done, feel unsure about how to define the occurrence, or are uncertain about whether the action qualified as abuse.

Date rape is considered a form of acquaintance rape, especially if the perpetrator and victim have not known one another for long and the abuse begins early in the relationship. In "Adolescent Dating Violence and Date Rape" (*Current Opinion in Obstetrics and Gynecology,* vol. 14, no. 5, October 2002), a review of the current research and literature about date rape, Vaughn Rickert,

TABLE 5.1

Change in marital status among married female victims who experienced a violent act by an intimate

Marital status over 6 months	Women married at the time of the earlier interview	
	Experienced intimate violence	Experienced non-intimate violence
Total	100%	100%
Still married	62	97
Divorced	8	1
Separated	30	1

Note: Percentages may not add to 100% due to rounding. Percentages exclude women who did not complete two consecutive interviews. Among married female respondents reporting having experienced a violent victimization, those who reported that an intimate had victimized them were substantially more likely to also report a change in their marital status.

SOURCE: Callie Marie Rennison, "Among married female respondents reporting having experienced a violent victimization, those who reported that an intimate had victimized them were substantially more likely to also report a change in their marital status," in *Intimate Partner Violence and Age of Victim, 1993–99,* U.S. Department of Justice, Bureau of Justice Statistics, Washington, DC, October 2001

Roger Vaughan, and Constance Wiemann observe that female teens age 16 to 19 years old and young adult women age 20 to 24 are not only 4 times as likely to be raped as women of other ages, but also that teens who have experienced rape or attempted rape during adolescence are twice as likely to experience an additional assault when they are college aged.

Rickert, Vaughan, and Wiemann also focus on high-risk subgroups of adolescents that, though less often studied, appear to experience high rates of date rape and other dating violence. They cite academically challenged teens as at high risk, with 67 percent of female students and 33 percent of male students in a high school dropout prevention program admitting to having perpetrated dating violence, including sexual abuse and rape.

Acts of Aggression

David Riggs and K. Daniel O'Leary, in their study "Aggression Between Heterosexual Dating Partners" (*Journal of Interpersonal Violence,* vol. 11, no. 4, December 1996), analyze questionnaires from 345 undergraduates and find that overall rates of aggression by men and women are quite similar. About one-third of both men and women report engaging in physical aggression in their current relationships, and nearly all have used at least one form of verbal aggression.

Men are somewhat more likely to use serious forms of aggression, while women are twice as likely to slap a partner and more than five times as likely to kick, hit, or bite. Women are more likely to engage in nearly all forms of verbal aggression. Riggs and O'Leary admit that their research does not reveal how much of the aggression reported by women was in self-defense.

The Influence of Alcohol on Sexual Assault

Alcohol reduces inhibitions and, in some cases, enhances aggression, so it is not surprising that researchers examine the link between alcohol and sexual assault. In "Alcohol and Sexual Assault in a National Sample of College Women" (*Journal of Interpersonal Violence,* vol. 14, no. 6, June 1999), Sarah E. Ullman, George Karabatsos, and Mary P. Koss examine how drinking prior to an assault influenced the severity of the attack.

The researchers administered a questionnaire to 3,187 college-age women, more than half of whom had been victims of rape, attempted rape, sexual contact, or sexual coercion. They measured the participants' alcohol use, the severity of the sexual attack, the social context in which the assault occurred, and the victims' familiarity with the offenders.

Ullman, Karabatsos, and Koss ranked the severity of the attack, the level of offender aggression, and the victims' resistance using a scale known as the Rasch Model Analysis. As expected, victims who reported getting drunk more often also reported more severe assaults than those who were drunk less often. Neither the victim's family income nor how well the victim knew the offender was related to the severity of the attack, although older women experienced more severe victimization.

The researchers also find that alcohol's role in predicting the severity of an attack did not vary according to how well the victim knew her attacker or whether a social situation, such as a party, was the setting for the assault— with one exception. Unplanned social situations were associated with more severe assaults when offenders were not drinking prior to the assault than when they were drinking. The victim's use of alcohol was related to the severity of the attack in cases where the rapist was not drinking. According to Ullman, Karabatsos, and Koss, this finding suggests that intoxicated victims may be targeted by offenders, who perceive an opportunity to engage in sex without using coercive behaviors.

As anticipated, the study finds that victims who abused alcohol or offenders and victims who used alcohol prior to the attack suffered higher rates of severe assaults. Drinking by both offenders and victims was associated with riskier, unplanned social situations in which victims did not know their assailants very well prior to the assaults. Ullman, Karabatsos, and Koss conclude that rape by known offenders who were drinking posed a greater risk when victims did not know the men very well.

The study also finds that offender drinking was related to more aggressive offender behavior and more severe victimization, suggesting that more violent assaults occurred when assailants had been drinking. Conversely, victim drinking was related to less offender aggression, possibly because force was not needed to complete the rape of intoxicated victims.

Sexual Coercion

Two studies examining the frequency of sexual coercion in dating relationships were undertaken by Lisa Waldner-Haugrud and Brian Magruder in "Male and Female Sexual Victimization in Dating Relationships: Gender Differences in Coercion Techniques and Outcomes" and Michele Poitras and Francine Lavoie in "A Study of Prevalence of Sexual Coercion in Adolescent Heterosexual Dating Relationships in a Quebec Sample" (both published in *Violence and Victims,* vol. 10, nos. 3–4, 1995).

Waldner-Haugrud and Magruder find that a "phenomenal" amount of sexual coercion was reported by 422 college students. Only 17 percent of the females and 27 percent of the males reported never experiencing any coercion. The most common coercion techniques experienced by both sexes were persistent touching and the use of alcohol and drugs. Together, these methods comprised more than half the reported incidents of coercion. Women were more likely to experience unwanted detainment, persistent touching, lies, and being held down.

Poitras and Lavoie questioned 644 adolescents between 15 and 19 years of age. The most frequently occurring unwanted sexual experiences were kissing, petting, and fondling. Verbal coercion was the most frequently used technique. Two in five girls reported sexual contact through verbal coercion, and one in five reported intercourse through verbal coercion. Approximately 1 out of 10 females reported intercourse through the use of force, alcohol, or drugs. Boys rarely reported the use of force, although 2.3 percent reported attempted penetration after giving their partners drugs or alcohol, and 2.9 percent reported intercourse as a result of verbal coercion. Poitras and Lavoie speculate that some of the differences in the reported rates of girls as the recipients of coercion and boys inflicting it may be attributed to the fact that adolescent girls frequently date older men, who may be more likely than boys to engage in coercive behaviors.

College Rape

According to *Preventing Alcohol-Related Problems on Campus: Acquaintance Rape* (Higher Education Center for Alcohol and Other Drug Prevention, Newton, MA, 1997), rape is the most common crime committed on college campuses. A 1985 survey of 6,159 students from 32 colleges found that 17 percent of the women had experienced rape or attempted rape in the past year. One out of 15 male students admitted raping or attempting to rape a female student during the year preceding the survey.

A national study of college students reported by the CDC found that 27.5 percent of women said they had suffered rape or attempted rape at least once since age 14, but just 5 percent of victims reported the incidents to the police. These numbers confirm researchers' suspicions that students frequently do not report acquaintance rapes or attempted rapes. According to the CDC, the term "hidden rape" has been used to describe this widespread finding of unreported and underreported sexual assault. Anecdotal reports from college and university administrators suggest that many female students who have been raped not only fail to report the offense, but also drop out of school.

In "Acquaintance Rape and the College Social Scene" (*Family Relations,* vol. 40, January 1991), Sally Ward et al. surveyed 518 women and 337 men at a large university. Thirty-four percent of the female respondents had experienced unwanted sexual contact, such as attempted or actual kissing, fondling, or touching; 20 percent had experienced unwanted attempted sexual intercourse; and 10 percent had unwanted intercourse, which was defined as any form of sexual penetration, including vaginal, anal, and oral. The majority of incidents were party related, and most involved alcohol, with 75 percent of the males and over half the females reporting alcohol consumption.

The majority of women reported that the men who perpetrated uninvited sexual contact or attempted intercourse simply initiated the acts without warning as did 46 percent of the men who engaged in forced intercourse. The percentage of cases involving force by men ranged from 8 percent for sexual contact to 21 percent for completed intercourse. Most of the women verbally protested, although 20 percent of victims said they were too frightened to protest. Victims most frequently chose to confide in a roommate or close friend, although 41 percent of the women told no one about the rape. Counselors were almost never told of any incidents.

The men reported a very different picture of unwanted sexual behavior on campus. Only 9 percent reported committing either unwanted sexual contact or attempted intercourse, and 3 percent admitted to incidents of unwanted sexual intercourse. Ward et al. propose that the reason for the different results is that men and women read sexual cues and form sexual expectations differently. Studies find that men are far more likely than women to interpret a woman's behavior as sexual and misconstrue it as an invitation to sexual intimacy.

Fraternities and Athletics

Fraternity members are frequently blamed as perpetrators of college rapes. Martin Schwartz and Carol Nogrady, in "Fraternity Membership, Rape Myths, and Sexual Aggression on College Campus" (*Violence Against Women,* vol. 2, no. 2, June 1996), think this characterization is false. They cite a 1993 study that alleged that men who are most likely to rape in college are frater-

nity pledges, along with an often-cited 1989 article postulating that fraternity members are more likely to have a narrow conception of masculinity, espouse group secrecy, and sexually objectify women. Schwartz and Nogrady assert that alcohol is the crucial variable, and because fraternity members are often heavy drinkers, researchers have mistakenly linked these men and sexually aggressive behavior.

Mary Koss and Hobart Cleveland, in "Athletic Participation, Fraternity Membership and Date Rape: The Question Remains—Self-Selection or Different Causal Processes?" (*Violence Against Women,* vol. 2, no. 2, June 1996), consider date rape and try to determine whether it is more likely perpetrated by athletes and fraternity members. They speculate that a fraternity-sponsored party draws acquaintances of the same social network together, while the fraternity controls the limited physical space with very little supervision. Together, these circumstances create an environment that legitimizes the actions of the members, thereby minimizing the chance of reporting as well as the credibility of women who do report sexual misconduct. Koss and Cleveland conclude that there is very low reporting of fraternity rape.

Several studies find that peer support of violence and social ties with abusive peers are predictors of abuse against women. In addition, training for violent occupations such as athletics and the military can "spill over" into personal life. Athletic training is sex-segregated, promotes hostile attitudes toward rivals, and rewards athletes for physically dominating others. Todd Crosset et al., in "Male Student-Athletes and Violence Against Women" (*Violence Against Women,* vol. 2, no. 2, June 1996), gather data from the judicial affairs offices of 10 Division I schools, which have the largest athletic programs. Although male student-athletes made up just 3 percent of the student population, they accounted for 35 percent of the reported perpetrators. It is not known whether these data are skewed because women assaulted by athletes are more likely to report attacks than women assaulted by other men on campus.

Crosset et al. contend that the special society of athletics promotes violent, woman-hating attitudes. In a July 1995 interview in *Sports Illustrated* ("Sports' Dirty Secret"), Crosset explains that it is an important aspect of male athleticism to not be considered feminine, meaning a "wimp" or a "sissy." Women are despised, degraded, and not respected. The athlete needs to "act like a man," and to be accused of acting like a woman is a grave insult.

While batterers are rarely identified in other professions, most Americans can name more than one athlete who has been charged with abuse. Among the well-known athletes charged with domestic violence are O. J. Simpson, Mike Tyson, Warren Moon, Lawrence Phillips, Darryl Strawberry, Jose Canseco, Jim Brown, and Penny Hardaway.

Alcohol on Campus

Alcohol has been implicated in most sexual assault cases on campuses. According to the Center on Addiction and Substance Abuse, in *Rethinking Rites of Passage: Substance Abuse on America's Campuses* (Columbia University, New York, 1994), 90 percent of all college rapes occur when either the victim or the rapist is under the influence of alcohol. Other studies estimate that one-third to three-quarters of all rapes and sexual assaults involve the use of alcohol by one or both parties.

Antonia Abbey et al., in "Alcohol and Dating Risk Factors for Sexual Assault Among College Women" (*Psychology of Women Quarterly,* vol. 20, 1996), conclude that having one's sexual intentions misperceived was directly related to experiencing sexual assault and that women tend to send misperceived messages when alcohol is consumed.

Researchers suggest that alcohol consumption increases the likelihood of sexual assault. In men, it appears to promote the expression of traditional gender beliefs about sexual behavior and creates expectancies associated with male sexuality and aggression, providing justification or a rationale for men to commit sexual assault. Furthermore, drinking increases the likelihood that men will misread women's friendly cues as signs of sexual interest.

For women, alcohol consumption limits the ability to correct men's misunderstanding of cues and misinterpretations. Drinking also decreases women's capacity to resist sexual assault and often prompts the victims to feel responsible for assaults.

In "Alcohol and Sexual Assault in a National Sample of College Women," Ullman, Karabatsos, and Koss polled a group of 3,187 college-age women about their own alcohol abuse, sexual victimization, sexual assault experience, and the social event surrounding their experience.

Of the 54.2 percent of women who had experienced some sexual victimization, 53.4 percent reported that their assailants were using alcohol at the time of the incident, and 42 percent reported that they themselves were using alcohol. Most of the assaults, 39.7 percent, occurred during dates with men that the women knew well or moderately well. Most assaults were committed without weapons, although 40 percent of the men used physical force. More than 90 percent of the victims said they attempted to resist the assault.

Ullman, Karabatsos, and Koss find that the victim's propensity to abuse alcohol, and the use of alcohol prior to the assault by both victim and assailant, were associated with more severe sexual victimization. The research reveals that a victim's preassault use of alcohol did not predict more severe sexual victimization, as hypothesized. Nor did alcohol's role in predicting the severity of sexual victimization vary in relationship to how well the victim knew the offender or whether a social situation was the setting for the assault. Since unplanned social situations were associated with more severe sexual victimizations when the offender was not drinking prior to the assault than when the offender was drinking, Ullman, Karabatsos, and Koss conclude that these assaults were opportunistic in nature, and therefore were not affected by offender drinking.

The researchers further speculate that victim drinking may have been related to less offender aggression, because force was not needed to complete the rape of an intoxicated victim. The study findings indicate that preassault alcohol use by victims and offenders plays direct and indirect roles in the severity of assaults, but generally the woman's drinking behavior contributes less strongly to the outcome of the attack.

Rohypnol—The "Date Rape Pill"

While alcohol abuse remains a significant problem on college campuses, other drugs, such as Rohypnol, have made resistance to attacks practically impossible. A hypnotic sedative 10 times more powerful than Valium, Rohypnol (known as "Roofies," "Roches," and "Ropies") has been used to obtain nonconsensual sex from many women. Mixed in a drink, it causes memory impairment, confusion, and drowsiness. A woman may be completely unaware of a sexual assault until she wakes up the next morning. The only way to determine if a victim has been given Rohypnol is to test for the drug within two or three days of the rape and few hospital emergency departments routinely screen for this drug. Health educators, high school guidance counselors, resident advisors at colleges, and scores of newspaper and magazine articles advise women not to accept drinks at parties or to leave drinks sitting unattended.

Although Rohypnol is legally prescribed outside of the United States for short-term treatment of severe sleep disorders, it is neither manufactured nor approved for sale in America. The importation of the drug was banned in March 1996, and the U.S. Customs Service began seizing quantities of Rohypnol at U.S. borders. In response to reported abuse, the manufacturers reformulated the drug as green tablets that can be detected in clear liquids and are visible in the bottom of a cup.

In October 1996 President Bill Clinton signed a bill amending the Controlled Substances Act to increase penalties for using drugs to disarm potential victims of violent crime. Anyone convicted of slipping a controlled substance, including Rohypnol, to an individual with intent to commit a violent act, such as rape, faces a prison term of up to 20 years and a fine as high as $2 million. The law also increases penalties for manufacturing, distributing, or possessing Rohypnol with the intent to distribute it.

Two other drugs are also used as date rape pills. Gamma hydroxybutyric acid (GHB, also known as "Liquid Ecstasy") enhances the effects of alcohol, which reduces the drinker's inhibitions. It also causes a form of amnesia. Ketamine hydrochloride (also known as "Special K") is an animal tranquilizer used to impair a person's natural resistance impulses. During 2002 anecdotal reports about another dangerous drug combination surfaced—3,4-methylenedioxymethamphetamine (known as "Ecstasy," "MDMA," or "crystal methamphetamine") and Viagra (a prescription drug used to treat erectile dysfunction)—dubbed "Sextasy." According to media reports, the drugs are taken together by male teens because Viagra offsets impotence, a potential side effect of methamphetamine use. Public health officials are alarmed by this "off-label" use of Viagra and fear that it may contribute to increased rates of STDs and sexual assault.

The Political Conflict: "One in Four"

The frequency of date rape has become a highly controversial subject. The most widely publicized rate of date rape, and the source of this dispute, is the declaration that "one in four" women are victims. This number originated in a study by Mary Koss, C. Gedycz, and N. Wisniewski.

In "The Scope of Rape: Incidence and Prevalence of Sexual Aggression and Victimization in a National Sample of Higher Education Students" (*Journal of Consulting and Clinical Psychology,* vol. 55, 1987), Koss, Gedycz, and Wisniewski interviewed more than 3,000 women nationwide about sexual violations. Among the 10 questions asked by the researchers were: "Have you had sexual intercourse when you didn't want to because a man gave you alcohol or drugs? Have you had sexual intercourse when you didn't want to because a man threatened or used some degree of physical force to make you? Have you had sexual acts (anal or oral intercourse or penetration by objects other than the penis) when you didn't want to because a man threatened or used some degree of physical force to make you?"

Koss, Gedycz, and Wisniewski determined that 15.4 percent of the women had been raped and 12.1 percent had been victims of attempted rape, making the total number of women who were victims of rape or attempted rape 27.5 percent. The women, however, saw things differently. Only 27 percent of the 15.4 percent Koss et. had labeled as "raped" agreed with that classification. Of the remainder, 49 percent said it was "miscommunication," 14 percent said it was a crime but not rape, and 11 percent said they didn't feel victimized. Furthermore, Koss, Gedycz, and Wisniewski found that 42 percent of the women they had classified as rape victims had sex again with their attackers on at least one other occasion.

Critics of this study faulted Koss, Gedycz, and Wisniewski for counting among their rape victims women who had intercourse as a result of alcohol or drugs. If a

woman passed out and her partner had intercourse with her, she had been raped, since the act was committed without her consent. But not everyone agreed that she had been raped if she had too much to drink and engaged in sex because her judgment was impaired, regardless of whether or not she regretted her actions later on.

Katie Roiphe, the author of *The Morning After: Sex, Fear and Feminism* (Back Bay, Boston, 1994), observed in an interview that date rape has become a synonym for bad sex, sex that is pressured, sex while drunk, or next-day regrets. If all these situations were called rape, she concluded, then almost everybody has been "raped" at one time or another.

If the women in Koss, Gedycz, and Wisniewski's study who did not identify themselves as raped while under the influence of drugs or alcohol were removed from the total, the rate of rape and attempted rape drops from 1 in 4 to 1 in 22 and 1 in 33, respectively.

Koss, Gedycz, and Wisniewski defended their inclusion of these women, citing the Ohio law that states, "No person shall engage in sexual conduct with another person . . . when . . . for the purpose of preventing resistance the offender substantially impairs the other person's judgment or control by administering any drug or intoxicant to the other person." But they later conceded that the question was ambiguously worded, because they omitted the portion of the statute that refers to "the situation where a person plies his intended partner with drink or drugs in hopes that the lowered inhibition might lead to a liaison."

Other critics charge that Koss, Gedycz, and Wisniewski's figures instill unnecessary fear in women and that the high rape statistics foster an image of women as helpless victims. Rather than empowering women, this portrayal belittles them. Neil Gilbert, in "Was It Rape?" (*The American Enterprise,* September–October 1994), cites the study as an example of "advocacy research" that demonizes men and characterizes common heterosexual relations as inherently violent and menacing.

Critics also claim Koss, Gedycz, and Wisniewski's data have been used in universities nationwide to institute expensive and unnecessary programs to combat rape. In 1992 Congress authorized $100 million to be used by the neediest colleges to fund rape education and prevention programs. According to statistics compiled by the *Chronicle of Higher Education,* 466 rapes and 448 sexual offenses were reported in 744 institutions in 1992. These numbers translated into slightly more than one sex offense per college. Based on these figures, Gilbert points out that the fund spent $10,000 for every reported campus rape, compared to $650 per reported rape spent in federal funds in the community at large—where most rapes occur.

Despite the firestorm of criticism that followed the widespread dissemination of the rates cited in Koss,

Gedycz, and Wisniewski's study, their research continues to be cited by credible providers of health and social policy data, including the CDC in the *Dating Violence Fact Sheet* and *Dating Violence* (National Center for Injury Prevention and Control, Atlanta, GA, 2002).

Rape Among Same-Sex Couples

Rape is not usually considered when talking about sexual abuse among gay and lesbian couples, but according to researchers it occurs at rates comparable to those in the heterosexual community.

In "Comparing Violence over the Lifespan in Samples of Same-Sex and Opposite Sex Cohabitants" (*Violence and Victims,* vol. 14, no. 4, 1999), researchers Patricia Tjaden, Nancy Thoennes, and Christine J. Allison find that cohabiting lesbians were nearly twice as likely as women living with male partners to have been forcibly raped as a minor (16.5 percent versus 8.7 percent) and nearly three times as likely to report being raped as an adult (25.3 percent versus 10.3 percent). The study also finds that 15.4 percent of cohabiting gays were raped as minors, while 10.8 percent were raped as adults. The rate of rape for heterosexual men living with female partners was insignificant.

The researchers find that cohabiting gays tended to be raped by strangers and acquaintances, while cohabiting females were raped by intimate partners. A vast majority of the rape victims, regardless of gender or sexual preference, were raped by men.

Gay and lesbian cohabitants were also significantly more likely to report being physically assaulted as a child by an adult caretaker. Among gays, 70.8 percent reported such violence, compared to 50.3 percent of heterosexual cohabitants. Among women, the figures were 59.5 percent and 37.5 percent, respectively. Gay and lesbian cohabitants also experienced higher levels of physical assault in adulthood.

The study also finds that same-sex cohabiting partners reported significantly more intimate partner violence than did cohabiting heterosexuals. About 32 percent of gay respondents said they were raped or physically assaulted by a spouse or cohabiting partner at some point in their lives, compared to just 7.7 percent of heterosexual men. Among lesbian cohabitants, 39.2 percent reported being physically assaulted by a spouse or cohabiting partner, compared to 20.3 percent of women living with male partners. Tjaden, Thoennes, and Allison note that lesbian cohabitants were also more than twice as likely to report being victimized by male intimate partners than by female intimate partners, with 30.4 percent of the lesbian cohabitants raped or physically assaulted by male intimates. Only 11.4 percent of that group said they were raped or physically assaulted by female intimate partners. The same group reported less violence by their female

partners than did heterosexual women living with males, leading the researchers to conclude that women are far more likely to be assaulted by male intimate partners than by female intimate partners.

The researchers also determine that gays and males with a history of same-sex cohabitation are significantly more likely to report histories of forcible rape as minors and adults, physical assaults as children by adult caretakers, and physical assaults as adults by all types of perpetrators, including intimate partners.

SEXUAL HARASSMENT

Guys were encouraged to get as drunk as they could, and do whatever they could to the women. If they felt like grabbing a woman by the boob or the ass, that was okay. They would use their power and authority to make you think you didn't have a job if you didn't go along.

—A former pharmaceutical company sales representative

Sexual harassment is hardly a new phenomenon. In the early days of Hollywood, it was generally accepted that many starlets auditioned for roles on the "casting couch," finding their way into films by acquiescing to the sexual demands of directors. The businessman chasing his secretary around the desk was a common theme of cartoonists. Until the 1970s, remarks laced with sexual innuendo were still considered acceptable in the workplace. But as women became more prominent in the workforce, behavior that had been condoned and even encouraged was redefined as sexual harassment.

Definitions

Sexual harassment is a form of sexual discrimination prohibited under Title VII of the Civil Rights Act of 1964. According to the U.S. Department of Justice, "[s]exual harassment has been defined as unwelcome sexual advances, requests for sexual favors, and other verbal or physical conduct that enters into employment decisions and/or conduct that unreasonably interferes with an individual's work performance or creates an intimidating, hostile, or offensive working environment."

Despite the legal definition, sexual harassment allegations remain difficult to prove and hard to refute, in part because the legal threshold varies with each case. Sexual harassment is based on the perceptions of the victim, rather than on the intent of the harasser. As a result, this form of abuse is in the eye of the beholder—one person's compliment is another person's offensive or even menacing remark.

There are two forms of harassment: quid pro quo, the Latin term meaning "this for that," and hostile-work-environment harassment.

Quid pro quo harassment occurs when an employee is pressured to choose between submitting to sexual advances or losing a job benefit, such as a promotion, raise, or the job itself. Hostile-work-environment harassment is unwelcome conduct that is so severe that it creates an intimidating or offensive work environment. For example, an employee who tells sexually explicit jokes that offend coworkers could be accused of creating a hostile work environment.

In 1986 the landmark U.S. Supreme Court case *Meritor Savings Bank v. Vinson* established the legal standard of a hostile work environment. The case originated when Michelle Vinson sued her employer, claiming her supervisor had harassed her constantly and raped her. A lower court ruled against Vinson, but the Supreme Court reversed the decision, focusing on the hostile environment clause of the law, which, the court found, "affords employees the right to work in an environment free from discriminatory intimidation, ridicule, and insult."

Cases

The Equal Employment Opportunity Commission (EEOC) is the federal agency responsible for investigating and resolving charges of sexual harassment. In 1990, 6,127 sexual harassment cases were filed with the EEOC. By 1997 that number reached its highest level, 15,889. The number dropped slightly in the following four years, to 15,618 in 1997, 15,222 in 1999, 15,836 in 2000, and 15,475 in 2001. But while the number of cases has remained about the same, the amount of money awarded to sexual harassment victims has grown steadily, from a total of $7.1 million in awards in 1990 to $53 million in 2001. Changes in the Civil Rights Act of 1991 gave women the right to jury trials, along with permission to sue for compensatory and punitive damages, opening the door for larger monetary awards. Some critics charge that the huge awards are excessive and disproportionate to the offenses.

When considering the merits of cases, courts apply a variety of tests to distinguish merely rude behavior from true instances of harassment. They ask whether the gesture, comment, or action was unwelcome and of a sexual nature. If it meets these criteria, they then examine the severity and prevalence of the behavior. Generally, the more extreme the behavior, the less frequently it has to have occurred to be deemed sexual harassment.

Some experts predicted that sexual harassment would be eliminated, or at least sharply reduced, as women became more accepted in the workplace. Instead, 1998 saw four major cases in the U.S. Supreme Court, three of which were brought under Title VII of the Civil Rights Act of 1964. These three cases clarified employer liability for sexual harassment in the workplace. The first involved Joseph Oncale, who was sexually assaulted by his coworkers and a supervisor on an oil rig off the coast of Louisiana. He filed a federal lawsuit alleging sexual harassment. Oncale lost to the lower court because he and

his harassers were male. But according to the unanimous ruling by the Supreme Court in *Oncale v. Sundowner Offshore Services,* same-sex sexual harassment constitutes legal discrimination.

In *Faragher v. City of Boca Raton,* Beth Faragher, who was employed for five years as a lifeguard for Boca Raton, Florida, alleged she endured repeated incidences of touching, sexual gestures, and sexual comments from two male bosses. Because Faragher feared retaliation, she never reported the abuse until after leaving her job, when she filed a sexual harassment suit against the city. The city responded that because it was never made aware of the events, it had no liability for the alleged actions of the supervisors. Although the city had a sexual harassment policy, it had not distributed that policy to Faragher or her department. The Supreme Court made it clear that any large employer must establish, distribute, and enforce a sexual harassment policy.

In *Burlington Industries v. Ellerth,* the court considered the case of Kimberly Ellerth, who claimed she was subjected to constant sexual harassment by a manager. Burlington Industries argued that Ellerth was not financially encumbered by the harassment and that as a result, Burlington was not liable. The Supreme Court held that an employer could be liable when a supervisor causes a hostile work environment, even when the employee suffers no tangible job consequences and the employer is unaware of the offensive conduct. The manager's numerous alleged threats were found to constitute severe or pervasive conduct.

In both the Faragher and Ellerth cases, the Supreme Court made it clear that a worker who is harassed has a duty to report it. Employers must have a sexual harassment policy that is compliant with the law, ensure that employees have effective avenues to file complaints, disseminate the policy so that all employees know about it and know how to use it, respond promptly and effectively to complaints, and enforce the policy with appropriate actions.

The fourth case, *Gebser v. Lago Vista Independent School District,* was brought under Title IX of the Education Amendments Act of 1972. It concerns a school district's liability for a teacher's sexual involvement with a 14-year-old student. Alida Gebser, a student in the Lago Vista, Texas, school district, claimed her relationship with the teacher was consensual, but she also said she was afraid to tell anyone about it, fearing she would be barred from the advanced-level courses the teacher taught. The teacher pled guilty to charges of statutory rape, and Gebser filed a civil suit against the school district. The Supreme Court ruled that a school district could not be held liable because the student had not told a supervisor, stating that a student must prove a school district acted with "deliberate indifference" to a complaint.

Sexual Harassment in the Military

Sexual harassment in the military captured the public's attention in 1991 when 83 female officers claimed they were abused at a convention of naval and marine pilots, which created an uproar that became known as the Tailhook Scandal.

In November 1996 four drill instructors and a captain at the U.S. Army's Aberdeen, Maryland, training center were charged with harassment and rape of female recruits. Within a month, more than 50 women had filed charges alleging sexual assault or rape. Sergeant Major Gene McKinney was tried on charges of coercing sexual favors from six women after they accused him of harassing or assaulting them. A month-long military trial resulted in McKinney's acquittal of all sex-related charges. He was, however, found guilty of a single count of obstructing justice and was subsequently demoted to master sergeant.

On July 7, 2000, the army inspector general confirmed charges of sexual harassment made by Lieutenant General Claudia Kennedy against Major General Larry Smith. Kennedy did not report the harassment until she learned Smith was to be selected to serve as deputy inspector general of the army, a position responsible for oversight of investigating instances of sexual harassment and directing programs to prevent and eliminate harassment. As a result of the substantiated charges, Smith did not assume the position of deputy inspector general and was issued an administrative memorandum of reprimand.

Military regulations forbid intimate relations between officers and enlisted personnel and between supervisors and their subordinates. The official army policy on sexual harassment calls for "zero tolerance" on the issue, and the edict is drilled into soldiers from their first day in the service. Nevertheless, violations continue throughout the armed services. Through the Department of Veterans Affairs, female veterans are counseled for sexual trauma. Caseloads are up sharply, from 2,090 in 1993 to more than 10,000 just nine years later.

The situation in the military is aggravated by the almost absolute power a superior has over a subordinate, especially in basic and advanced training units. From the moment recruits enter basic training, they learn that they must always obey their drill sergeants. With such absolute, unquestioned power, the drill sergeant can easily make a purposely difficult situation even worse.

Therapist and editor of *For Love of Country: Confronting Rape and Sexual Harassment in the Military* (Haworth Maltreatment and Trauma, September 2002), Teri Spahr Nelson estimates that "two-thirds of female service members experience unwanted, uninvited sexual behavior in the military. The problems of sexual harassment and sexual assault in the U.S. military are epidemic." Nelson writes that in one year alone, an estimated 9 percent

of women in the Marines, 8 percent in the Army, 6 percent in the Navy, and 4 percent in the Air Force and Coast Guard have very likely been victims of rape or attempted rape.

HARASSMENT IN THE FEDERAL WORKPLACE

In the study *Sexual Harassment in the Federal Workplace* (U.S. Merit Systems Protection Board, Washington, DC, 1995), federal workers were polled about sexual harassment in 1980, 1987, and 1994. According to these polls, rates of sexual harassment remained fairly stable over the 14-year period. In 1987, 14 percent of men and 42 percent of women reported harassment, compared to 19 percent of men and 44 percent of women in 1994. These rates included behavior that ranged from pressure for dates or sexual jokes to rape.

In the 1980 survey, 91 percent of women and 84 percent of men thought it was harassment for a supervisor to pressure for sexual favors. When a coworker pressured for sexual favors, 81 percent of women and 65 percent of men thought it was harassment. In 1994 nearly all of the respondents thought pressure for sexual favors from a supervisor was harassment, with 99 percent of the women and 97 percent of the men agreeing with this description. Of the women, 98 percent also thought it was harassment when the behavior originated with a coworker, compared to 93 percent of the men.

Some portion of the observed shift in thinking and apparent heightened awareness of these issues may be attributable to Anita Hill's 1991 appearance before the U.S. Senate during Clarence Thomas's Supreme Court confirmation hearing. Hill, who had worked as Thomas's assistant at the EEOC, alleged that Thomas had repeatedly pressured her for dates and made lurid remarks during her employment. An estimated 30 million households watched the three-day televised proceedings, which made sexual harassment one of the year's most hotly debated topics. In the year following that hearing, the EEOC recorded a 50 percent increase in sexual harassment complaints.

Different Perceptions

The Merit Systems Protection Board study reveals that men and women see harassment differently when it comes to sexual teasing, jokes, and remarks. In 1987 less than half the men, or 47 percent, thought this behavior was harassment when it was done by a coworker, compared to 64 percent of women. In 1994 these percentages rose to 64 percent for men and 77 percent for women. (See Table 5.2.) More than twice as many women as men reported experience with every form of sexual harassment, and in the 1994 survey twice as many women as men reported harassment by their supervisors. (See Table 5.3 and Table 5.4.)

This difference in perception is at the heart of a legal controversy about how to define sexual harassment.

TABLE 5.2

Is it sexual harassment?*

Type of uninvited behavior by a supervisor	Percentage of women who consider it harassment		
	1980	1987	1994
Pressure for sexual favors	91	99	99
Deliberate touching, cornering	91	95	98
Suggestive letters, calls, materials	93	90	94
Pressure for dates	77	87	91
Suggestive looks, gestures	72	81	91
Sexual teasing, jokes, remarks	62	72	83
	Percentage of men who consider it harassment		
	1980	1987	1994
Pressure for sexual favors	84	95	97
Deliberate touching, cornering	83	89	93
Suggestive letters, calls, materials	87	76	87
Pressure for dates	76	81	86
Suggestive looks, gestures	59	68	76
Sexual teasing, jokes, remarks	53	58	73

Type of uninvited behavior by a coworker	Percentage of women who consider it harassment		
	1980	1987	1994
Pressure for sexual favors	81	98	98
Deliberate touching, cornering	84	92	96
Letters, calls, other materials	87	84	92
Pressure for dates	65	76	85
Suggestive looks, gestures	64	76	88
Sexual teasing, jokes, remarks	54	64	77
	Percentage of men who consider it harassment		
	1980	1987	1994
Pressure for sexual favors	65	90	93
Deliberate touching, cornering	69	82	89
Letters, calls, other materials	76	67	81
Pressure for dates	59	66	76
Suggestive looks, gestures	47	60	70
Sexual teasing, jokes, remarks	42	47	64

*Based on the percentage of respondents who indicated that they "definitely" or "probably" would consider the identified behavior sexual harassment.

SOURCE: "Table 1. Is It Sexual Harassment?," *Sexual Harassment in the Federal Workplace: Trends, Progress, Continuing Challenges,* U.S. Merit Systems Protection Board, Washington, DC, 1995

TABLE 5.3

Forms of sexual harassment

Percentage of respondents who experienced the indicated behaviors during the preceding 2 years

	Men	Women
Sexual remarks, jokes, teasing	14	37
Sexual looks, gestures	9	29
Deliberate touching, cornering	8	24
Pressure for dates	4	13
Suggestive letters, calls, materials	4	10
Stalking	2	7
Pressure for sexual favors	2	7
Actual/attempted rape, assault	2	4

SOURCE: "Table 4. Forms of Sexual Harassment," in *Sexual Harassment in the Federal Workplace: Trends, Progress, Continuing Challenges,* U.S. Merit Systems Protection Board, Washington, DC, 1995

TABLE 5.4

Who are the harassers?

Percentage of victims sexually harassed by supervisors and others

Harasser	1980		1987		1994	
	Men	Women	Men	Women	Men	Women
Coworker or other employee	76	65	77	69	79	77
Immediate and/or higher level supervisor	14	37	19	29	14	28
Subordinate	16	4	10	2	11	3
Other or unknown*	5	6	10	10	6	7

*E.g., contractor personnel, anonymous person(s)
Note: Because some victims reported harassment from more than one source, these percentages cannot be added together to obtain aggregate percentages.

SOURCE: "Table 5. Who Are the Harassers?," in *Sexual Harassment in the Federal Workplace: Trends, Progress, Continuing Challenges,* U.S. Merit Systems Protection Board, Washington, DC, 1995

TABLE 5.5

Opinion poll regarding the amount of attention given to issue of sexual harassment in recent years

1994 Survey Item: "Too much attention has been paid to the issue of sexual harassment in the past several years."

Response	Men	Women
Agree	32	17
Disagree	43	64
Neither agree nor disagree	23	16
Don't know/can't judge	3	3

Note: Percentages have been rounded

SOURCE: "Table 2. 1994 Survey Item: Too much attention has been paid to the issue of sexual harassment in the past several years," in *Sexual Harassment in the Federal Workplace: Trends, Progress, Continuing Challenges,* U.S. Merit Systems Protection Board, Washington, DC, 1995

TABLE 5.7

How did victims react?

Percentage of victims who said they took the indicated informal action in response to sexual harassment, 1994

Ignored it/did nothing	44
Asked or told harasser to stop	35
Avoided the harasser	28
Made a joke of it	15
Reported it to a supervisor or other official	12
Threatened to tell/told others	10
Went along with the behavior	7

Note: Some respondents took more than one action.

SOURCE: "Table 7. How Did Victims React?," *Sexual Harassment in the Federal Workplace: Trends, Progress, Continuing Challenges,* U.S. Merit Systems Protection Board, Washington, DC, 1995

TABLE 5.6

What is sexual harassment's impact on victims?

Percentage of respondents who experienced sexual harassment and took or experienced the indicated action, 1987 and 1994

	1987	1994
Used sick leave	13	8
Used annual leave	12	8
Took leave without pay	2	1
Received medical and/or emotional help	2	3
Would have found medical or emotional help beneficial	12	7
Were reassigned or fired	2	2
Transferred to a new job	5	2
Quit without a new job	0.6	0.1
Suffered a decline in productivity	14	21

SOURCE: "Table 6. What Is Sexual Harassment's Impact on Victims?," in *Sexual Harassment in the Federal Workplace: Trends, Progress, Continuing Challenges,* U.S. Merit Systems Protection Board, Washington, DC, 1995

TABLE 5.8

What should targets of sexual harassment do?

Percentage of all 1994 respondents who believe the indicated action would be most effective in stopping sexual harassment

Ask or tell the person to stop	88
Report the behavior	83
File a formal complaint	66
Threaten to tell or tell others	23
Avoid the person	23
Ignore the behavior	17

Note: Respondents could choose more than one action.

SOURCE: "Table 8. What Should Targets of Sexual Harassment Do?," *Sexual Harassment in the Federal Workplace: Trends, Progress, Continuing Challenges,* U.S. Merit Systems Protection Board, Washington, DC, 1995

Normally, a court defines behavior as harassment if a "reasonable person" views the situation as harassment. Some advocates insist that harassment should be defined on a "reasonable woman" standard instead. The U.S. Court of Appeals for the 9th Circuit, in the 1991 case *Ellison v. Brady,* advocated a "reasonable woman" standard when it argued that words and actions men might consider mild harassment, women found threatening and perhaps a prelude to more serious sexual assault. The libertarian think tank the Cato Institute in Washington, D.C., disagreed, charging that this standard would have the effect of "gutting the concept of neutrality under the law."

Differences between male and female perceptions are underscored by findings in the Merit Systems Protection Board study that survey respondents disagreed about whether enough or too much attention was being paid to the issue of sexual harassment. Table 5.5 shows that nearly twice as many men felt the issue had been overemphasized, while nearly one-third more women than men disagreed with the assertion that too much attention had been paid to harassment.

The study calculates the economic impact of sexual harassment—a staggering $327.1 million in job turnover, sick leave, and lost or diminished individual and work group productivity over a two-year period during the mid-1990s. Table 5.6 shows the impact of harassment on individuals and the increased percentage of victims who reported suffering a decline in productivity.

Handling Harassment

The most frequent response to harassment was to ignore it and about 44 percent of harassment victims did just that. The reason for some of this inaction may be related to the perceived insignificance of the offense. For some, however, the harassing behavior was quite serious, and yet they did nothing. The next most common reaction to unwanted sexual attention was to ask or tell the harasser to stop. About 35 percent of harassment victims said this was the approach they used. Another 28 percent responded by avoiding the harasser. (See Table 5.7.) The survey finds that respondents felt that the most effective methods of dealing with harassment were to ask or tell the person to stop and to report the

TABLE 5.9

Why are victims of sexual harassment reluctant to take formal action?

Percentage of victims who chose the indicated reason for not taking formal action in response to unwanted sexual attention, 1994

Did not think it was serious enough	50
Other actions resolved the situation satisfactorily	40
Thought it would make my work situation unpleasant	29
Did not think anything would be done	20
Thought the situation would not be kept confidential	19
Did not want to hurt the person who had bothered me	17
Thought it would adversely affect my career	17
Was too embarrassed	11
Thought I would be blamed	9
Did not think I would be believed	8
Supervisor was not supportive	6
Did not know what actions to take or how to take them	5
Would take too much time or effort	5
Other	4

Note: Respondents could choose more than one reason.

SOURCE: "Table 11. Why Are Victims of Sexual Harassment Reluctant to Take Formal Action?," in *Sexual Harassment in the Federal Workplace: Trends, Progress, Continuing Challenges,* U.S. Merit Systems Protection Board, Washington, DC, 1995

TABLE 5.10

What do employees view as effective preventative measures for agencies to take against harassment?

Percentage of all 1994 survey respondents who believe that the indicated action would be among the most effective an organization could take

Establish and publicize policies	81
Provide training for all employees	76
Publicize penalties that can be imposed	72
Publicize complaint channels	70
Protect victims from reprisal	67
Provide training for managers and supervisor	66
Enforce strong penalties	66

Note: Respondents could choose more than one action.

SOURCE: "Table 13. What Do Employees View as Effective Preventive Measures for Agencies to Take Against Harassment?," in *Sexual Harassment in the Federal Workplace: Trends, Progress, Continuing Challenges,* U.S. Merit Systems Protection Board, Washington, DC, 1995

situation to a supervisor. (See Table 5.8.) While avoidance may be successful, it can also have a negative effect on work performance when employees spend considerable time, energy, and effort attempting to avoid their harassers.

One-quarter of victims filed grievances or adverse action appeals, 30 percent filed discrimination complaints or suits, and 42 percent requested an investigation by the employing organization. Less than 15 percent of victims requested an investigation by an outside organization, and 17 percent took other actions. Although some victims took more than one action to report and seek recourse against their harassers, others chose to take no action at all. Half of the victims who chose not to take formal action said they did not consider the offense serious enough, 40 percent felt other actions resolved the situation, and 29 percent feared that taking formal action would worsen their work situations. (See Table 5.9.)

There are sharp penalties for violating federal agency sexual harassment policies. Employees risk suspension, demotion, and even losing their jobs. Victims opting to sue the federal government for on-the-job harassment may seek as much as $300,000 in compensation for the abuse.

The strategies that survey respondents considered most effective for preventing harassment largely relied on the adequacy of communication and the organization's ability to get the word out to employees at every level. (See Table 5.10.) Interestingly, federal agencies have employed a wide range of activities to disseminate information about sexual harassment, ranging from sending copies of official policies about harassment to each employee via fact sheets to airing radio and television stories about how to combat sexual harassment.

CHAPTER 6

TREATMENT FOR MALE BATTERERS

Batterer intervention programs were established in the late 1970s when activists working with battered women realized that no real progress could be made in reducing domestic violence unless there was some way to change the behavior of the batterer. As a result, criminal justice agencies responded by referring an increasing number of batterers to intervention programs in an effort to deter further violence. Several hundred intervention and treatment programs for batterers now exist throughout the United States.

Studies of the effectiveness of male batterer treatment programs are inconclusive and many are discouraging about the programs' effectiveness. Some follow-up studies performed 4 to 24 months after batterers complete programs indicate nonviolence rates of between 53 and 85 percent. Other reports find no difference in outcomes between those attending batterer programs and control groups that did not. In assessing whether these programs work, many factors must be considered, including the type of batterer and the kind of treatment that works best. Although researchers are beginning to identify different types of abusers, they have not yet identified the treatment approach that is most effective with each group.

STANDARDS FOR BATTERER INTERVENTION PROGRAMS

Most states have developed battering intervention programs to deal with violent batterers. But state program standards differ over the type of batterers who must attend and the penalties they incur if they fail to attend. Critics contend that state-mandated standards for participation and program type produce inflexible programs that fail to take into account research demonstrating the need for different approaches to deal with different batterers.

Some critics charge that these standards were written by those who felt regulation was necessary to ensure that male batterers were held accountable. They believe such

standards focus on domestic violence as a crime that requires criminal sanctions. Mental health professionals, however, view domestic abuse as a dysfunctional disorder that is best treated with mental health treatment and therapy. Other critics feel that the standards may result in a limited treatment approach, even though research has not yet determined the effectiveness of any one program in deterring future abuse.

In "Standards for Batterer Intervention Programs: In Whose Interest?" (*Violence Against Women,* vol. 5, no. 1, 1999), Larry Bennett and Marianne Piet find that much of the conflict over program standards results from a misunderstanding about the purpose of these standards. Rather than focusing on program content and potentially preventing creation and implementation of innovative practices, they feel standards should be designed to hold men accountable for their actions, hold providers accountable for their programs, and increase the safety of the victims of domestic violence.

The Battered Women's Justice Project (State Batterers Programs, Minneapolis, MN, 1995) compares standards in 11 states and finds that almost all are in consensus when it comes to treatment options, with group treatment specified in 80 percent of the standards. There is also consensus concerning the legal duty that treatment providers have to warn victims of impending violence, ensure their safety, and conduct mandatory substance abuse assessments. There is little agreement, however, about aspects of service delivery, such as providing affordable services, using mental status exams, requiring professional credentials for program staff, or evaluating program outcomes.

A NATIONAL INSTITUTE OF JUSTICE STUDY

In *Batterer Intervention: Program Approaches and Criminal Justice Strategies* (National Institute of Justice,

Washington, DC, 1998), Kerry Healey and Christine Smith report on their study of batterer intervention programs. The study is designed to help criminal justice personnel better understand the issues surrounding batterer intervention to enable them to make appropriate referrals to programs and communicate effectively with program providers. Healey and Smith look at both "mainstream" programs and innovative approaches across the country. Although many programs are structurally similar, there is considerable diversity in terms of the theoretical approaches used to treat perpetrators of intimate partner violence.

The Feminist Model

The feminist model, which was used by early intervention programs, attributes domestic violence to social values that legitimize male control. In this view, violence is a way to maintain male dominance of the family. Feminist programs attempt to raise consciousness about sex-role conditioning and how it influences men's emotions and behavior. These programs use education and skill building to resocialize batterers and help them learn to build relationships based on trust instead of fear. Most feminist approaches also support confronting men about their misuse of power and control tactics.

Detractors of this approach claim that the feminist perspective overemphasizes sociocultural factors to the exclusion of individual factors, such as growing up abused or witnessing family violence. Some observers argue that the feminist approach is too confrontational and alienates the batterer, thereby increasing his hostility.

The Family Systems Model

The family systems model is based on the theory that violent behavior stems from dysfunctional family interactions. It focuses on cultivating communication and conflict-resolution skills within the family. According to this model, both partners may contribute to the escalation of conflict, with each attempting to dominate the other. Either partner may resort to violence, although the male's violence will likely have greater consequences. From this perspective, interactions produce violence; therefore, no one is considered to be a perpetrator or victim.

Critics of the family systems model do not think that the majority of partner abuse involves shared responsibility. They believe batterers bear full responsibility for the violence. Many also fear that counseling of the couple may place the victim at risk if the woman expresses complaints during a counseling session. In fact, couples counseling is expressly prohibited in 20 state standards.

Psychological Approaches

The psychological perspective views abuse as a symptom of underlying emotional problems. This approach emphasizes therapy and counseling to uncover and resolve a batterer's subconscious problems. Proponents of this approach believe that other interventions are superficial and only suppress violence temporarily. Critics argue that attaching psychiatric labels to batterers provides them with an excuse for their behavior.

Another psychological approach is cognitive-behavioral group therapy. This therapy is intended to help individuals function better by changing how they think and act. According to the theory underlying this approach, behaviors are learned as a result of positive and negative reinforcements, and interventions should focus on changing thought patterns and building skills. Feminist proponents criticize this approach, however, saying it fails to explain why batterers are not violent in other relationships and why some men continue to abuse women even when their behavior is not rewarded.

Investigators use the psychological model to study battering behavior. In "Neuropsychological Correlates of Domestic Violence" (*Violence and Victims,* vol. 14, no. 4, Winter 1999), researchers Ronald A. Cohen et al. studied the neurological functioning of 39 male abusers and 63 nonviolent subjects to determine whether there was any relationship between neurological functioning and domestic abuse. They divided the groups into those who suffered from head injuries and those who did not, and measured both groups for general intelligence and neurological functioning. The subjects were tested to assess their marital satisfaction, using the Locke-Wallace Short Marital Adjustment Test, and their current level of emotional distress, using the Symptom Checklist-90 Revised. The subjects were also tested to diagnose antisocial personality disorders, using the Structured Clinical Interview.

Cohen et al. find that the batterers had less formal education than the nonbatterers but that neither group differed in the amount of alcohol they consumed, nor in the number of times they used illegal drugs. The batterers did, however, have past problems with aggression while under the influence of alcohol.

The study also reveals a higher incidence of head injury among batterers, with 46.2 percent of that group reporting head injuries, compared to 20.6 percent of nonbatterers. In addition, batterers had a higher incidence of prior academic problems.

Cohen et al. conclude that there is a strong relationship between neurological functioning and domestic violence. Batterers with head injuries also show a higher level of frontal lobe dysfunction, which is among the clinical variables most strongly associated with violence and aggressive behavior.

Emotional distress is also strongly associated with battering. This finding is not surprising, the researchers assert, given the relationship between emotional distress, marital discord, and the propensity for intimate partner violence.

Cohen et al. conclude that brain dysfunction may contribute to the propensity for violence and other aggressive behaviors, however, they caution that while dysfunction contributes to the propensity for domestic violence among some batterers, it is not involved in all cases of domestic violence, nor does it explain all types of aggression. Nonetheless, they believe that the relationship between brain dysfunction and domestic violence has significance for planning preventive and therapeutic interventions for some batterers. By identifying cognitive defects, patients with a propensity for aggression may be taught behavioral and cognitive strategies to inhibit aggressive behaviors. The results of this research also indicate the need to investigate the efficacy of biological and pharmacological (prescription drug) treatment of domestic violence.

Content of Batterer Intervention Programs

Among the batterer programs Healy and Smith study, most combine elements of different theoretical models. Of the three mainstream programs they review, the Duluth Curriculum uses a classroom format and focuses on issues of power and control. The development of critical thinking skills is emphasized to help batterers understand and change their behavior. In contrast, the other two mainstream models, EMERGE and AMEND, involve more in-depth counseling and are of longer duration.

THE DULUTH CURRICULUM. The Duluth model was developed in the early 1980s by the Domestic Abuse Intervention Project of Duluth, Minnesota. The classroom curriculum focuses on the development of critical thinking skills relating to the themes of nonviolence, nonthreatening behavior, respect, support, trust, honesty, partnership, negotiation, and fairness. Two or three sessions are devoted to exploring each theme. For example, the first session begins with a video demonstration of specific controlling behaviors. The video is followed by discussion of the actions used by the batterer in the video. Each participant contributes by describing his particular use of the controlling behavior. The group then identifies and discusses alternative behaviors that can build healthier, more equal relationships.

EMERGE. EMERGE, a 48-week batterer intervention program in Cambridge, Massachusetts, begins with 8 weeks of educational and skill-building sessions. Program members who complete this phase and admit to domestic violence then progress to an ongoing group that blends cognitive behavioral techniques with group therapy centered on personal accountability.

In the group, new members describe the events and actions that brought them to the program, answer questions about their behavior, and accept responsibility for their violence. Regular group members also talk about their actions during the previous week. There may also be discussion of particular incidents disclosed by members of the group.

EMERGE focuses not only on the abusive behavior, but also on the broader relationship between the batterer and the victim. Each member formulates goals related to his control tactics, and the group helps him develop ways to address these concerns.

AMEND. The professionals who created AMEND, a program in Denver, Colorado, share the same commitment to long-term treatment as the founders of EMERGE. The purpose of AMEND is to establish client accountability, increase awareness of the social context of battering, and build new social skills. AMEND group leaders serve as "moral guides" who take a firm position against violence and vigorously describe their clients' behavior as unacceptable and illegal.

The program's long-term approach has four stages. The first two stages consist of several months of education and confrontation to break through the batterer's denial and resistance. Several months of advanced group therapy follow during which the batterer identifies his own rationalizations for abusive behavior and admits the truth about his actions. This stage includes ongoing contact with the partner, who can reveal relapses or more subtle forms of abuse. During this stage, the client develops a plan that includes participation in a support network to prevent future violence. The fourth stage, which is optional, consists of involvement in community service and political action to stop domestic violence.

OTHER APPROACHES. Most observers conclude that a single intervention program cannot accommodate the staggering diversity of batterers. Unlike mainstream programs, innovative approaches focus on the individual profile and characteristics of a batterer and some programs tailor their interventions to the various categories of batterers.

The criminal justice system, for example, categorizes offenders based on their potential danger, history of substance abuse, psychological problems, and risk of dropout and rearrest. Interventions focus on the specific type of batterer and the approach that will most effectively produce results, such as linking a substance abuse treatment program with a batterer intervention program. Other program approaches focus on specific sociocultural characteristics, such as poverty, race, ethnicity, and age.

One such program, currently in use in Somerset, New Jersey, is based on the Cultural Context Model (CCM), an intervention method that acknowledges a cultural basis for battering among some ethnic groups. While this treatment model requires accountability from batterers and supports the empowerment of abused spouses and their children, it also recognizes the impact that social forces have in cultures where battering is considered acceptable.

Rhea V. Ameida and Ken Dolan-Delvecchio contend that the impact of culture is often overlooked or minimized by people who work with batterers in traditional treatment programs. In "Addressing Culture in Batterers Intervention: The Asian Indian Community As an Illustrative Answer" (*Violence Against Women,* vol. 5, no. 6, June 1999), Ameida and Dolan-Delvecchio suggest that if program workers are trained in cultural differences, they will be better able to serve the needs of both the abuser and his family. The CCM works by providing treatment not only to the batterer, but also to the victims of abuse, generally in a family therapy atmosphere.

As part of their therapy, participants are shown videos that illustrate abusive situations and are encouraged to talk about the video incidents and their own instances of abuse. The participants then study power and control wheel illustrations, which give them graphic, visual perspectives about how a variety of factors interact to create abusive situations. Figure 6.1 is a version of this graphic tool that has been customized to address issues specific to members of racial and ethnic minority groups.

The treatment model attempts to reeducate the abused and abuser by raising their consciousness about gender, race, culture, and sexual orientation. One desired outcome of this therapy, Ameida and Dolan-Delvecchio explain, is to make participants more aware of the social impact of their actions.

Which Treatment Settings Are Effective?

In the study "The San Diego Navy Experiment: An Assessment of Interventions for Men Who Assault Their Wives" (*Journal of Consulting and Clinical Psychology,* vol. 68, no. 3, June 2000), Franklyn W. Dunford compares three different yearlong interventions for men who had physically assaulted their wives. The study involved randomly assigning 861 couples to 1 of 4 groups: a men's group, a conjoint group (men and women), a rigorously monitored group, and a control group. The men's and conjoint groups received cognitive-behavioral therapy and outcomes were measured every six months using several reliable measures.

The men's group met weekly for six months, and then monthly for the second six months. Group leaders covered a wide range of perpetrator attitudes and values and taught skills believed to be important to ending the abuse of women, such as enhancing empathy and communication, as well as managing anger and jealousy. Along with instruction, participants practiced their newly acquired skills and developed plans to assume complete responsibility for their behavior.

Using the same curriculum used by the men's group, the conjoint group, composed of victims and perpetrators, was a controversial treatment approach since most conventional programs do not believe it is useful or effective to treat victims and their abusers together. But the navy was interested in finding out if couple therapy would be effective and anticipated some benefits from the presence of the wives, such as less "women bashing" and more realistic opportunities to engage participants in role-playing to help them practice more constructive behaviors.

The rigorous monitoring intervention aimed to inhibit abuse by making service members' commanding officers aware of every instance of abuse. By closely monitoring and reporting their behavior, this approach attempted to increase scrutiny of the perpetrators' life, creating a situation Dunford calls a "fishbowl" effect.

Men assigned to the control group received no treatment; however, to ensure their wives' safety, the wives were given preliminary stabilization and safety planning counseling to help prevent additional instances of abuse.

The results of the interventions were measured using demographic variables—age, rank, family size, ethnicity, education, and income—and outcome assessments. Outcomes were evaluated using self-reports and spouse reports, and the Modified Conflict Tactics Scale (MCTS), which looked at 42 items relating to the type and frequency of abuse. Official police and court records, as well as reports of new injuries, were also considered outcome measures.

The study finds no significant differences in the prevalence or frequency of abuse, as reported by the wives or their spouses, between the treatment groups. This finding suggests that none of the three treatment approaches was any more effective at reducing abuse than participation in the control group.

No significant differences are found among the four groups in MCTS scores and the differences that appear are attributed to a few extreme scores, rather than a statistically significant variation. The study also finds no differences in terms of new arrests among the perpetrators in all four groups.

Dunford concludes that the cognitive-behavioral model is ineffective as an intervention for spouse abuse, at least in this military setting. He calls for further research to confirm his study's findings and hypothesizes that the one-size-fits-all approach to treatment may be responsible for the ineffectiveness of treatment.

Program Procedures

Regardless of an intervention program's philosophy or methods, program directors and criminal justice professionals generally monitor the offenders' behavior closely. Most batterers enter intervention programs after having been charged by the police with a specific incident of abuse. As a requirement of probation, most courts will order a batterer into an intervention program.

At the court, the batterer is first interviewed to determine the type of program that may be most effective.

FIGURE 6.1

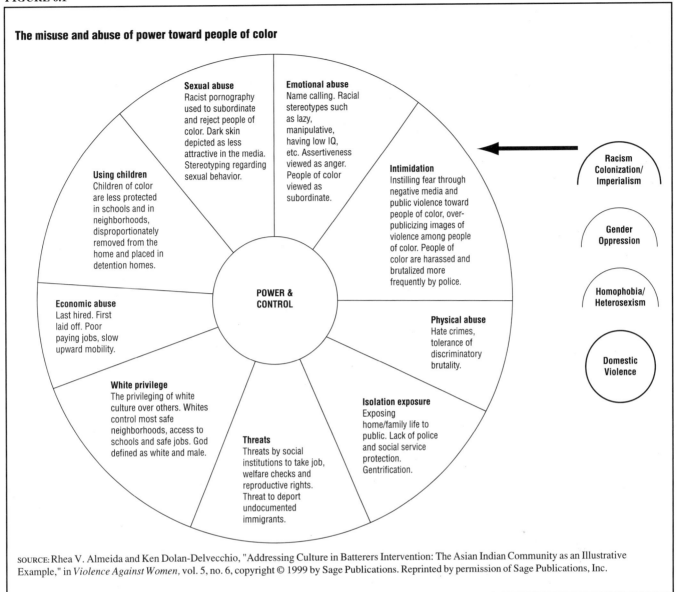

The misuse and abuse of power toward people of color

Sexual abuse
Racist pornography used to subordinate and reject people of color. Dark skin depicted as less attractive in the media. Stereotyping regarding sexual behavior.

Emotional abuse
Name calling. Racial stereotypes such as lazy, manipulative, having low IQ, etc. Assertiveness viewed as anger. People of color viewed as subordinate.

Using children
Children of color are less protected in schools and in neighborhoods, disproportionately removed from the home and placed in detention homes.

Intimidation
Instilling fear through negative media and public violence toward people of color, over-publicizing images of violence among people of color. People of color are harassed and brutalized more frequently by police.

Economic abuse
Last hired. First laid off. Poor paying jobs, slow upward mobility.

POWER & CONTROL

Physical abuse
Hate crimes, tolerance of discriminatory brutality.

White privilege
The privileging of white culture over others. Whites control most safe neighborhoods, access to schools and safe jobs. God defined as white and male.

Threats
Threats by social institutions to take job, welfare checks and reproductive rights. Threat to deport undocumented immigrants.

Isolation exposure
Exposing home/family life to public. Lack of police and social service protection. Gentrification.

Racism Colonization/ Imperialism

Gender Oppression

Homophobia/ Heterosexism

Domestic Violence

SOURCE: Rhea V. Almeida and Ken Dolan-Delvecchio, "Addressing Culture in Batterers Intervention: The Asian Indian Community as an Illustrative Example," in *Violence Against Women,* vol. 5, no. 6, copyright © 1999 by Sage Publications. Reprinted by permission of Sage Publications, Inc.

Known as an "intake assessment," this process that may take as long as eight weeks. During this time, the batterer agrees to the terms of the program, his behavior is assessed, and he is screened for other problems, such as substance abuse or mental illness. If other problems are detected, he may be referred to a program or treatment that specifically addresses those issues. Not all batterers are accepted at intake. Some programs consider batterers inappropriate for treatment if they deny having committed violence.

Several states require that the victim be notified at various points of the intervention, and programs with a strong advocacy policy make victim contact every two or three months. Victims may be asked for additional information about the relationship, given information about the program's goals and methods, and helped with safety planning. In addition, the batterer's counselor will inform the victim if further abuse appears imminent.

Batterers leave the program either because of successful completion or because they are asked to leave. Reasons for termination include failure to cooperate, nonpayment of fees, revocation of parole or probation, failure to attend group sessions regularly, or violation of program rules.

Successful completion of a program means that the offender has attended the required sessions and accomplished the program's objectives. With court-mandated clients, a final report also is made to probation officials.

The Criminal Justice Response

To be successful, batterer intervention programs must have the support of the criminal justice system, which includes coordinated efforts between police, prosecutors, judges, victim advocates, and probation officers. Healey and Smith suggest that authorities can reinforce the message that battering is a crime and further support the efforts of batterer programs by taking the following steps:

- Expedite domestic violence cases though the court system

- Use special domestic violence prosecution and probation units and centralize dockets where all aspects of domestic violence may be managed in one location in order to improve services to victims and better coordinate prosecution, sentencing, and supervision

- Gather offender information quickly, including previous arrests and convictions, substance abuse history, child welfare contacts, and victim information

- Take advantage of culturally competent or specialized interventions and find appropriate interventions for batterers who are indigent, high-risk, or mentally ill

- Coordinate batterer intervention with substance abuse treatment and mandate treatment where appropriate, making sure it is monitored intensively

- Be alert to the risks to children in abusive households by coordinating with child protective services to ensure that the batterer's children are safe and receiving appropriate services

- Create a continuum of support and protection for victims by using victim advocates to assist victims with the criminal justice system and to monitor their safety while their batterers are sentenced to treatment programs

- Encourage interagency cooperation by organizing formal committees of probation officers, prosecutors, battered women advocates, child protection workers, and batterer intervention providers to discuss referral and monitoring policies

THE ABUSER WHO SEES HIS WIFE AS AN OBJECT

Violence does not always mean physical assault. David Adams, the president and cofounder of EMERGE, considers battering any act that forces the victim to do something she does not want to do, prevents her from doing something she wants to do, or causes her to be afraid.

Violence is not a series of isolated blowups. It is a process of deliberate intimidation intended to coerce the victim to comply with the victimizer's wishes. According to Adams, the abuser's level of control can be seen in how agreeable he can be with police, bosses, neighbors, and others with whom it is in his best interest to appear reasonable.

Even when abusive men are supposed to be working on their relationships, EMERGE counselors have observed that the men devalue and denigrate their partners. Ellen Pence of Duluth notices that men rarely call the women they abuse by name, because they refuse to see them as people in their own right. In one group session,

she counted 97 references to women, many of them obscene, before someone used his partner's name. When Pence insisted program participants use the names of their partners, she reported that many could hardly speak.

PTSD AND SHAME

Donald Dutton, a psychology professor and author of *The Batterer: A Psychological Profile* (Basic, New York, 1995), finds that many of his clients suffer the same symptoms manifested in posttraumatic stress disorder (PTSD), a psychological response to extreme trauma. These symptoms include depression, anxiety, sleep disturbances, disassociation, flashbacks, and out-of-body experiences. Dutton's batterers had psychological profiles surprisingly similar to Vietnam War veterans who had been diagnosed with PTSD. Abusers are rarely seen as victims, yet their psychological profiles reveal they suffer the same trauma. Dutton feels that the batterers' chronic anger and abusiveness point to a common source of early childhood trauma.

Researching his clients' childhood experiences, Dutton determines that the crucial factor in abusive behavior is the shame the men suffered as children. Shame, Dutton feels, is an emotional response to an attack on the global sense of self. Dutton finds that the men had experienced a childhood characterized by humiliation, embarrassment, and shame. Through his research, he discovers that physical abuse alone did not predict abusive behavior but that the combination of shame and abuse was a dangerous mix.

According to Dutton, shame attacks his entire identity and teaches the child that he is worthless. Punishing a child at random also poses a serious attack on his identity. Because the punishment does not relate to a particular behavior, it tells the child that his very being is wrong and unlovable. The child has no outlet for his rage and shame until he enters an intimate relationship. When his bravado—the "tough guy" mask—risks being uncovered by his girlfriend or wife, he responds with rage. The shame of his rage is too great to bear, so he blames the woman and the destructive pattern is established.

Dutton lists the early childhood experiences he believes make the strongest contributions to predicting wife assault in order of importance: feeling rejected by one's father, a lack of warmth from one's father, physical abuse from one's father, verbal abuse by one's father, and feeling rejected by one's mother.

ABUSER TYPES

Daniel G. Saunders, in "A Typology of Men Who Batter: Three Types Derived from Cluster Analysis" (*American Journal of Orthopsychiatry,* vol. 62, no. 2, 1992), surveys 165 abusive men, using such psychological measures as childhood victimization, severity of violence, psychological abuse, domestic decision making, level of conflict, anger, jealousy, depression, the ability to make a good impression on others, and alcohol use. His pioneering work defines three types of batterers:

- Type I men are characterized as "family-only" aggressors. These men report low levels of anger, depression, and jealousy, and are the least likely to have been severely abused as children. They claim the most satisfaction in their relationships, the least marital conflict, and the least psychological abuse. Their violence is associated with alcohol about half the time. Members of this group suppress their anger until alcohol or stress triggers its release.

- Type II men are "generally violent" and are the most likely to be violent inside and outside the home. The majority have been severely abused as children, yet they report low levels of depression and anger. Their lower anger may reflect an attitude of "I don't get mad, I get even." Their violence is usually associated with alcohol, and they report the most frequent severe violence. Their attitudes about sex roles are more rigid than those of Type I men.

- Type III men report the highest levels of anger, depression, and jealousy. They are characterized as "emotionally volatile" aggressors. They are most likely to fear losing their partners and feel suicidal and angry. These men are not as physically aggressive as Type II men, but they are the most psychologically abusive and the least satisfied with their relationships. They also have the most rigid sex-role attitudes. About half of these men have previously received counseling and are thought to be the most likely to complete treatment.

Based on these three categories of batterers, Saunders proposes different types of counseling that would be most effective for each type. The family-only aggressor, Type I, might gain the most from an emphasis on the communication aspects of assertiveness training. He needs to learn how to express anger and understand his rights. He may be helped by couples counseling if his past violence level is low enough and if he remains nonviolent and committed to the relationship.

The Type II man may need help dealing with the psychic wounds of his childhood, stopping his abuse of alcohol, and learning how to express his feelings rather than by exploding. He also needs to recognize that his rigid sex-role notions are harmful. Saunders proposes that this type of abuser will probably require more than the standard three- to six-month treatment program.

The emotionally volatile man, Type III, must learn to express his feelings in nonaggressive ways and to accept his "weaker" feelings of jealousy and depression rather than express them through anger. He also needs to understand the damage caused by his psychological abuse and rigid sex-role beliefs.

Antisocial Men

John Gottman and Neil Jacobson, in "The Relationship Between Heart Rate Reactivity, Emotionally Aggressive Behavior and General Violence in Batterers" (*Journal of Family Psychology,* vol. 9, 1995), completed the first laboratory study of couples in which wife battering is common. Gottman and Jacobson are among the first to observe and report that many of the most vicious husbands become physiologically calmer when they argue with their wives. As their anger mounts, their heart rates drop and their attention sharpens, making their violence an act of calculated terrorism designed to control their wives through fear. These "antisocial" men are about 15 times more likely than other abusive husbands to be violent outside their marriage.

Gottman and Jacobson define two types of violent husbands.

Type I:

- Heart rate drops as the argument proceeds, making the violence more deliberate

- In arguments, abusers are highly belligerent, insulting, and threatening

- They use a general strategy of controlling their wives by instilling fear

- Forty-four percent are violent toward family members and others

- Fifty-six percent had fathers who abused their mothers

- None of the men in the study were divorced

Type II:

- Heart rate climbs as they become angrier, making their violence more impulsive

- In arguments, they are less emotionally abusive

- They fear abandonment or rejection or feel jealous

- Only 3 percent are violent outside the marriage

- Thirteen percent had fathers who abused their mothers

- Twenty-eight percent of the men in the study were divorced or separated

During the course of the two-year study, none of the wives of these most abusive men left their husbands. Gottman and Jacobson theorize that some of the women married to Type I men were genuinely afraid to leave them. Type I men may be successful in inhibiting their wives' anger, an emotion that presumably might give the wives the impetus to leave. Support for this hypothesis comes from the observation that the wives of Type I men showed remarkably low levels of anger during arguments.

On the other hand, a significant proportion of women married to Type I men are themselves antisocial and may be more habituated to violent relationships than other women. Gottman and Jacobson do not think that any form of marital therapy or counseling could help these couples.

PROGRAM DROPOUT RATES

Dropout rates in battering programs are high, even though most clients have been ordered to attend by the courts. Several studies indicate that 20 to 30 percent of the men who begin short-term treatment programs do not complete them. A 1990 survey of 30 programs of differing lengths finds a wide range in completion rates. Half of the programs reported completion rates of 50 percent or less. If dropout rates are based on attendance at the intake session, rather than the first treatment session, noncompletion rates are even higher. A 1999 study that documents the dropout rate after the initial assessment finds that 59 percent of those who completed the initial assessment never attended a single session and that 75 percent dropped out before the 10-week program was over.

High dropout rates in batterer intervention programs make it difficult to evaluate their success. Evaluations based on men who complete these programs focus on a very select group of highly motivated men who likely do not reflect the composition of the group when it began. Since a follow-up is not conducted with program dropouts, the men most likely to continue their violence, research generally fails to accurately indicate the success or failure of a given treatment program.

Certain characteristics are generally related to dropout rates. Unemployment is the one characteristic most consistently related to dropping out of treatment. Other factors include youth, not being legally married, low income and little education, unstable work histories, criminal backgrounds, and excessive drinking. Voluntary clients, especially those with college educations, remain in treatment longer. Some researchers find better attendance among college-educated men, regardless of whether their enrollment in a program is court ordered or voluntary.

Dropout rates are high, in part, because the courts rarely impose penalties for noncompliance. One researcher reports that 45 percent of surveyed programs indicated that the courts' failure to penalize those who did not attend was a problem. In addition, many court-ordered participants resisted the counseling and dropped out because they saw it as a form of punishment.

Nearly all professionals involved in domestic violence prevention and treatment programs concur that batterer intervention programs must address the issue of dropouts. Reducing or eliminating intake sessions and immediately engaging batterers in useful interventions may help to promote attendance and participation by immediately engaging participants in the treatment program. Counselors should provide more information about the purpose of the program and the preprogram orientation sessions. Other suggested retention measures include courtroom assistance, mentors, and stiffer and quicker punishment for dropouts. One study finds that home visits after a batterer misses a meeting also help decrease dropout rates.

RECIDIVISM RATES

Recidivism, the tendency to relapse to old ingrained patterns of behavior, is a well-documented problem among persons in intimate partner violence treatment programs. In "Pattern of Reassault in Batterer Programs" (*Violence and Victims,* vol. 12, no. 4, 1997), Edward Gondolf reports his evaluation of four well-established batterer programs to assess the pattern of reassault or a return to battering. All the research sites had operated for five years or more and received at least 40 to 50 referrals per month. Located in Pittsburgh, Pennsylvania, Dallas and Houston, Texas, and Denver, Colorado, the programs' lengths ranged from three to nine months.

At each site, 840 batterers, 210 per site, were recruited and tested during program intake. Of the 840 batterers, 82 percent were referred to the program by court order, and 18 percent entered the program voluntarily. Both batterers and their partners were interviewed by phone every 3 months for 15 months after intake. The female partners of 79 percent of the batterers were interviewed at least once during the 15-month follow-up.

In follow-up reports on 662 batterers, 32 percent of the female partners reported at least one reassault during the 15 months. Of the 210 reassault cases, 61 percent resulted in bruises or injuries, and 12 percent of victims required medical attention. Not surprisingly, the reassault rate was significantly higher for program dropouts than for participants who completed the program. Voluntary participants were also more likely to reassault their partners than court-ordered participants.

While the proportion of women who were reassaulted was relatively low, 70 percent of the women were subjected to verbal abuse, 45 percent were subjected to controlling behaviors, and 43 percent experienced threats. Nonetheless, 66 percent of the women said their "quality of life" improved, and 73 percent reported feeling "very safe" during the follow-up periods.

Fourteen percent of first-time reassaults occurred in the first three months of the program, and 8 percent occurred within six months. Early reassault appeared to be a high-risk marker for continued abuse. Men who reassaulted their partners within the first three months were much more likely to repeat their attacks than were men who reassaulted for the first time after the first three months. The repeat offenders were also highly likely to use severe tactics and inflict injuries. Gondolf speculates that intervention may have been less effective for this group of men because of previous contact with the criminal justice system and/or severe psychological disorders.

Gondolf feels that the rate of those who stopped their violence after participating in batterer programs was noteworthy, considering their previous histories and psychological problems. He concludes that well-established programs seem to contribute to the cessation of assault, at least in the short term. For "resistant batterers," he encourages more extensive monitoring and intervention.

Other Studies

Saunders, in "Husbands Who Assault: Multiple Profiles Requiring Multiple Responses" (*Legal Response to Wife Assault,* Sage, Newbury Park, CA, 1993), reviews the available information on male batterers and finds that the recurrence of violence six months or more after treatment averages 35 percent across a number of studies. For men who do not complete treatment, the average is 52 percent. The men most likely to return to violence are on average, younger, report alcohol problems, score higher for narcissism (excessive self-involvement) on psychological tests, and have longer histories of pretreatment violence.

Julia C. Babcock and Ramalina Steiner report some cautiously optimistic findings in "The Relationship Between Treatment, Incarceration, and Recidivism of Battering: A Program Evaluation of Seattle's Coordinated Community Response to Domestic Violence" (*Journal of Family Psychology,* vol. 13, no. 1, March 1999). Their research measured recidivism of domestic violence after arrest and mandatory completion, or noncompletion, of a coordinated program of treatment involving the courts, probation officers, and treatment providers.

Babcock and Steiner followed 387 people arrested for misdemeanor domestic violence offences, 31 of whom were women. More than three-quarters of participants had no prior domestic violence convictions and 69 percent had no prior criminal history. The average age of participants was 32.7 years, 45 percent had graduated from high school, and 36 percent had attended college or were college graduates. About 41 percent of participants were white, 36 percent were African American, 6.6 percent were Hispanic, 8.6 percent were Asian American, and 7.8 percent identified themselves as "other." Half of the participants were employed and 31 percent were married.

Participants were referred to 1 of 11 certified domestic violence treatment programs. The majority attended programs that use the Duluth model, while the remainder participated in feminist, psychoeducational, and cognitive-behavioral men's groups. About 31 percent completed at least 24 sessions of treatment, and those considered to have completed treatment attended an average of 32 sessions. In contrast, those who did not complete treatment attended an average of just 5.8 sessions. Treatment completers were generally first-time offenders, better educated, employed, and had less prior criminal involvement. Of the noncompleters, 58 percent did not attend any sessions,

but the majority were not legally punished, despite their failure to attend court-ordered treatment.

Program completion was related to lower rates of recidivism—treatment completers had significantly fewer domestic violence arrests at follow-up than noncompleters, and this difference remained even when the researchers controlled for differences in prior criminal record and history. Batterers who had been court ordered to attend treatment and failed to complete it were more likely to commit further offenses than treatment completers. Babcock and Steiner conclude that their findings support the premise that completing treatment is directly related to reduced rates of domestic violence, thereby necessitating police involvement. They caution, however, that participants who completed treatment were probably not representative of the entire population of batterers—they likely had more to lose as a result of failure to complete treatment than the treatment dropouts.

SIMILARITIES BETWEEN BATTERERS AND ALCOHOLICS

Adams observes that the men he treats typically deny their violence. Like substance abusers, batterers compare themselves to the worst-case abuser, the man who is severely abusive on a daily basis, and conclude that since they are not that bad, they do not really have a problem. EMERGE also finds that men will lie outright about the violence or minimize or rationalize it, calling choking or punching self-defense.

Adams, in "Identifying the Assaultive Husband in Court: You Be the Judge" (*Response to the Victimization of Women and Children,* vol. 13, no. 1, 1990), finds similarities between the alcoholic and the abuser:

- Perhaps the most common manipulation pattern of the abusive man is to project blame for his violence onto his wife. In treatment programs for abusers, statements like "she drove me to it," "she provoked me," and "she really knows how to push my buttons" are common. Statements like these reveal the abuser's attempts to divert attention away from his behavior and choices. During the early stages of treatment, abusers resist self-criticism by projecting responsibility for their violence onto others. This is similar to the alcoholic's tendency to blame other people, events, and circumstances for his drinking. The abusive husband, like the alcoholic, presents himself in treatment as a victim.

- Fifty percent of EMERGE clients drop out of treatment within the first month, a figure similar to that of other programs. This is attributed to a "quick-fix" mentality on the part of the batterer—not unlike the attitude many alcoholics bring to treatment. Their desire to restore the status quo overrides their desire to change.

CHAPTER 7

THE RESPONSE OF LAW ENFORCEMENT
TO VIOLENCE AND ABUSE

THE POLICE RESPONSE

According to the 2000 National Crime Victimization Survey (NCVS), the police came to the aid of victims for about three-quarters of all violent crimes. In about two-thirds of incidents of rape and sexual assault, police came to victims and 12.4 percent of victims went to police. Table 7.1 shows that police came to the aid of more victims of aggravated assault, simple assault, and robbery than victims of rape and sexual assault.

The police are often the victim's initial contact with the judicial system, making the police response particularly important. The manner in which the police handle a domestic violence complaint will likely color the way the victim views the entire judicial system. Not surprisingly, when police project the blame for intimate partner violence on victims, the victims may be reluctant to report further abuse.

Family disturbance calls constitute the majority of calls received by police departments throughout the country. In the mid-1960s, Detroit police dispatchers were instructed to screen out family disturbance calls unless they suspected "excessive" violence. A 1975 police guide, *The Function of the Police in Crisis Intervention and Conflict Management*, taught officers to avoid arrest at all costs and to discourage the victim from pressing charges by emphasizing the consequences of testifying in court, the potential loss of income, and other detrimental aspects of prosecution.

Arrest policies have changed significantly in the past 25 years. By 2002 all but one state (West Virginia) had moved to authorize probable cause arrests—arrest before the completion of the investigation of the alleged violation or crime—without a warrant in domestic violence cases. Police departments have adopted proarrest or

TABLE 7.1

Percent distribution of police response to a reported incident, by type of crime, 2000

Type of crime	Number of incidents	Percent of incidents						
		Total	Police came to victim	Victim went to police	Contact with police-don't know how	Police did not come	Not known if police came	Police were at the scene
Crimes of violence	**2,577,300**	**100 %**	**76.4 %**	**7.0%**	**0.1 %***	**10.8 %**	**1.4%**	**4.4%**
Rape/Sexual assault[1]	118,880	100	63.2	12.4 *	0.0 *	22.0	2.4 *	0.0 *
Robbery	369,490	100	80.5	4.8 *	0.0 *	7.8	4.3 *	2.7 *
Aggravated assault	568,510	100	78.0	7.3	0.1 *	11.6	1.3 *	1.7 *
Simple assault	1,520,420	100	75.9	7.0	0.0 *	10.3	0.7 *	6.1
Purse snatching/Pocket picking	95,860	100	49.5	16.8 *	0.0 *	33.6	0.0 *	0.0 *
Property crimes	**6,731,790**	**100 %**	**65.5 %**	**7.4%**	**0.0 %***	**23.7 %**	**1.9%**	**1.5%**
Household burglary	1,706,960	100	82.5	3.8	0.0 *	11.6	1.3 *	0.8 *
Motor vehicle theft	719,820	100	73.0	4.3	0.0 *	18.9	2.1 *	1.7 *
Theft	4,305,020	100	57.5	9.3	0.0 *	29.3	2.0	1.7

Note: Detail may not add to total shown because of rounding.
*Estimate is based on about 10 or fewer sample cases.
[1]Includes verbal threats of rape and threats of sexual assault.

SOURCE: "Table 106. Percent distribution of police response to a reported incident, by type of crime," in *Criminal Victimization in the United States, 2000 Statistical Tables*, U.S. Department of Justice, Bureau of Justice Statistics, National Crime Victimization Survey, Washington, DC, August 2002 mandatory arrest policies. Proarrest strategies include a range of sanctions from issuing a warning, to mandated treatment, to prison time.

WHO CALLS THE POLICE?

In the past, most women did not report incidents of abuse to the police. Several studies estimate that only about 10 percent of battering incidents are ever reported to authorities. The 1985 National Family Violence Survey (NFVS) finds that only 6.7 percent of all husband-to-wife assaults were reported to police. When the assaults are categorized by severity as measured on a Conflict Tactics Scale, only 3.2 percent of minor violence cases and 14.4 percent of severe violence cases were reported.

There is some evidence that over time, slightly higher percentages of female victims have reported instances of intimate partner violence to the police. In "The 'Drunken Bum' Theory of Wife Beating" (*Physical Violence in American Families*, Transaction, Piscataway, NJ, 1990), Glenda Kaufman Kantor and Murray Straus estimate that between 7 and 14 percent of intimate partner assaults are reported to police. A 1995 study using NCVS data made the most optimistic projections, estimating that 56 percent of battering incidents were reported to the police. By 2000 the estimate drawn from the NCVS data was that slightly more than half of female victims filed police reports.

The women who chose not to report their abuse cite a variety of reasons, including fear of retaliation, loss of income, or loss of their children to child protective authorities. When abuse is reported to law enforcement agencies, it is often by health care professionals from whom the woman has sought treatment for her injuries. In many states, health professionals are mandated by law to report all instances of domestic violence to law enforcement authorities.

In an examination of the law enforcement response to mandated reporting by health professionals, Laura E. Lund surveyed domestic violence experts at 39 police agencies in California. She finds that almost all had standard procedures for responding to domestic violence reports from health practitioners. But while the law mandates health practitioners to make these reports by telephone and in writing, she finds that fewer than one-quarter of the police agencies consistently received both types of reports from health care providers.

In "What Happens When Health Practitioners Report Domestic Violence Injuries to the Police? A Study of the Law Enforcement Response to Injury Reports" (*Violence and Victims*, vol. 14, no. 2, September 1999), Lund questions whether California law enforcement agencies have policies and procedures in place to respond to domestic violence complaints from health practitioners. She finds that hospital emergency departments are the source of many of the abuse complaints filed with police, even

though these complaints make up only a fraction of the domestic violence caseload of police agencies.

Of the 39 law enforcement agencies, 30 reported that when they receive a handwritten domestic violence report from a health care provider, they first search their own records to see whether the case is already under investigation. Many agencies also search for previous domestic violence cases or other crimes involving the alleged perpetrator.

Twenty-five law enforcement agencies said that in many cases the written reports from health practitioners cannot be matched to a previous report of the incident. They said that if the health care professional does not report the abuse by telephone, it may be days or even weeks before police receive a handwritten abuse report. Often, the agencies noted, the reports lack essential information, such as a contact number for the victim, making it even more difficult for investigators to match the incident with a crime report.

Most law enforcement agencies said they attempt to conduct investigations when they receive these reports, known as "unmatched reports," because they do not correspond to police reports of the incidents. The most common agency response to these reports was to contact the victims. Fifteen agencies said this was their usual response or their only response to unmatched reports. Of these 15 agencies, only 2 said they also attempt to contact the health practitioner who made the report and only 1 agency said it sends an officer to talk to the victim if the health practitioner provides an address but no phone number. It was unusual for agencies to have a policy of dispatching an officer based on an unmatched health practitioner report.

Lund feels that since law enforcement agencies receive relatively few health practitioner reports, with most of the reports received from hospital emergency rooms, this indicates some problems in the implementation of mandatory reporting. The scarcity of the reports may be due, in part, to a lack of understanding of the law by health professionals, insufficient training in reporting techniques, or an unwillingness to report.

Lund also faults police responses to reports from health practitioners, asserting that simply reporting and responding is not adequate. Rather, health practitioners must report effectively and agencies must respond appropriately in order to help, rather than harm, domestic violence victims.

NATIONAL CRIME VICTIMIZATION SURVEYS

The NCVS are ongoing, nationwide surveys that gather data on criminal victimizations from a national sample of 80,000 household respondents, ages 12 and older. The surveys provide a biannual estimate of crimes experienced by the public, whether or not a law enforcement agency was contacted about the crime.

It is well established that much intimate partner violence is unreported or underreported. Using seven years of data from the NCVS, statistician Callie Rennison examines trends, including police notification, in *Intimate Partner Violence and Age of Victim, 1993–99* (Bureau of Justice Statistics, Washington, DC, 2001). Table 7.2 shows that nearly three-quarters of intimate partner violence against females aged 12 to 15 is not reported to police, and more than half of females aged 16 to 19 and over 50 do not make police reports.

According to the 2000 NCVS, about half of the victims of rape or sexual assault (48.1 percent) report the crime to the police. (See Table 7.3.) Women are slightly more likely to report violent victimizations involving nonstrangers (55.8 percent) than strangers (52.4 percent). (See Table 7.4.) The percentage is virtually unchanged from 1993 when 48 percent of women who were victims of intimate partner violence reported the incidents to the police. The survey also finds that black females are most likely to report victimizations to the authorities—55.8 percent of black women reported the violent victimizations, compared to 42.1 percent of non-Hispanic men. (See Table 7.5.)

The reasons given for reporting victimizations to the police are shown in Table 7.6. For all personal crimes, the highest proportion of victims (16.1 percent) said they reported the incident because it was a crime. Of the other reasons, 8.5 percent said they wanted to prevent others from assaults by the offender and 8.1 percent said they hoped to punish the offender.

The reason offered most frequently for not reporting all types of personal crimes to the police was that the offense was a private or personal matter (18.2 percent). Almost one-quarter of victims of rape or sexual assault cited this reason for failing to report the crime. (See Table 7.7.) This reason was given more often by victims who chose not to report offenses committed by nonstrangers, except for instances of rape and sexual assault, where about the same percentage said the crime went unreported because the matter was personal, whether the offender was a stranger or nonstranger. (See Table 7.8.)

DETERMINING POLICE RESPONSE

In "Determining Police Response to Domestic Violence Victims" (*American Behavioral Scientist,* May 1993), a landmark study of four precincts of the Detroit Police Department, Eve Buzawa and Thomas Austin document several factors that affected police decisions to arrest offenders:

- The presence of bystanders or children during the abuse

TABLE 7.2

Intimate partner violence against females and reporting to police, by age, 1993–99

| | | Intimate partner violence against women | | |
| | Average annual number | Percent reported to the police | | |
Age of victim		Yes	No	Did not know
Total	902,240	53.7%	46.1%	0.3%*
12-15	17,870	27.9	72.1	0.0*
16-19	123,760	45.9	54.1	0.0*
20-24	185,590	53.2	46.6	0.2*
25-34	306,550	57.3	42.7	0.0*
35-49	239,370	56.8	42.5	0.7*
50 or older	29,110	41.7	57.3	1.1*

*Based on 10 or fewer sample cases.

SOURCE: Callie Rennison, "Table 7. Intimate partner violence against females and reporting to police, by age, 1993–99," in *Intimate Partner Violence and Age of Victim, 1993–99,* U.S. Department of Justice, Bureau of Justice Statistics National Crime Victimization Survey, Washington, DC, September 18, 2001

- The presence of guns and sharp objects as weapons

- An injury resulting from the assault

- The offender and victim sharing the same residence whether they were married or not

- The victim's desire to have the offender arrested (of those who expressed such a desire, arrests were made in 44 percent of the cases; when the victim did not want the offender arrested, arrests were made in only 21 percent of the cases)

Interviewing 110 victims, Buzawa and Austin find that 85 percent of victims were satisfied with the police response. Not surprisingly, they were particularly satisfied when the police responded to their preferences for arresting or not arresting the offenders.

Lynette Feder, in "Police Handling of Domestic and Nondomestic Assault Calls: Is There a Case for Discrimination?" (*Crime and Delinquency,* vol. 44, no. 2, April 1998), finds that domestic assault calls are nearly twice as likely to result in arrests than are nondomestic assault calls. However, overall rates of arrest are fairly low—23 percent of domestic assault calls and 13 percent of nondomestic assault calls. Feder's study identifies four variables that determine the probability of arrest: the presence of the offender when the police arrive, the victim's desire for the arrest of the offender, the extent of the victim's injuries, and the offender's disrespectful demeanor toward police.

VICTIMS' DISSATISFACTION

Raquel Kennedy Bergen interviewed 40 women who had been physically abused and raped by their husbands. In *Wife Rape: Understanding the Response of Survivors*

TABLE 7.3

Percent distribution of victimizations, by type of crime and whether or not reported to the police, 2000

		Percent of victimizations reported to the police			
Sector and type of crime	Number of victimizations	Total	Yes[1]	No	Not known and not available
All crimes	**25,893,340**	**100%**	**38.7%**	**60.3%**	**1.0%**
Personal crimes	**6,596,690**	**100%**	**47.4%**	**51.3%**	**1.4%**
Crimes of violence	6,322,730	100	47.9	50.7	1.4
Completed violence	2,044,050	100	58.2	41.0	0.8*
Attempted/threatened violence	4,278,690	100	43.0	55.3	1.7
Rape/Sexual assault	260,950	100	48.1	49.8	2.1*
Rape/Attempted rape	147,160	100	61.9	38.1	0.0*
Rape	92,440	100	57.9	42.1	0.0*
Attempted rape[2]	54,720	100	68.8	31.2*	0.0*
Sexual assault[3]	113,790	100	30.2	65.0	4.8*
Robbery	731,780	100	56.3	43.7	0.0*
Completed/property taken	520,120	100	61.8	38.2	0.0*
With injury	160,480	100	75.8	24.2	0.0*
Without injury	359,640	100	55.6	44.4	0.0*
Attempted to take property	211,660	100	42.7	57.3	0.0*
With injury	65,700	100	38.5*	61.5	0.0*
Without injury	145,960	100	44.6	55.4	0.0*
Assault	5,330,010	100	46.7	51.7	1.6
Aggravated	1,292,510	100	56.7	41.0	2.3
With injury	346,090	100	63.9	36.1	0.0*
Threatened with weapon	946,420	100	54.0	42.8	3.1
Simple	4,037,500	100	43.6	55.1	1.3
With minor injury	989,020	100	56.8	42.2	1.0*
Without injury	3,048,480	100	39.3	59.3	1.5
Purse snatching/Pocket picking	273,960	100	35.0	65.0	0.0*
Completed purse snatching	57,040	100	59.8	40.2*	0.0*
Attempted purse snatching	8,850*	100*	25.6*	74.4*	0.0*
Pocket picking	208,060	100	28.6	71.4	0.0*
Property crimes	**19,296,650**	**100%**	**35.7%**	**63.4%**	**0.9%**
Household burglary	3,443,700	100	50.7	48.6	0.7*
Completed	2,909,460	100	52.4	46.9	0.7*
Forcible entry	1,037,860	100	74.4	24.6	1.0*
Unlawful entry without force	1,871,600	100	40.2	59.3	0.5*
Attempted forcible entry	534,240	100	41.8	57.8	0.4*
Motor vehicle theft	937,050	100	80.4	19.4	0.2*
Completed	641,850	100	90.7	9.3	0.0*
Attempted	295,200	100	58.2	41.2	0.6*
Theft	14,915,900	100	29.5	69.5	1.0
Completed	14,299,970	100	29.3	69.8	0.9
Less than $50	4,707,270	100	14.8	84.7	0.5*
$50 - $249	5,296,630	100	26.7	72.4	0.9
$250 or more	3,176,630	100	53.7	45.4	0.9
Amount not available	1,119,440	100	33.6	63.9	2.5
Attempted	615,930	100	33.4	63.3	3.3*

Note: Detail may not add to total shown because of rounding.
*Estimate is based on about 10 or fewer sample cases.
[1]Figures in this column represent the rates at which victimizations were reported to the police, or "police reporting rates."
[2]Includes verbal threats of rape.
[3]Includes threats.

SOURCE: "Table 91. Percent distribution of victimizations, by type of crime and whether or not reported to the police," in *Criminal Victimization in the United States, 2000 Statistical Tables*, U.S. Department of Justice, Bureau of Justice Statistics National Crime Victimization Survey, Washington, DC, August 2002

and Service Providers (Sage, Thousand Oaks, CA, 1996), she reports that only 37 percent of the women, or 15 out of 40, contacted the police for help on at least one occasion. Three women in the study felt it was impossible to call the police because their spouses were members of the police department. One participant reported that during several interviews with the police, the officers made a point of asking embarrassing questions and repeatedly asked for intimate details. Another woman who found the police unresponsive lied to get them to come to her aid.

About 80 percent of those who did call the police were not satisfied with the officers' response. Ultimately, only eight of the spouses were charged with rape.

A SOURCE OF FRUSTRATION

There can be little doubt that "domestic quarrels" cause great frustration to the police. According to the *FBI Law Enforcement Bulletin* (October 1997), domestic violence calls repeatedly involve the same homes, diverting

TABLE 7.4

Percent of victimizations reported to the police, by type of crime, victim-offender relationship and gender of victims, 2000

	Percent of all victimizations reported to the police								
	All victimizations			Involving strangers			Involving nonstrangers		
Type of crime	Both genders	Male	Female	Both genders	Male	Female	Both genders	Male	Female
Crimes of violence	**47.9%**	**42.9%**	**54.5%**	**47.4%**	**45.1%**	**52.4%**	**48.4%**	**39.7%**	**55.8%**
Completed violence	58.2	52.6	63.9	60.9	58.9	64.9	55.9	43.2	63.5
Attempted/threatened violence	43.0	39.1	48.9	41.8	39.6	46.7	44.3	38.3	50.5
Rape/Sexual assault[1]	48.1	56.4*	47.6	48.7	28.9*	50.3	47.6	100.0*	45.5
Robbery	56.3	48.8	71.8	56.7	50.3	73.9	54.7	41.3	67.8
Completed/property taken	61.8	55.8	72.3	65.9	60.5	77.7	47.4	31.1*	61.2
With injury	75.8	69.8	88.1	70.2	66.2	81.6	100.0	100.0*	100.0*
Without injury	55.6	48.9	66.3	63.9	57.5	76.3	28.9*	11.6*	45.1*
Attempted to take property	42.7	35.1	69.9	34.1	29.9	55.9*	72.6	60.9*	88.7*
With injury	38.5*	35.8*	53.8*	29.3*	27.8*	46.8*	80.9*	100.0*	59.2*
Without injury	44.6	34.7	74.2	36.4	31.1	57.6*	69.8*	49.5*	100.0*
Assault	46.7	41.9	53.5	45.2	44.0	48.2	48.1	39.4	56.1
Aggravated	56.7	53.7	64.0	55.9	53.1	65.2	58.0	54.9	62.8
With injury	63.9	61.0	69.6	66.8	68.5	59.0*	61.2	50.4	73.4
Threatened with weapon	54.0	51.2	61.5	53.0	48.7	66.5	56.1	56.9	54.5
Simple	43.6	37.0	51.3	40.2	38.9	42.7	46.0	35.1	55.1
With minor injury	56.8	45.8	66.4	54.7	51.0	64.0	57.6	41.8	66.9
Without injury	39.3	34.6	45.3	37.3	36.2	39.3	41.0	32.9	48.8

Note: Detail may not add to total shown because of rounding.
*Estimate is based on about 10 or fewer sample cases.
[1]Includes verbal threats of rape and threats of sexual assault.

SOURCE: "Table 93. Percent of victimizations reported to the police, by type of crime, victim–offender relationship and gender of victims," in *Criminal Victimization in the United States, 2000 Statistical Tables,* U.S. Department of Justice, Bureau of Justice Statistics National Crime Victimization Survey, Washington, DC, August 2002

resources from other areas while resulting in no legal action against offenders. Police claim 90 percent of domestic violence calls are repeat calls and that police typically know the callers by the location. Both victims and police officers find these situations frustrating. Battered women think the police are sometimes insensitive and the officers become exasperated after responding to multiple calls from the same woman.

Research finds that few women will file complaints against their batterers. In spite of significant legislative changes, police officers still meet victim resistance to arresting the abusive partner. Furthermore, researchers document the fact what many battered women have long suspected: that arrests do not decrease repeat offenses.

Kathleen Ferraro and Lucille Pope, in "Battered Women, Police and the Law" (*Legal Responses to Wife Assault,* Sage, Thousand Oaks, CA, 1993), examine the cultural context of law enforcement's attitude to arrest. Based on 440 hours of field observation of the Phoenix, Arizona, police, Ferraro and Pope conclude that among the most influential factors in police attitudes are the officers' background beliefs about race and class. Women from low-income, minority communities are more likely to be seen as "enmeshed in a culture of violence." A specific violent event is likely to be viewed as part of a larger pattern of culture and therefore beyond the scope of police intervention.

TABLE 7.5

Percent of victimizations reported to the police, by type of crime and gender and race or ethnicity of victims

	Percent of all victimizations reported to the police	
Characteristic	Crimes of violence[1]	Property crimes
Total	**47.9%**	**35.7%**
Male		
White	42.2	35.7
Black	45.6	35.5
Female		
White	54.6	35.4
Black	55.8	37.6
Male		
Hispanic	47.7	33.8
Non-Hispanic	42.1	35.8
Female		
Hispanic	61.2	31.1
Non-Hispanic	53.7	36.6

Note: Excludes data on persons of "Other" races. Excludes data on persons whose ethnicity was not ascertained.
[1]Includes date rape and sexual assault, not shown separately.

SOURCE: "Table 91b. Percent of victimizations reported to the police, by type of crime and gender and race or ethnicity of victims," in *Criminal Victimization in the United States, 2000 Statistical Tables,* U.S. Department of Justice, Bureau of Justice Statistics National Crime Victimization Survey, Washington, DC, August 2002

Ferraro and Pope find in past research that while the police express frustration that women refuse to press charges, the proportion of cases dropped because of the

TABLE 7.6

Percent of reasons for reporting victimizations to the police, by type of crime, 2000

Type of crime	Number of reasons for reporting	Total	Percent of reasons for reporting				
			Stop or prevent this incident	Needed help due to injury	To recover property	To collect insurance	To prevent further crimes by offender against victim
All personal crimes	**2,772,120**	**100%**	**17.9%**	**1.6%**	**4.2%**	**0.5%***	**18.6%**
Crimes of violence	2,668,410	100	18.3	1.7	3.6	0.6*	19.2
Completed violence	958,610	100	15.9	2.9	8.0	0.5*	18.1
Attempted/threatened violence	1,709,800	100	19.6	1.0*	1.1*	0.6*	19.8
Rape/Sexual assault[1]	121,160	100	22.0	2.0*	0.0*	0.0*	26.7
Robbery	403,220	100	7.1	1.9*	19.1	1.3*	8.3
Completed/property taken	362,260	100	6.3*	2.1*	21.3	1.4*	6.2*
With injury	98,160	100	11.2*	2.2*	15.0*	0.0*	7.2*
Without injury	264,100	100	4.5*	2.1*	23.6	1.9*	5.8*
Attempted to take property	40,960	100	13.4*	0.0*	0.0*	0.0*	26.9*
With injury	3,250*	100*	0.0*	0.0*	0.0*	0.0*	0.0*
Without injury	37,710	100	14.6*	0.0*	0.0*	0.0*	29.2*
Assault	2,144,040	100	20.2	1.6	0.9*	0.5*	20.8
Aggravated	617,670	100	15.5	1.2*	1.9*	0.9*	17.3
Simple	1,526,370	100	22.1	1.8	0.5*	0.3*	22.2
Purse snatching/Pocket picking	103,710	100	9.2*	0.0*	18.9*	0.0*	5.2*
All property crimes	**7,464,350**	**100%**	**7.3%**	**0.2%***	**26.4%**	**5.2%**	**7.4%**
Household burglary	2,039,020	100	7.5	0.3*	22.9	3.5	10.1
Completed	1,840,550	100	7.0	0.4*	25.1	3.8	9.9
Forcible entry	914,930	100	7.5	0.3*	21.4	4.4	9.5
Unlawful entry without force	925,620	100	6.6	0.4*	28.8	3.2	10.2
Attempted forcible entry	198,470	100	12.2*	0.0*	2.5*	0.8*	12.6*
Motor vehicle theft	882,860	100	6.4	0.0*	34.0	9.0	5.0
Completed	628,180	100	4.0*	0.0*	46.4	9.4	5.0
Attempted	254,690	100	12.3	0.0*	3.4*	8.0*	5.2*
Theft	4,542,470	100	7.3	0.2*	26.5	5.2	6.6
Completed	4,367,350	100	7.0	0.2*	27.4	5.1	6.4
Attempted	175,120	100	14.3*	0.0*	4.4*	8.1*	11.8*

victim's reluctance—13 percent—is not much higher than the 10 percent dropped because of the inadequacy of police reports documenting the evidence.

Police blame not only the women for refusing to file charges, but also the courts for undermining the seriousness of the crime by failing to impose jail sentences or probation. A review of court cases cited by Ferraro and Pope finds that only 1 out of 250 cases of wife assault actually ended up with a report to police, a court conviction, and a serious sentence.

Ferraro and Pope observe that some officers resent the time it takes to process an arrest. They view domestic violence calls as a time-consuming effort that could be better devoted to other police work. One officer complained that she was unable to respond to an armed robbery call because she was transporting a woman to a shelter. Police officers are not often rewarded or promoted for their efforts to prevent intimate partner violence but are recognized for their work on high-profile crimes, such as illegal drug trafficking or armed robberies.

TRADITIONAL ATTITUDES PREVAIL

George Rigakos, in "Constructing the Symbolic Complainant: Police Subculture and the Nonenforcement of

Protective Orders from Battered Women" (*Violence and Victims,* vol. 10, no. 3, 1995), studies how police officers' attitudes influenced the treatment women received in a suburb of Vancouver, British Columbia. He finds that a traditional masculine culture contributed to negative stereotypes of women as liars, manipulators, and unreliable witnesses.

According to Rigakos, interviews with police officers and justice officials reveal four major themes. First, justice officials and police felt they were doing all they could for women but contended that other institutions impeded their work. Police officers blamed the legal system, charging the courts with liberally issuing unenforceable restraining and protective orders. In addition, judges issued these orders incorrectly, according to the police. For their part, the justices blamed the police for lack of enforcement. They believed the police misunderstand the law and failed to respond adequately.

Second, the police in this study held conservative attitudes about marriage that resulted in their excusing men's behavior. Officers expressed preferences for women who adhered to traditional behaviors, such as mothering and housekeeping.

Third, since traditional beliefs influenced police attitudes toward the victims, many male officers seemed determined to make the women's behavior appear "unreliable."

TABLE 7.6

Percent of reasons for reporting victimizations to the police, by type of crime, 2000 [CONTINUED]

| | | | | | | | Percent of reasons for reporting | |
Type of crime	To prevent crime by offender against anyone	To punish offender	To catch or find offender	To improve police surveillance	Duty to notify police	Because it was a crime	Some other reason	Not available
All personal crimes	**8.5%**	**8.1%**	**5.4%**	**3.5%**	**6.7%**	**16.1%**	**7.3%**	**1.5%**
Crimes of violence	8.8	8.4	5.5	3.6	6.7	15.0	7.2	1.6
Completed violence	7.1	11.7	6.4*	1.9	4.2	16.4	5.7	1.2*
Attempted/threatened violence	9.7	6.5	4.9	4.6	8.1	14.3	8.1	1.8
Rape/Sexual assault[1]	12.6*	14.7*	4.6*	2.7*	4.2*	10.6*	0.0*	0.0*
Robbery	8.7	10.6	13.2*	2.3*	5.7	17.6	2.6*	1.7*
Completed/property taken	8.9	11.9	14.0*	1.8*	6.4	15.0	2.9*	1.8*
With injury	7.9*	15.0*	14.3*	0.0*	4.7*	19.9*	0.0*	2.7*
Without injury	9.2*	10.7	13.9*	2.4*	7.0	13.3	4.0*	1.5*
Attempted to take property	6.8*	0.0*	5.8*	6.8*	0.0*	40.2*	0.0*	0.0*
With injury	0.0*	0.0*	0.0*	0.0*	0.0*	100.0*	0.0*	0.0*
Without injury	7.4*	0.0*	6.3*	7.4*	0.0*	35.0*	0.0*	0.0*
Assault	8.6	7.6	4.0	3.9	7.0	14.8	8.5	1.6
Aggravated	12.8	7.5	6.5	6.8	9.0	15.5	3.8*	1.3*
Simple	6.9	7.6	3.1	2.8	6.2	14.5	10.4	1.8
Purse snatching/Pocket picking	2.8*	0.0*	4.9*	0.0*	7.3	43.1	8.6*	0.0 *
All property crimes	**4.7%**	**3.5%**	**5.5%**	**6.5%**	**7.1%**	**21.9%**	**3.1%**	**1.2%**
Household burglary	5.5	3.6	6.7	8.4	7.5	20.1	2.9	0.9*
Completed	5.4	3.8	6.6	7.6	7.5	19.4	2.7	0.8*
Forcible entry	5.2	3.6	6.6	8.6	7.1	21.2	4.2	0.5*
Unlawful entry without force	5.6	4.1	6.7	6.6	7.9	17.6	1.3*	1.1*
Attempted forcible entry	7.0*	0.9*	7.4	15.8*	7.4	26.9	4.6*	2.0*
Motor vehicle theft	3.5	5.2	7.4	3.8	5.6	19.4	0.5*	0.0
Completed	2.6*	4.7	4.2*	3.0	4.4	15.8	0.4*	0.0*
Attempted	5.6*	6.5*	15.4*	6.0*	8.5	28.2	0.8*	0.0 *
Theft	4.6	3.2	4.7	6.2	7.2	23.1	3.7	1.6
Completed	4.4	3.1	4.6	6.3	7.2	23.1	3.7	1.4
Attempted	7.3*	4.9*	6.4*	3.5*	7.2	24.6	2.4*	5.1*

Note: Detail may not add to total shown because of rounding.
Some respondents may have cited more than one reason for reporting victimizations to the police.
*Estimate is based on about 10 or fewer sample cases.
[1]Includes verbal threats of rape and threats of sexual assault.

SOURCE: "Table 101. Percent of reasons for reporting victimizations to the police, by type of crime," in *Criminal Victimization in the United States, 2000 Statistical Tables,* U.S. Department of Justice, Bureau of Justice Statistics National Crime Victimization Survey, Washington, DC, August 2002

Some felt that the women were using restraining orders to manipulate their husbands to give them advantages in custody battles and divorces. Even some female officers blamed the women.

Fourth, according to Rigakos, the officers made generalizations that were supported by their beliefs about the women but were not substantiated by official court records. The officers' perception was that after they spent tremendous amounts of time and effort to prepare a case, the women frequently did not pursue the charges. These negative perceptions of the women produced "selective memory" that magnified every instance of a battered woman failing to appear to testify against a partner and diminished the number of times when the women followed through with legal action.

A survey of the court records for 1993 finds that out of 49 cases, 5 women were "uncooperative," 3 were no-shows, 1 refused to testify, and 1 stated she had lied. Rigakos concludes that the feelings of betrayal engendered by the small number of women who became reluc-

tant witnesses tended to overshadow the hundreds of successful prosecutions. These few cases stood out because of their strong personal effect on the witnessing officers and their consistency with the officers' prevailing patriarchal views.

NOT ALL VICTIMS WHO SEEK POLICE ATTENTION ARE THE SAME

Investigators Robert Apsler, Michelle Cummins, and Steven Carl speculate that the female victims who seek police aid are very likely the most frightened women, and that they are seeking assistance to prevent future instances of abuse. In "Fear and Expectations: Differences Among Female Victims of Domestic Violence Who Come to the Attention of Police" (*Violence and Victims,* vol. 17, no. 4, August 2002), they review police officers' interviews of 95 consecutive victims who came to the attention of a police department in a suburb of Boston, Massachusetts.

The study participants had either contacted the police department via telephone or by personal appearance at the

TABLE 7.7

Percent of reasons for not reporting victimizations to the police, by type of crime, 2000

Type of crime	Number of reasons for not reporting	Percent of reasons for not reporting					
		Total	Reported to another official	Private or personal matter	Object recovered; offender unsuccessful	Not important enough	Insurance would not cover
All personal crimes	**4,006,480**	**100 %**	**15.4 %**	**18.2 %**	**16.8 %**	**5.6 %**	**0.1 %***
Crimes of violence	3,771,620	100	15.2	19.1	16.7	5.9	0.0 *
Completed violence	982,770	100	12.1	15.6	9.0	3.1	0.0 *
Attempted/threatened violence	2,788,840	100	16.3	20.4	19.4	6.9	0.0 *
Rape/Sexual assault[1]	155,320	100	3.0 *	24.2	3.1 *	2.0 *	0.0 *
Robbery	422,810	100	3.9 *	8.3	16.7	3.1 *	0.0 *
Completed/property taken	245,650	100	3.5 *	4.8 *	7.6 *	2.6 *	0.0 *
With injury	58,910	100	0.0 *	0.0 *	0.0 *	0.0 *	0.0 *
Without injury	186,750	100	4.6 *	6.4 *	10.0 *	3.4 *	0.0 *
Attempted to take property	177,160	100	4.3 *	13.1 *	29.4	3.7 *	0.0 *
With injury	66,160	100	3.5 *	12.9 *	34.9 *	3.8 *	0.0 *
Without injury	111,000	100	4.8 *	13.2 *	26.2	3.7 *	0.0 *
Assault	3,193,490	100	17.3	20.3	17.3	6.5	0.0 *
Aggravated	646,370	100	10.8	20.1	13.7	5.4	0.0 *
Simple	2,547,120	100	18.9	20.4	18.2	6.8	0.0 *
Purse snatching/Pocket picking	234,860	100	18.8	3.0 *	18.9	1.2 *	0.9 *
All property crimes	**14,895,390**	**100 %**	**10.9 %**	**5.7 %**	**27.0 %**	**3.1 %**	**2.2 %**
Household burglary	2,059,110	100	3.8	7.2	23.9	4.3	1.9
Completed	1,660,510	100	3.2	8.1	20.9	3.6	2.3
Forcible entry	319,330	100	3.4 *	11.9	16.4	2.9 *	3.1 *
Unlawful entry without force	1,341,180	100	3.1	7.2	22.0	3.8	2.2
Attempted forcible entry	398,600	100	6.5	3.6 *	36.5	7.0	0.0 *
Motor vehicle theft	219,280	100	1.9 *	10.7 *	29.8	3.6 *	3.4 *
Completed	66,550	100	3.0 *	27.5 *	15.9 *	3.4 *	0.0 *
Attempted	152,730	100	1.5 *	3.4 *	35.8	3.6 *	4.9 *
Theft	12,617,010	100	12.2	5.3	27.5	2.8	2.2
Completed	12,174,440	100	12.5	5.2	26.8	2.9	2.2
Attempted	442,560	100	4.5 *	8.9	46.1	1.9 *	2.2 *

police station to request intervention in a violent intimate partner dispute. Police officers administered a standardized questionnaire that included questions about the severity of the abuse victims had experienced, their level of fear, and their expectations about the future. About half the victims were living with their abusers at the time the incident occurred.

Apsler, Cummins, and Carl find that just one-quarter of respondents said they were very afraid of their abusers. Another 6 percent were fairly afraid, 12 percent said they were slightly afraid, and 36 percent claimed they were not at all afraid of their abusers. Taken together, these latter two groups accounted for nearly half of participants reporting little or no fear of their abusers.

The results were similar in terms of participants' expectations of future abuse. Instead of a high proportion anticipating future violence, Apsler, Cummins, and Carl find that just 21 percent thought future abuse was very likely and well over half of those surveyed said future abuse was not at all likely or only slightly likely. These findings challenge long-standing beliefs that the greatest proportion of victims who come to the attention of the police are those who most fear future abuse.

Interestingly, there are no statistically significant relationships found between victims' expectations of future

violence and whether they lived with their abusers, had children under 18 years old, or were able to support themselves financially. A less surprising result is that victims' expectations of future abuse strongly influenced their desired future relationships with their offenders. A strong majority of the participants (90 percent) who thought future abuse was fairly or very likely wanted to permanently separate from the offenders. In contrast, only about half of those who thought further abuse was not at all likely wanted permanent separations.

Apsler, Cummins, and Carl conclude that the differences between victims of domestic violence and their varied expectations when seeking police attention point to a need for law enforcement agencies to offer a variety of police responses tailored to individual victim's needs. For example, Apsler, Cummins, and Carl suggest that mandatory arrest of victims' aggressors might not be a universally applicable strategy for all victims, especially those who are not at all fearful of further abuse. On the other hand, very fearful victims might be reassured and experience greater security if police maintained regular, ongoing contact with them following the incident. Apsler, Cummins, and Carl add that police follow-up might also send a powerful message to perpetrators—that they are under surveillance and that future violations will not be tolerated.

TABLE 7.7

Percent of reasons for not reporting victimizations to the police, by type of crime, 2000 [CONTINUED]

| | Percent of reasons for not reporting | | | | | | | |
Type of crime	Not aware crime occurred until later	Unable to recover property; no ID no.	Lack of proof	Police would not want to be bothered	Police inefficient, ineffective, or biased	Fear of reprisal	Too inconvenient or time consuming	Other reasons
All personal crimes	**0.7%**	**0.7%**	**4.7%**	**4.8%**	**4.0%**	**4.7%**	**3.3%**	**21.0%**
Crimes of violence	0.4 *	0.3 *	4.1	4.6	4.1	4.9	3.3	21.5
Completed violence	0.0 *	1.2 *	6.0	5.1	6.2	8.2	4.2	29.4
Attempted/threatened violence	0.5 *	0.0 *	3.5	4.5	3.3	3.7	3.0	18.7
Rape/Sexual assault/[1]	0.0 *	0.0 *	4.1 *	6.7 *	5.1 *	7.0 *	5.9 *	39.1
Robbery	1.2 *	2.7 *	11.6	7.9	11.4	7.0	3.4 *	22.9
Completed/property taken	0.0 *	4.6 *	15.6	10.1 *	13.8	9.4 *	3.3 *	24.8
With injury	0.0 *	0.0 *	14.4 *	11.9 *	39.1 *	6.2 *	4.3 *	24.3 *
Without injury	0.0 *	6.1 *	16.0	9.5 *	5.8 *	10.4 *	3.0 *	25.0
Attempted to take property	2.9 *	0.0 *	6.2 *	4.8 *	8.2 *	3.7 *	3.5 *	20.2
With injury	0.0 *	0.0 *	12.8 *	3.8 *	0.0 *	3.8 *	0.0 *	24.6 *
Without injury	4.7 *	0.0 *	2.2 *	5.4 *	13.0 *	3.6 *	5.6 *	17.6 *
Assault	0.3 *	0.0 *	3.1	4.1	3.0	4.5	3.2	20.4
Aggravated	0.4 *	0.0 *	4.8	5.8	7.6	4.4	3.5 *	23.3
Simple	0.2 *	0.0 *	2.7	3.7	1.9	4.5	3.1	19.7
Purse snatching/Pocket picking	6.3 *	7.2 *	14.9	7.6 *	3.7 *	1.2 *	3.4 *	13.0
All property crimes	**5.5%**	**6.4%**	**11.0%**	**7.6%**	**3.1%**	**0.7%**	**3.3%**	**13.4%**
Household burglary	8.2	4.9	11.7	9.0	5.7	0.5 *	3.0	15.8
Completed	9.0	5.9	11.0	9.7	5.8	0.6 *	3.2	16.7
Forcible entry	6.0 *	7.5 *	10.8	11.4	12.2	1.2 *	2.8 *	10.3
Unlawful entry without force	9.7	5.6	11.0	9.3	4.2	0.5 *	3.3	18.2
Attempted forcible entry	5.1 *	0.4 *	14.6	6.2 *	5.2 *	0.0 *	2.4 *	12.3
Motor vehicle theft	6.8 *	0.0 *	11.3 *	12.7	3.2 *	0.0 *	2.7 *	13.9
Completed	6.3 *	0.0 *	8.3 *	4.3 *	4.3 *	0.0 *	0.0 *	27.0 *
Attempted	7.0 *	0.0 *	12.6 *	16.4 *	2.8 *	0.0 *	3.8 *	8.2 *
Theft	5.0	6.8	10.9	7.2	2.7	0.7	3.4	13.0
Completed	5.1	7.0	11.0	7.3	2.7	0.7	3.4	13.1
Attempted	2.5 *	0.5 *	9.3	5.4 *	4.3 *	0.5 *	2.6 *	11.2

Note: Detail may not add to total shown because of rounding.
Some respondents may have cited more than one reason for not reporting victimizations to the police.
*Estimate is based on about 10 or fewer sample cases.
[1]/Includes verbal threats of rape and threats of sexual assault.

SOURCE: "Table 102. Percent of reasons for not reporting victimizations to the police, by type of crime," in *Criminal Victimization in the United States, 2000 Statistical Tables,* U.S. Department of Justice, Bureau of Justice Statistics National Crime Victimization Survey, Washington, DC, August 2002

INNOVATIONS IN POLICE DEPARTMENTS

In recent years, a number of police departments have developed programs to improve their responsivity to spousal abuse calls and to handle these calls more effectively and consistently. These programs train officers to recognize that a crime has been committed, arrest the abuser, and provide some form of protection for the victim.

The Duluth Curriculum is a strong antiabuse policy. More than 15 years after its creation, the Duluth program is still driven by its original goal to ensure that every agent of the justice system, including police officers, prosecutors, probation officers, and judges, delivers the same message: that domestic violence is a crime and that the community will not tolerate it. Police are instructed to arrest batterers. Representatives from battered women's shelters and batterer treatment programs are sent to talk with the offenders immediately after arrest. Typically, a first-time offender is sentenced to 30 days in jail and probation until completion of a 26-week treatment program. If the offender misses classes, he is usually sent to jail.

Elements of this program have been duplicated throughout the country.

POLICE RESPONSE CAN EMPOWER VICTIMS

Researchers Carolyn Hoyle and Andrew Sanders contend that police intervention in cases of domestic violence can further intimidate women or actually help them to improve their own circumstances. In "Police Response to Domestic Violence: From Victim Choice to Victim Empowerment? "(*British Journal of Criminology,* vol. 40, 2000), they examine the views of victims about the value of criminal justice interventions in light of proarrest policies and the establishment of specially trained domestic violence units and officers.

Hoyle and Sanders interviewed 65 women in 3 communities in Thames, England, to find out what the victims wanted when they called the police to intervene in domestic disputes. In earlier studies, Hoyle and Sanders characterized the police policy as "victim's choice"—the police approached each instance of domestic violence according to

TABLE 7.8

Percent of reasons for not reporting victimizations to the police, by victim-offender relationship and type of crime, 2000

Relationship and type of crime	Number of reasons for not reporting	Percent of reasons for not reporting						
		Total	Reported to another official	Private or personal matter	Object recovered; offender unsuccessful	Not important enough	Insurance would not cover	Not aware crime occurred until later
Involving strangers								
Crimes of violence	1,853,320	100 %	12.5 %	16.7 %	20.3 %	5.8 %	0.0 % *	0.6 % *
Rape/Sexual assault[1]	79,600	100 %	2.7 *	23.8 *	2.8 *	3.9 *	0.0 *	0.0 *
Robbery	295,930	100 %	2.5 *	6.2 *	18.6	4.4 *	0.0 *	1.8 *
Assault	1,477,790	100 %	15.0	18.5	21.6	6.2	0.0 *	0.4 *
Involving nonstrangers								
Crimes of violence	1,918,300	100 %	17.8	21.4	13.1	6.0	0.0 *	0.2 *
Rape/Sexual assault[1]	75,720	100 %	3.2 *	24.5 *	3.4 *	0.0 *	0.0 *	0.0 *
Robbery	126,880	100 %	7.1 *	13.2 *	12.2 *	0.0 *	0.0 *	0.0 *
Assault	1,715,700	100 %	19.2	21.9	13.6	6.7	0.0 *	0.2 *

Relationship and type of crime	Percent of reasons for not reporting						
	Unable to recover property; no ID no.	Lack of proof	Police would not want to be bothered	Police inefficient, ineffective, or biased	Fear of reprisal	Too inconvenient or time consuming	Other reasons
Involving strangers							
Crimes of violence	0.4 % *	6.9 %	5.2 %	5.5 %	3.3 %	4.0 %	18.7 %
Rape/Sexual assault[1]	0.0 *	8.0 *	9.0 *	9.9 *	7.5 *	2.8 *	29.6 *
Robbery	2.6 *	14.9	4.6 *	11.8	5.9 *	3.5 *	23.3
Assault	0.0 *	5.3	5.1	4.0	2.6	4.2	17.2
Involving nonstrangers							
Crimes of violence	0.2 *	1.4	4.1	2.7	6.4	2.6	24.2
Rape/Sexual assault[1]	0.0 *	0.0 *	4.3 *	0.0 *	6.4 *	9.1 *	49.1
Robbery	2.9 *	4.1 *	15.4 *	10.5 *	9.5 *	3.1 *	21.8
Assault	0.0 *	1.3 *	3.2	2.2	6.2	2.3	23.3

Note: Detail may not add to total shown because of rounding.
Some respondents may have cited more than one reason for not reporting victimizations to the police.
*Estimate is based on about 10 or fewer sample cases.
[1]Includes verbal threats of rape and threats of sexual assault.

SOURCE: "Table 104. Percent of reasons for not reporting victimizations to the police, by victim–offender relationship and type of crime," in *Criminal Victimization in the United States, 2000 Statistical Tables*, U.S. Department of Justice, Bureau of Justice Statistics National Crime Victimization Survey, Washington, DC, August 2002

the woman's preferences about pursuing legal action. This policy was widely criticized because it allowed victims to decide on actions without consideration of the consequences of nonprosecution on perpetrators and victims. Critics also felt that many women were not actually expressing their true wishes and that their choices were coerced or influenced by fear of retribution from their abusers.

Since 1993 Thames police policy has shifted from victim's choice to proarrest, on the premise that arrest and prosecution better serve the interests of victims and the community at large. The policy changed in response to U.S. research findings that arrest correlates with short-term reductions in domestic violence among certain populations, such as employed men living in cities. Hoyle and Sanders believe that the new policy is not only proarrest, but also procharge. In other words, the new policy favors immediate intervention in the form of arresting the abusers and longer-term intervention by pressing charges that presumably might result in sentences of rehabilitation

or incarceration. Furthermore, they argue that this policy is the opposite of the previous one since it assumes that policy makers are more capable of deciding on correct courses of action than the victims themselves.

More than half (31) of the survey participants called the police with the intent of having the offender arrested, but the majority of these women did not wish to pursue prosecution. The balance either wanted the offender removed from the scene—simply to get a break from the abuse—or wanted the police to calm the agitated man. The women cited a wide range of reasons for their choices, from fear of retaliation, to a desire to remain married, to genuine sympathy for a substance-abusing or otherwise impaired spouse.

Hoyle and Sanders find that arrest, with or without prosecution, might in some instances act as a deterrent, but it does not reduce violence. They assert that arrest is most effective when combined with other strategies, such as treatment programs, incentives to reduce recidivism, and social supports for women. They term this the "victim empowerment model" and propose that it might prove more effective than the exclusively legal remedies provided by either the victim's choice or proarrest policies.

Hoyle and Sanders conclude that battered women are a diverse group in need of different kinds of support. They also observe that victims' preferences are shaped by a variety of factors and that an ideal approach would be to support each victim to change her circumstances in order to reduce coercion and to help her to make different choices, including the decision to end the violent relationship.

DOES ARREST HELP?

The Bureau of Justice Statistics (BJS), in the 1997 fact sheet *Preventing Domestic Violence Against Women*, finds that about one out of four of all violent offenders incarcerated in local jails had committed their offense against an intimate. These same violent offenders were also about twice as likely to be convicted of assault than if the same act was committed against a stranger. (See Figure 7.1.)

Of the violent offenders convicted of a crime against an intimate, the majority, 72.3 percent, were serving time for assault, 12.3 percent were incarcerated for rape or sexual assault, and 4.7 percent were convicted of homicide. The remaining 2.4 percent were convicted of robbing an intimate.

The study also finds that half of all inmates serving time in local jails had been previously placed under a restraining or protective order. Four out of 10 of these inmates had criminal justice status or a protective order in effect against them at the time of the offense.

Among violent offenders in state prison, women were about three times as likely as men to have committed their crime against an intimate. State prison inmates serving time for intimate violence were more likely to be white, and 8 out of 10 of these inmates either killed or injured their victims. An estimated 29 percent of these state prison inmates were armed with a gun at the time of the offense.

The BJS report also notes that more than half of inmates in state prisons or local jails had been drinking or using drugs when they violently assaulted their partners, and many had been drinking for six hours or more. About 4 out of 10 of the inmates in local jails said they consumed the equivalent of a 6 pack of beer before the attack; about 1 out of 4 reported drinking the equivalent of 24 or more beers.

The BJS report supports arrest, stating that it could:

- Prevent future criminal behavior

- Prevent further injury to the victim

- Demonstrate to the offender that he will face legal consequences

- Demonstrate to the victim, the offender, and the community that domestic violence is criminal behavior

FIGURE 7.1

Profile of convicted violent offenders in local jails

Convicted violent offenders in local jails

Intimate violence 23.6%	Other relatives violence 8.6%	Friend/ acquaintance violence 25.9%	Stranger violence 41.9%
Homicide 4.7%	Homicide 2.0%	Homicide 8.6%	Homicide 7.5%
Rape/ sexual assault 12.3%	Rape/ sexual assault 52.4%	Rape/ sexual assault 23.5%	Rape/ sexual assault 3.6%
Robbery 2.4%	Robbery 3.7%	Robbery 14.1%	Robbery 46.8%
Assault 72.3%	Assault 34.4%	Assault 46.4%	Assault 36.6%

Note: Intimate violence includes violent offenses committed against current and former spouses, boyfriends, and girlfriends.

SOURCE: "Profile of convicted violent offenders in local jails," in *Violence by Intimates: Analysis of Data on Crimes by Current or Former Spouses, Boyfriends, and Girlfriends,* U.S. Department of Justice, Bureau of Justice Statistics, Washington, DC, 1998

- Increase the number of offenders subject to prosecution, court supervision, treatment, and other community intervention

Arrest gained popularity as a tactic after the publication of the influential National Institute of Justice study "The Specific Deterrent Effects of Arrest for Domestic Assault" (*American Sociological Review,* April 1984). Over an 18-month period, criminologists Lawrence Sherman and Richard Berk examined the effectiveness of various police actions in domestic violence cases in Minneapolis.

The police randomly selected from among three different approaches: arrest, advice or mediation, or ordering the offender to leave the house for an eight-hour period. Sherman and Berk found that offenders not arrested were responsible for nearly twice the repeat violence during a six-month follow-up period. Almost all offenders were released shortly after their arrest, so this difference was not because they were in jail and could not commit violence. In addition, only 3 of the 136 arrested offenders were actually punished by fine or imprisonment, so it appeared that it was not punishment, but the actual arrest that contributed to the decline.

Although Sherman and Berk cautioned about generalizing from the results of a small study dealing with a single police department in which few police officers properly followed the test procedure, they concluded that in instances of domestic violence, an arrest is advisable except in cases where it would be clearly counterproductive. At the same time, Sherman and Berk recommended allowing police a certain amount of flexibility when making decisions about individual situations, on the premise that police officers must be permitted to rely on professional judgment based on experience.

Arrest Is Not More Effective

Sherman and Berk's study had a tremendous impact on police practices. A survey conducted two years after their report found more than a fourfold increase in the number of police departments reporting arrest as their preferred policy in domestic violence disputes.

In an effort to further validate the results of the Minneapolis study, the National Institute of Justice funded experiments in six other cities. J. David Hirschel et al. report on the results of the Charlotte, North Carolina, study in "The Failure to Deter Spouse Abuse" (*Journal of Research in Crime and Delinquency,* vol. 29, no. 1, 1992). In Charlotte, three police procedures were measured: advising and possibly separating the couple, issuing a citation requiring the offender to appear in court to answer charges, and arresting the offender. The experiment involved the entire police force and was in effect 24 hours a day. Of the 686 cases that met all the study criteria, all were followed for six months after the original intervention through interviews and police records.

In about 18 percent of the cases in which the officer had arrested the offender, the offender was rearrested for abuse during the six-month follow-up period. The rate for those who had been cited was 19 percent, while those who received advice or had been separated reoffended at a rate of nearly 12 percent. Interviewing the victims, Hirschel et al. find that 59 percent reported further abuse after the original arrest and 31 percent of these victims reported five times or more instances of abuse. Rates were comparable for the other two interventions with 65 percent of the citation offenders and 60 percent of the advise/separate offenders repeating their violence during the six-month period.

The study concludes that arrest was no more effective than any other measure used by police. Furthermore, police data suggest that repeat offenses were the exception, while interview data with victims show that reoffending was the rule and not the exception. Hirschel et al. propose several reasons why their data does not support the findings of the Minneapolis study:

- The majority (69.4 percent) of the offenders in the sample had previous criminal records, so arrest was not an unusual occurrence for them.

- For many of the couples in the study, abuse is a common occurrence and it is unrealistic to expect one arrest to deter chronic behavior.

- Arrest alone may not be a strong enough deterrent, because time spent in jail is often minimal. The medi-

an amount of time between the incident and release from jail was 9.4 hours, with over a quarter of the men spending less than 4 hours in jail.

- In only 35.5 percent of the cases in which the offender was either arrested or issued a citation was he ultimately prosecuted, and in less than 1 percent of cases did the offender spend any time in jail beyond the initial arrest.

Hirschel et al. conclude with an observation of one of the economic realities faced by the criminal justice system: as jails become more and more overcrowded, it is not difficult for offenders to realize that premium jail space will not be devoted to misdemeanor spouse abusers.

While this study demonstrates that arrest is not a deterrent in misdemeanor spouse abuse cases, it does not address the issues of whether arrest would be effective in cases of felony assault or for lower levels of abuse that are not considered misdemeanors.

Arrest Does Deter Some Men

Sherman et al. are among the first investigators to examine and report rates of recidivism in a Milwaukee police study in "Crime, Punishment and Stake in Conformity: Legal and Extralegal Control of Domestic Violence" (*American Sociological Review,* vol. 57, 1992). The study finds that arrest deters men with strong attachments to their local communities, perhaps through employment, friends, or family. Those who have little "stake in conformity," such as the unemployed and unmarried, have a tendency to become more violent in response to arrest. However, this benchmark study does not consider other variables that might have influenced the results. For example, employed offenders might have less violent histories, less stressful home life, or may be older—all factors that might affect their rates of recidivism.

Peter G. Jaffe et al., in "The Impact of Police Laying Charges" (*Legal Responses to Wife Assault—Current Trends and Evaluations,* Sage, Newbury Park, CA, 1993), study the effect of police intervention in London, Ontario. The participants were 90 female victims of assault, 52 of whom had called for police intervention and filed criminal charges, 14 received police intervention but no charges were filed, and 24 had neither police help nor filed charges.

Although arrest alone did not decrease the violence in this study, it was a significant deterrent when charges were filed. Jaffe et al. urge that police support be integrated into a community response that includes all aspects of support for battered women.

Warrantless Probable Cause Arrests

In the early 1970s, it was legal for the police to make probable cause arrests without a warrant for felonies, but only 14 states permitted it for misdemeanors. Because the crime of simple assault and battery is a misdemeanor in most states, family violence victims were forced to initiate their own criminal charges against a batterer. By 2002 West Virginia was the only state that did not authorize warrantless probable cause misdemeanor arrests in domestic violence cases. However, more than half of the states have added qualifiers, such as visible signs of injury or report of the violence within eight hours of the incident. Most state codes authorizing warrantless arrests require police to inform victims of their rights, which include the acquisition of protection orders, as well as referral to emergency and shelter facilities and transportation.

Mandatory Arrests

By 1992, 15 states, the District of Columbia, and dozens of municipalities had instituted a mandatory arrest policy whenever police are called to a domestic violence situation. Some battered women's advocates do not support mandatory arrest. They fear that poor and minority families are treated more harshly than middle-class families and that if the police arrive and both spouses are bloodied by the fight, both will be arrested, forcing the children into foster care. In Connecticut, where a strict arrest policy is mandatory, the dual arrest rate is 14 percent.

Recent data suggest that mandatory arrests may actually increase violence, especially if the batterer is unemployed or has a criminal record. Some observers suggest that mandatory arrest should be replaced with mandatory action, such as providing transportation to a shelter or granting the victim the option to have the offender arrested. Mandatory action would allow police officers to make decisions appropriate to each individual case.

Some police departments have adopted a presumptive arrest policy. This policy means that an arrest should be made unless clear and compelling reasons exist not to arrest. Presumptive arrest provisions forbid officers from basing the decision to arrest on the victim's preference or on a perception of the victim's willingness to testify or participate in the proceedings. Proponents point out that arresting an offender gives the victim a respite from fear and an opportunity to look for help. Furthermore, they claim it prevents bias in arrests.

Evan Stark, in "Mandatory Arrest of Batterers: A Reply to Its Critics" (*Do Arrests and Restraining Orders Work?* Sage, Newbury Park, CA, 1996), offers reasons for a mandatory arrest policy other than deterrence. Stark asserts that the policy provides:

- A standard against which to judge variation in police responses

- Immediate protection from current violence and time for victims to consider their options

- Measurable reductions in the overall incidence of domestic violence directly (because arrest might deter recidivism) and indirectly, by sending a clear message that battering is unacceptable

- Victims with access to services and protection that would not be available outside the criminal justice system

Pros and Cons for Arrest

Richard Berk, in "On the Average, We Can Do No Better Than Arrest" (*Current Controversies on Family Violence,* Sage, Newbury Park, CA, 1993), supports the use of arrest in certain circumstances. Follow-up studies to the Minneapolis study find that arrest is no more effective in preventing subsequent violence than any other approach. Berk observes that this finding may also be interpreted as one can do no better than by arresting the offender. On the other hand, Sherman et al.'s Milwaukee study finds that arrest is beneficial in the case of offenders with strong attachments to their communities. If arrest is effective for some offenders, then it cannot be said that arrest does not work at all. It is useful to consider it as one strategy that has limited benefits for a specific population.

Eve Buzawa and Carl Buzawa, in "The Scientific Evidence Is Not Conclusive" (*Current Controversies on Family Violence,* Sage, Newbury Park, CA, 1993), disagree about the effectiveness of arrest. They contend that studies repeatedly demonstrate increased violence after arrest, especially when the offender is released soon after arrest. They cite Sherman et al., who theorize that the anger engendered by arrest may overpower any deterrent effect of the arrest, especially for those who have little to lose.

Buzawa and Buzawa charge that the focus on arrest diverts limited funds away from shelters, based on the mistaken belief that arrests deter the violence prior to the need for shelter. Furthermore, Buzawa and Buzawa and other victims' advocates argue that rather than safeguard and empower them, mandatory arrest may further disable battered women because it is a strategy that ignores their wishes and is patronizing.

The actual cost of arrest is high and the indirect costs in terms of fractured community relations may be greater. Mandatory arrest undermines efforts to build trust between the police and the poor and minority groups who are likely to have experienced confrontations with the police. Some minority women fear that if they call the police, their partners will be beaten by arresting officers.

Instead, Buzawa and Buzawa would prefer to see the federal government fund services for victims and offenders. They believe that well-placed and properly funded rehabilitation programs, including substance abuse treatment, might dramatically decrease the need for arrests. Buzawa and Buzawa believe that long-term counseling and other rehabilitation measures may ultimately prove

TABLE 7.9

FIGURE 7.2

Percentage and estimated number of men and women stalked in previous 12 months, 1995–96

	Persons stalked in previous 12 months	
Group	Percentage*	Estimated Number**
Men (N = 8,000)	0.4	370,990
Women (N = 8,000)	1.0	1,006,970

* Differences between men and women are significant at ≤.001.
** Based on estimates of men and women aged 18 years and older, U.S. Bureau of the Census, Current Population Survey, 1995.

SOURCE: "Exhibit 2. Percentage and Estimated Number of Men and Women Stalked in Previous 12 Months," in *Stalking and Domestic Violence: The Third Annual Report to Congress under the Violence Against Women Act*, U.S. Department of Justice, Violence Against Women Grants Office, Washington, DC, July 1998

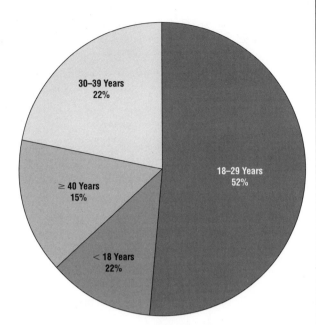

Victim's age when first stalked

Note: Based on responses from 797 male and female victims. Percentages do not total 100 due to rounding.

SOURCE: "Victim's Age When First Stalked," in *Stalking and Domestic Violence: The Third Annual Report to Congress under the Violence Against Women Act*, U.S. Department of Justice, Violence Against Women Grants Office, Washington, DC, July 1998

more effective than arrest in deterring future intimate partner violence.

STALKING

Many abused women who leave their partners feel threatened and remain in physical danger of further attacks. One form of threatening behavior is known as stalking, and it is generally defined as harassment that involves repeated visual or physical proximity, nonconsensual communication, verbal, written, or implied threats, or a combination of these acts that would cause a reasonable person fear. Stalking is a series of actions, usually escalating from legal but annoying acts, such as following or repeatedly phoning the victim, to violent or even fatal actions.

Not all stalking incidents involve abusive couples or intimate relationships. A stalker may fixate on an acquaintance or a stranger as the object of obsession. Celebrity stalking cases have been highly publicized but they account for a very small percentage of stalking incidents. Stalking most often involves intimates or former intimates and starts or continues after a victim leaves the relationship.

In a report to Congress *Stalking and Domestic Violence: The Third Annual Report to Congress Under the Violence Against Women Act* (Violence Against Women Grants Office, U.S. Department of Justice, Washington, DC, 1998), researchers estimate that 8.1 million women and more than 2 million men have been stalked in their lifetime.

Using National Violence Against Women Survey (NVAWS) data, researchers estimate that 1 out of 12 American women and 1 out of 45 American men have been stalked at some point in their life, with 90 percent of the victims being stalked by the same person. An estimated 1 percent of all women respondents and 0.4 percent of all male respondents were stalked in the 12 months prior to the NVAWS. These percentages represent more than 1 million women and 370,000 men who are stalked annually in the United States. (See Table 7.9.)

Stalkers: Who Are They?

Although stalking is considered a "gender-neutral" crime, the majority of victims are women and the primary perpetrators are men. Young adults are the primary targets—52 percent of victims were between the ages of 18 and 29. Another 22 percent were between 30 and 39 years old when the stalking began and 15 percent were 40 years old or older. (See Figure 7.2.)

As suspected, the survey finds that most victims knew their stalker. Strangers stalked only 23 percent of the female victims and 36 percent of male victims, the survey reports. Most women were stalked by intimate partners. Overall, current or former intimates stalked 62 percent of women and 32 percent of male victims. Figure 7.3 shows the relationship between stalkers and victims—women were stalked by spouses and former spouses nearly three times as often as men.

Most stalkers follow or spy on their victims, place unwanted phone calls, and send unwanted letters or items. The pattern of harassment is the same whether the victim is male or female. Eighty-two percent of all female stalking victims and 72 percent of all male stalking victims reported being followed or spied on, or found the stalker standing outside their home or workplace. Sixty-one percent of the

FIGURE 7.3

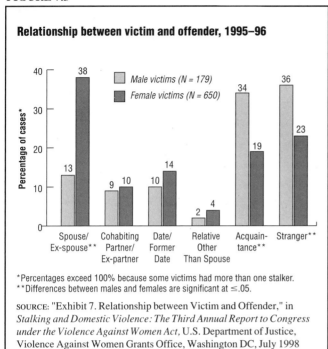

Relationship between victim and offender, 1995–96

*Percentages exceed 100% because some victims had more than one stalker.
**Differences between males and females are significant at ≤.05.

SOURCE: "Exhibit 7. Relationship between Victim and Offender," in *Stalking and Domestic Violence: The Third Annual Report to Congress under the Violence Against Women Act,* U.S. Department of Justice, Violence Against Women Grants Office, Washington DC, July 1998

FIGURE 7.4

Stalking activities engaged in by stalkers

* Differences between males and females are significant at ≤.05.
** Differences between males and females are significant at ≤.001.
*** Percentages exceed 100% because the question had multiple responses.

SOURCE: "Stalking activities engaged in by stalkers," in *Stalking and Domestic Violence: The Third Annual Report to Congress under the Violence Against Women Act,* U.S. Department of Justice, Violence Against Women Grants Office, Washington, DC, July 1998

females and 42 percent of the males reported receiving phone calls from the stalker. Twenty-nine percent of the women and 30 percent of the men reported property damage by the stalker, while 9 percent of the women and 6 percent of the male victims said the stalker either killed or threatened to kill their family pet. (See Figure 7.4.)

When the Violence Occurs

Victims' advocates and counselors have long held that women are at the greatest risk of violence when they end the relationship with the batterer. This assumption is based on findings that divorced or separated women report more intimate partner violence than married women. In addition, interviews conducted with men who killed their wives reveal that the violence escalated or was precipitated by separation or threats of separation from their partners.

Many female stalking victims (43 percent) reported that they were stalked after ending their relationship with intimate partners, although 36 percent said they were stalked both before and afterwards. Twenty-one percent of the victims said the stalking began before they terminated their relationships. (See Figure 7.5.)

According to findings released in *Extent, Nature, and Consequences of Intimate Partner Violence: Findings from the National Violence Against Women Survey* (National Institute of Justice and Centers for Disease Control and Prevention, Washington, DC, July 2000), separated women are nearly four times more likely to report rape, physical assault, or being stalked by their spouses

FIGURE 7.5

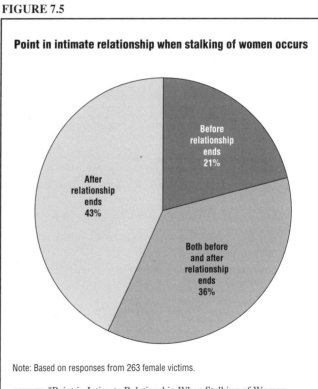

Point in intimate relationship when stalking of women occurs

Note: Based on responses from 263 female victims.

SOURCE: "Point in Intimate Relationship When Stalking of Women Occurs," in *Stalking and Domestic Violence: The Third Annual Report to Congress under the Violence Against Women Act,* U.S. Department of Justice, Violence Against Women Grants Office, Washington DC, July 1998

FIGURE 7.6

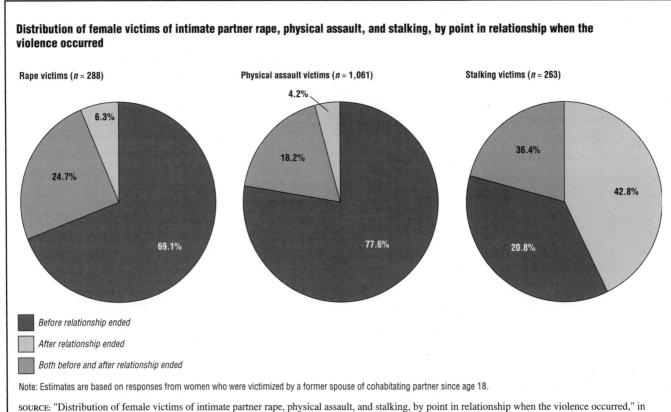

Distribution of female victims of intimate partner rape, physical assault, and stalking, by point in relationship when the violence occurred

Rape victims (*n* = 288)

6.3%

24.7%

69.1%

Physical assault victims (*n* = 1,061)

4.2%

18.2%

77.6%

Stalking victims (*n* = 263)

36.4%

42.8%

20.8%

◼ *Before relationship ended*

◼ *After relationship ended*

◼ *Both before and after relationship ended*

Note: Estimates are based on responses from women who were victimized by a former spouse of cohabitating partner since age 18.

SOURCE: "Distribution of female victims of intimate partner rape, physical assault, and stalking, by point in relationship when the violence occurred," in *Extent, Nature, and Consequences of Intimate Partner Violence: Findings From the National Violence Against Women Survey,* National Institute of Justice and Centers for Disease Control and Prevention, Washington, DC, July 2000

than women who live with their husbands. In comparison, men who lived apart from their spouses were nearly three times as likely to report being victimized by their wives than men who lived with their spouses. These findings support the widely held belief that there is an increased risk of partner violence for both men and women once the relationship ends. (See Figure 7.6.)

While 43 percent of all stalking victims said the stalking began after they ended their relationship, only 6.3 percent of the rape victims and 4.2 percent of the physical assault victims reported victimization after they terminated their relationship. These findings suggest that most rapes and violent assaults against women by their partners occur during the relationship but stalking is more likely to occur after the relationship is terminated.

Legal Response to Stalking

Table 7.10 shows that about half of the victims reported stalking to the police. In most cases, the victim made the report. Of the cases reported, police responded most often by taking a report. Police were significantly more likely to arrest or detain a suspect stalking a female victim than one stalking a male. Other responses included referrals to the prosecutor, court, or victim services and advice on self-protective measures. In 18.9 percent of the cases, police did nothing.

Of those who reported their stalking to the police, half of the victims were satisfied with the actions taken by the police, and about the same proportion indicated they felt police interventions had improved their situations or that the police had done all it could. (See Figure 7.7.) Victims who thought police actions were inadequate hoped that their assailants would have been jailed (42 percent) and that their complaints were treated more seriously (20 percent). Another 16 percent wanted police to do more to protect them from their assailants. (See Figure 7.8.)

Victims who chose not to report their stalking to the police said they felt their stalking was not a police matter, they believed police would be unable to help them, or they feared reprisal from their stalkers. (See Figure 7.9.)

Not unexpectedly, since women were more likely to be stalked by intimate partners with a history of violence, female victims were significantly more likely than male victims to obtain protective or restraining orders. According to *Stalking and Domestic Violence: The Third Annual Report to Congress Under the Violence Against Women Act,* (U.S. Department of Justice, Washington, DC, July 1998), of those who obtained protective orders, 68.7 percent of the women and 81.3 percent of the men said their stalker violated the order.

According to Table 7.11, about 12 percent of all stalking cases resulted in criminal prosecutions. Of the cases reported to police, 13.1 percent of the stalkers of female victims and 9 percent of the stalkers of male victims were prosecuted. More than half the stalkers who were prosecuted were convicted and 63 percent of those convicted were sentenced to jail or prison. Although a larger percentage of persons stalking female victims was prosecuted, a higher proportion of those stalking male victims was convicted.

TABLE 7.10

Percentage and characteristics of stalking cases reported to the police, by sex of victim

Reported to police/response	Stalking victims (%)		
	Male	Female	Total
Was case reported to the police?	(N = 178)	(N = 641)	(N = 819)
Yes	47.7	54.6	53.1
No	52.3	45.4	46.9
Who reported the case?[a]	(N = 84)	(N = 350)	(N = 434)
Victim	75.0	84.0	82.3
Other	25.0	16.0	17.7
Police Response[a,b]	(N = 84)	(N = 350)	(N = 434)
Took report	66.7	68.6	68.0
Arrested or detained perpetrator[c]	16.7	25.1	23.5
Referred to prosecutor or court	19.0	24.3	23.3
Referred to victim services[c]	8.3	15.1	13.8
Gave advice on self-protective measures	29.8	34.0	33.2
Did nothing	16.7	19.4	18.9

[a]Based on responses from victims whose stalking was reported to the police.
[b]Percentages exceed 100 percent because of multiple responses.
[c]Differences between males and females are significant at ≤.05.

SOURCE: Patricia Tjaden and Nancy Thoennes, "Percentage and characteristics of stalking cases reported to the police, by sex of victim," in *Extent, Nature, and Consequences of Intimate Partner Violence: Findings From the National Violence Against Women Survey,* National Institute of Justice and Centers for Disease Control and Prevention, Washington, DC, July 2000

FIGURE 7.7

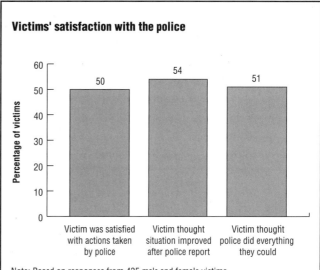

Victims' satisfaction with the police

Note: Based on responses from 435 male and female victims.

SOURCE: "Exhibit 17. Victims' Satisfaction with the Police," in *Stalking and Domestic Violence: The Third Annual Report to Congress under the Violence Against Women Act,* Violence Against Women Grants Office, U.S. Department of Justice, Washington, DC, July 1998

FIGURE 7.8

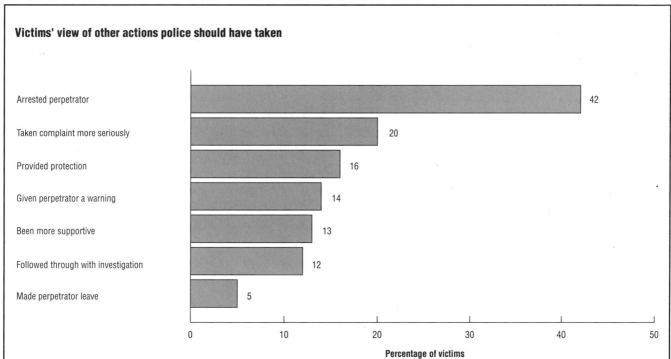

Victims' view of other actions police should have taken

Note: Based on responses from 201 male and female victims who thought police should have done more.

SOURCE: "Exhibit 18. Victims' View of Other Actions Police Should Have Taken," in *Stalking and Domestic Violence: The Third Annual Report to Congress under the Violence Against Women Act,* Violence Against Women Grants Office, U.S. Department of Justice, Washington, DC, July 1998

FIGURE 7.9

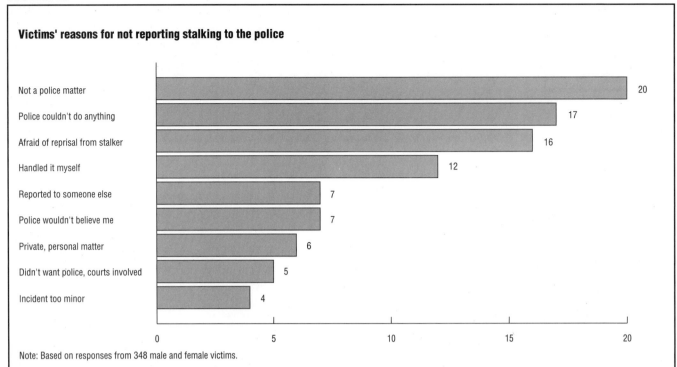

Victims' reasons for not reporting stalking to the police

Note: Based on responses from 348 male and female victims.

SOURCE: "Exhibit 16. Victims' Reasons for Not Reporting Stalking to Police," in *Stalking and Domestic Violence: The Third Annual Report to Congress under the Violence Against Women Act,* U.S. Department of Justice, Violence Against Women Grants Office, Washington DC, July 1998

TABLE 7.11

Percentage and outcomes of criminal prosecution in stalking cases, by sex of victim

	Stalking victims (%)		
Outcome	Male	Female	Total
Was perpetrator prosecuted?	(*N* = 178)	(*N* = 645)	(*N* = 823)
Yes	9.0	13.1	12.1
No	91.0	86.9	87.9
Was perpetrator convicted?[a]	(*N* = 15)	(*N* = 72)	(*N* = 87)
Yes	60.0	52.8	54.0
No	40.0	47.2	46.0
Was perpetrator sentenced to jail or prison?[b]	(*N* = 9)	(*N* = 37)	(*N* = 46)
Yes	77.8	59.5	63.0
No	22.2[c]	40.5	37.0

[a] Based on responses from victims whose perpetrator was prosecuted.
[b] Based on responses from victims whose perpetrator was convicted.
[c] Based on five or fewer sample cases.

SOURCE: "Percentage and outcomes of criminal prosecutions in stalking cases, by sex of victim," in *Stalking and Domestic Violence: The Third Annual Report to Congress under the Violence Against Women Act,* U.S. Department of Justice, Violence Against Women Grants Office, Washington, DC, July 1998

Antistalking Legislation

All states and the District of Columbia have laws making stalking a crime, but whether it is a felony or a misdemeanor varies by state. In 1996 the Interstate Stalking Punishment and Prevention Act, part of the National Defense Authorization Act for 1997, made interstate stalking a felony. This federal statute addresses "cases that cross state lines"—interstate offenses that in the past made it difficult for the state law enforcement agencies to take action.

Several state legislatures have amended their antistalking laws after constitutional challenges or judicial interpretations of the law made it difficult to prosecute alleged stalkers. For example, in 1996 the Texas Court of Criminal Appeals, in *Long v. Texas,* ruled that the 1993 Texas antistalking law was unconstitutional since it addressed conduct protected by the First Amendment. Legislators amended the statute in January 1997 to stipulate that to violate the statute, an alleged offender must knowingly engage in conduct that the offender "knows or reasonably believes the other person will regard as threatening."

According to the U.S. Department of Justice Office for Victims of Crime, the variation in state stalking laws is generally in the type of repeated behavior that is prohibited, whether by definition stalking must include a threat, the victim's reaction to the stalking, and the stalker's intent. The U.S. Department of Justice legal series bulletin *Strengthening Antistalking Statutes* (January 2002) details state legislative changes to better define prohibited conduct so that supreme courts would not find the statutes "unconstitutionally vague." For example, the Oregon legislature removed the term "legitimate purpose" from its statute when its supreme court determined it did not adequately describe the prohibited behavior. Similarly, the Supreme Court of Kansas sought increased precision when it requested that the state's stalking statute provide measures of behaviors such as "alarm, annoy and harassment," arguing that actions that alarm or annoy one person may not alarm or annoy another.

Stalking Interventions

Criminal justice officials and victim service providers continue to develop and refine programs, strategies, and protocols to address stalking with an emphasis on enhancing victim safety. According to *Domestic Violence and Stalking: The Second Annual Report to Congress Under the Violence Against Women Act* (U.S. Department of Justice, Washington, DC, 1997), intervention strategies must strike a balance between stopping the stalking and protecting the victim.

"Suspect intervention" and "victim intervention" are important aspects of the Los Angeles Police Department (LAPD) Stalking and Threat Assessment Team response to stalking cases. Suspect intervention is the process of gathering, documenting, and analyzing information to assess the potential danger of the stalker. It also includes arrests, protection orders, confiscation of weapons, and face-to-face meetings with stalking suspects. Victim intervention includes educating the victims about stalking, instructing victims about self-protective measures and how they can assist police to establish and pursue cases, and recommending therapeutic interventions, such as support groups or self-defense training, to help the victims regain control over their life. The LAPD Stalking and Threat Assessment Team and a comparable program in New York City have been lauded for their properly trained personnel and dedication of resources to pursue and combat stalking crimes.

As police departments and victim service agencies implement new and modified strategies, those that prove to be effective deterrents to stalking will serve as models. The U.S. Department of Justice is committed to support basic research to better understand intimate partner violence and stalking. Evaluation of these efforts will better inform public policy decision makers and guide officials to develop effective prevention and intervention programs.

Cyberstalking

Cyberstalking—online harassment and threats that can escalate to frightening and even life-threatening offline violence—is a relatively recent phenomenon. Although the extent of the problem is difficult to measure, by 1999 it had generated enough concern to warrant the report from the U.S. attorney general *Cyberstalking: A New Challenge for Law Enforcement and Industry* to then vice president Al Gore.

The attorney general's report cautioned that although cyberstalking does not involve physical contact, it should not be considered less dangerous than physical stalking. In fact, the ease and anonymous nature of online communication coupled with increased access to personal information may pose a greater threat because potential stalkers unable or unwilling to confront victims in person may not hesitate to send menacing e-mail (electronic mail) messages. Finally, although there is no research to support or refute the contention that cyberstalking leads to more serious violent relationships, recent incidents investigated by representatives of the media and reports from law enforcement agencies underscore the potential for dire consequences.

CASES MAKE HEADLINE NEWS. The attorney general's report recounted three of many serious instances of cyberstalking that attracted attention in the media and among policy makers. The first successful prosecution under California's cyberstalking law was in Los Angeles, where a 50-year-old man stalked a 28-year-old woman who had refused his advances by posting her name and telephone number along with messages saying she wanted to be raped. The Internet posts prompted men to knock on the woman's door, often during the night, in the hopes of fulfilling the fantasy her stalker had posted. In April 1999, the accused pled guilty to stalking and solicitation of sexual assault and was sentenced to a six-year prison term.

Another California case involved an honors graduate student at the University of San Diego who entered a guilty plea after sending, over the course of a year, hundreds of violent and menacing e-mail messages to five female university students he had never met. He also faces up to six years in prison. The third case cited in the report was prosecuted in Massachusetts, where a man repeatedly harassed coworkers via e-mail and attempted to extort sexual favors from a coworker.

In July 2002 the CBS News program *48 Hours* investigated a lethal case of cyberstalking that shocked the nation. In 1999 Amy Boyer was killed by a cyberstalker she had met, but never befriended or dated, in the eighth grade. The 20-year-old New Hampshire resident's stalker had constructed a Web site that described his stalking of Boyer and his plans to kill her. Her killer discovered where she worked, ambushed her as she left work, and then killed himself. Boyer's death inspired her parents to speak out and champion anticyberstalking laws, which as of July 2002 were in place in 20 states.

Law Enforcement Response

Cyberspace has become a fertile field for illegal activity. By the use of new technology and equipment, which cannot be policed by traditional methods, cyberstalking has replaced traditional methods of stalking and harassment. Since cyberstalking has led to offline incidents of violent crime, police and prosecutors have cooperated to devise strategies to resolve these problems through the criminal justice system.

—Linda Fairstein, chief of the Sex Crimes Prosecution Unit, Manhattan District Attorney's Office

Cyberstalking presents some unique law enforcement challenges. Offenders are often able to use the anonymity of online communication to avoid detection and account-ability for their actions. Appropriate interventions and recourse are unclear because often the stalker and his victim have never been in physical proximity to one another. Complicating the situation, the identity of the stalker may be difficult to determine. In Dallas a judge issued a temporary restraining order to stop an alleged offender from stalking his victim over the Internet. According to an October 1996 article that appeared in the *Dallas Morning News*, because the alleged stalker's address was unknown, the restraining order was served through e-mail and posted on the Internet.

Furthermore, in many jurisdictions law enforcement agencies are unprepared to investigate cyberstalking cases because they lack the expertise and training. The attorney general's study found that some victims had been advised by law enforcement agents to simply "turn off their computers" or to "come back should the offender confront or threaten them offline." Finally, some state and local law enforcement agencies are frustrated in their efforts to track down cyberstalkers by the limits of their statutory authority. For example, the Cable Communications Policy Act of 1984 bars the release of cable subscriber information to law enforcement agencies without advance notice to the subscriber and a court order. Since a growing number of Internet users receive services via cable, the act inadvertently grants those wishing to remain anonymous for purposes of cyberstalking some legal protection from investigation. The attorney general's report called for modifications to the act to include provisions to help law enforcement agents gain access to the identifying information they need while maintaining privacy safeguards for cable customers.

CHAPTER 8
DOMESTIC VIOLENCE—THE LAWS AND THE COURTS

At one time, turning to the judicial system for help was unlikely to produce or result in assistance or justice for victims of spousal abuse. The judicial system tended to view wife abuse as a matter to be resolved within the family. After all, "a man's home is his castle," and the U.S. government has been traditionally reluctant to violate the sanctity of the home. Furthermore, many legal authorities persisted in "blaming the victim," maintaining that the wife was, to some degree, responsible for her own beating by somehow inciting her husband to lose his temper.

Alcohol, and later illegal drug abuse, was sometimes considered the root of the problem. Authorities encouraged substance abusers to seek treatment on the assumption that curing a drinking or drug problem would bring an end to the abuse. Several recent studies, including "The Relationship Between Treatment, Incarceration, and Recidivism of Battering: A Program Evaluation of Seattle's Coordinated Community Response to Domestic Violence" (*Journal of Family Psychology,* vol. 13, no. 1, March 1999), soundly refute the hypothesis that completing substance abuse treatment programs effectively serves to reduce rates of intimate partner violence or prevent recurrences of battering.

While appealing to the judicial system for help will not solve all the problems facing an abused victim, the reception a battered woman can expect from the system has improved markedly over the past several years. The Violence Against Women Act (VAWA), signed into law by President Bill Clinton in September 1994, did much to help. The act simultaneously strengthened prevention and prosecution of violent crimes against women and provided law enforcement officials with the tools they needed to prosecute batterers. Although the system is far from perfect, legal authorities are far more likely to view abuse complaints as legitimate and serious than they had in the past.

KEY DOMESTIC VIOLENCE LEGISLATION

The Violence Against Women Internet (VAWnet) Library is an online resource center for information about issues of interest to victims and advocates working to end domestic violence. The organization maintains a law library containing descriptions and provisions of rules established by the U.S. Code of Federal Regulations, as well as interim, unenacted, and proposed legislation. It also details U.S. federal and state statutes, known as "acts," codes, and provisions that relate to prevention and prosecution of domestic violence, as well as services for victims.

Rules and Regulations

The following are among the rules and regulations aimed at addressing violent crimes against women that were finalized between 1999 and 2001:

- Grants to Combat Violent Crimes Against Women on Campuses: Final Rule (published July 22, 1999)—The regulation summary states, "This authorization provides funds to institutions of higher education for two broad purposes: To develop and strengthen effective security and investigation strategies to combat violent crimes against women on campuses, particularly domestic violence, sexual assault, and stalking and to develop, enlarge, and strengthen victim services in cases involving violent crimes against women on campuses."

- Postal Service, Release of Information, Final Rule (published January 25, 2000, effective February 24, 2000)—If an individual postal customer presents the U.S. Postal Service with a court order of protection, then the postal service may not disclose identifying information such as address, location, or post office box, unless ordered by the court.

- Visas: Documentation of Immigrants and Nonimmigrants—Visa Classification Symbols: Final Rule (published June 18, 2001)—This rule amended PL

106-386 to create new nonimmigrant categories for victims of trafficking for illicit sexual purposes and slavery and those who have suffered abuse, such as battering, and other forms of violence.

Also during 1999 and 2000 two rules to develop tribally operated programs and reduce the incidence of family violence in tribally governed communities were published. During 2000 the Asylum and Withholding Definitions: Proposed Rule sought to amend U.S. Immigration and Naturalization Service regulations to recognize circumstances in which battered women and victims of domestic violence might qualify for asylum.

In addition, on January 26, 2001, the U.S. Sentencing Commission published the Sentencing Guidelines for United States Courts: Notice, which increases the base levels of offenses and stricter sentences for stalking, domestic violence, and cases involving the use of gamma hydroxybutyric acid (GHB, also known as "Liquid Ecstasy").

U.S. Federal Statutes

Two key acts were published during the 1990s. The Family Violence Prevention and Services Act of 1992 supports the development and expansion of shelters and other services for victims as well as programs to prevent family violence. The VAWA of 1994 was landmark legislation that was enacted as Title IV of the Violent Crime Control and Law Enforcement Act of 1994 to provide additional safeguards for victims of domestic violence.

The Hillory J. Farias and Samantha Reid Date Rape Drug Prohibition Act of 2000 made it illegal to manufacture, distribute, or dispense GHB and created a special unit to evaluate abuse and trafficking of GHB and other drugs associated with instances of sexual assault. The Victims of Trafficking and Violence Protection Act of 2000 reauthorized the VAWA by allocating $3.3 billion over 5 years to fund traditional support services along with prevention and education about dating violence and rape and stalking via the Internet, new programs for transitional housing, and expanded protection for immigrant women.

Domestic Violence Gun Ban

The Omnibus Consolidated Appropriations Act of 1997 included a domestic violence gun ban. The law prohibits batterers convicted of domestic violence crimes or those with domestic violence protection orders filed against them from owning or carrying guns. During 1997 background checks of potential handgun buyers prevented an estimated 69,000 purchases. Most of those rejected (62 percent) had been convicted of a felony or were under felony indictment. Domestic violence misdemeanor convictions represented nearly 10 percent of the rejections, while domestic violence restraining orders accounted for 2 percent.

On November 30, 1998, the permanent provisions of an even tighter handgun ban, the Brady Handgun Prevention Act, went into effect. These provisions require background checks for anyone seeking to transfer ownership of a gun, which includes pawnshop transactions as well as purchases from retail gun shops.

From the inception of the Brady Act on March 1, 1994, through December 31, 2001, about 38 million applications for firearm permits or transfers were subjected to background investigations. Of these applications, about 840,000 were rejected (*Background Checks for Firearm Transfers,* Bureau of Justice Statistics, Washington, DC, 2002). In 2001 about 14 percent were rejected because the Federal Bureau of Investigation or state or local police agencies found that applicants had been either convicted of a domestic violence misdemeanor or had a protective order issued against them. (See Table 8.1.) After prior felony convictions, domestic violence was the second leading reason for rejecting applicants' gun permit requests.

The passage of the domestic violence gun ban was a victory for the battered women's movement but generated an outcry in the law enforcement community. Because the ban applied retroactively, anyone, including police officers, convicted of domestic violence before passage of the law on September 30, 1996, lost the right to possess and carry firearms.

The law has been hotly debated. Some people feel that law enforcement officers and military personnel who use firearms in their professional duties should be exempt from the prohibition. Others want to apply the ban only to those convicted of domestic violence after the date when the gun ban was enacted. Still others maintain that all persons convicted of such offenses should be prohibited from carrying firearms. Legislation has been introduced that would apply the ban only to those convicted after September 30, 1996, and that would exempt government employees, such as military and police.

Responses to the Ban

After the domestic violence gun ban passed, John W. Magaw of the Bureau of Alcohol, Tobacco, and Firearms advised police officers to turn over their firearms to a third party if they had ever been convicted of a domestic violence misdemeanor. Most police groups claimed that the law unfairly punished officers who committed domestic violence offenses in the past, and requested that exceptions be made for police officers who would be unable to conduct their law enforcement duties without firearms.

In 1998, at the request of the U.S. Department of Justice, the International Association of Chiefs of Police drafted the *Model Policy on Police Officer Domestic Violence.* In an attempt to address the domestic violence problem before it cost an officer his or her job, the policy takes a "continuum" approach, including:

• Prevention, education, and training

TABLE 8.1

Reasons for rejections of firearm transfer applications, 1996–2001

Reason for rejection	State and local agencies					
	2001	2000	1999	1998	1997	1996
Total	100%	100%	100%	100%	100%	100%
Felony indictment/conviction	57.7	57.6	72.5	63.3	61.7	67.8
Domestic violence						
Misdemeanor conviction	10.6	8.9	9.0	9.9	9.1	—
Restraining order	3.7	3.3	2.1	3.4	2.1	—
State law prohibition	7.0	4.7	3.5	6.6	6.1	5.5
Fugitive	5.8	4.3	5.0	6.1	5.9	6.0
Mental illness or disability	1.2	1.0	0.5	0.7	0.9	3.9
Drug addiction	1.0	0.7	1.0	0.9	1.6	1.2
Local law prohibition	0.5	0.2	0.2	0.3	0.9	0.7
Other*	12.5	19.4	6.2	8.8	11.7	13.4

—Not available or not applicable.

*Includes illegal aliens, juveniles, persons dishonorably discharged from the Armed Services, persons who have renounced their U.S. citizenship, and other unspecified persons.

SOURCE: "Table 4. Reasons for rejection of firearm transfer applications, 1996–2001," in *Background Checks for Firearm Transfers, 2001*, U.S. Department of Justice, Bureau of Justice Statistics, Washington, DC, September 2002

- Early warning and intervention

- Incident response protocols

- Victim safety and protection

- Postincident administrative and prosecutorial actions

Though the policy focuses on early prevention and intervention strategies, it also states that officers convicted of domestic abuse are to be removed from their enforcement positions and either terminated or reassigned. It calls on police departments to screen recruits for any indications of violent or abusive tendencies and to conduct background checks for histories of domestic violence or abuse.

FILING CHARGES

In the past, the burden of filing charges in domestic violence cases was typically with the victims. Historically, prosecutors and the courts offered victims little support or protection. Currently, the decision to charge offenders in cases of domestic violence is notable for having less to do with legal criteria than with evaluation of the victims' and offenders' personal attributes. Prosecutors are more likely to charge in cases where victims suffer serious injuries and defendants have a record of previous arrests.

Negative characteristics in the offender, such as alcohol or drug use and the failure to comply with the police and courts, increase the likelihood that charges will be pressed. Yet, the same attributes in the abused woman call into question her status as an innocent "victim." Eve Buzawa and Carl Buzawa, in *Current Controversies on Family Violence* (Sage, Newbury Park, CA, 1993), claim that more than a third of misdemeanor domestic violence cases would have been felony offenses of rape, robbery, or aggravated assault had they been committed by strangers rather than intimates.

Who should file the charges: The state through the prosecutor or the victim? In *Confronting Domestic Violence: A Guide for Criminal Justice Agencies* (National Institute of Justice, Washington, DC, 1986), advocates for the state filing the charges indicate that this policy would:

- Clearly establish spouse abuse as a crime

- Force prosecutors to take domestic violence cases seriously and eliminate their reluctance to handle these cases because of their view that victims tend to seek dismissals or refuse to testify

- Protect the community as a whole, since presumably innocent bystanders might be injured during future violence

- Strengthen the criminal justice system's control over prosecution and increase the number of batterers convicted and held accountable for their actions (either through incarceration or court-ordered intervention)

- Reduce the likelihood that batterers will intimidate and harass victims because they hold the victims responsible for their prosecution

Those recommending that victims file the charge argue:

- Battered women, when given full information, have the right and the ability to decide whether they want criminal justice intervention. For example, a battered woman might choose not to prosecute because she prefers civil remedies, faces life-threatening danger, fears race-biased sentencing, or would lose critical financial support.

- Civil remedies may be appropriate in some cases. If batterer counseling is viewed as a critical intervention, then it can be mandated through properly monitored and enforced civil protection orders, as well as through criminal action.

- There are other ways to address the potential for victim intimidation and harassment, including statutes that make intimidation of a witness a substantive crime and the use of protection orders a condition of release.

- Policies that eliminate victim discretion may serve to alienate battered women and discourage them from calling police or seeking other legal intervention in the future, thereby placing them in jeopardy of extreme injury or death.

Should a Woman Be Forced to File?

Those who favor the victim filing charges agree that when the lives of others are clearly endangered, battered women must be expected to cooperate with the prosecution. To pressure women to testify, some prosecutors have charged them with filing false police reports and perjury or lying to the court. In rare instances, they have also been jailed. Some prosecutors see this as a further abuse of an already demoralized woman, while others claim that allowing the woman to drop charges sends the message that the court does not take her problems seriously.

Victims' advocates claim that when the courts help women file charges and support them throughout the process, many more women follow through. In Brockton, Massachusetts, a court found that 71 percent of women who obtained restraining orders did not appear at their hearings 10 days later. In comparison, in a Quincy, Massachusetts, court with a separate office for restraining orders and support groups for the women, only 2.8 percent of the women failed to show at their hearings.

THE COURTS

An appeal to the American judicial system is intended to be an effective method of obtaining justice. For battered women, however, this has not always been the case. In the past, ignorance, social prejudices, and uneven attention from the criminal justice system conspired to diminish the importance of domestic violence. Although society has become significantly less tolerant of domestic violence, and laws in many states criminalize behavior previously considered acceptable, old attitudes and biases continue to plague intimate partner violence and spouse abuse cases in the courts.

Intimate partner abuse cases are often complicated by evidence problems because domestic violence usually takes place behind closed doors. The volatile and unpredictable emotions and motivations influencing the behavior of both the abuser and victim may not always fit neatly into the organized and systematic framework of legal case presentation. Finally, training mandates to ensure that prosecutors and judges are better informed about the social and personal costs of domestic violence, along with society's changing attitudes toward abuse, influence the responses of the judicial system.

Keeping the Family Together

Traditionally, the family has been the basis of American society. While the value of an intact family cannot be underestimated, the traditional family is one of the fastest changing aspects of our culture. Preserving a marriage "for the children's sake" is much less common than it was just two generations ago. Nonetheless, there are still many women, police, lawyers, judges, and other community opinion leaders, such as members of the clergy, politicians, and social scientists, who feel that only the most extreme instances of abuse justify breaking up the family.

In the past, with a view toward maintaining the family unit, many judges backed away from the responsibility to punish batterers under the pretense of protecting and preserving the family. *Confronting Domestic Violence* cites a judge who claimed, "Even if the woman shows up in my court with visible injuries, I don't really have any way of knowing who is responsible or who I should kick out of the house. Yes, he may have beaten her but nagging and a sharp tongue can be just as bad. Maybe she used her sharp tongue so often . . . she provoked him to hit her."

Confronting Domestic Violence also offers evidence that attitudes are changing and cites several judges' statements from the bench. "I don't care if she's your wife or not," one judge declared. "A marriage license is not a hitting license. If you think that the courts can't pin you for assaulting your wife, you are sadly mistaken." When another defendant claimed his girlfriend had provoked a beating, the judge warned, "This is your problem, not your girlfriend's. You will damage your next relationship in the same way if you don't get help." Another judge took the pressure off a wife testifying against her abusive husband by saying, "It's not your wife's fault that she's here to testify. She has no choice. I could have arrested her to make her come. She's not prosecuting you. The city is. She's required to tell the truth. It's perjury if she doesn't."

Obstacles to Prosecuting Abusers

One of the most formidable problems in prosecuting abusers is the victim's reluctance to bring her abuser to justice. In "Obstacles to Victims' Cooperation with the Criminal Prosecution of Their Abusers: The Role of Social Support" (*Violence and Victims,* vol. 14 no. 4, Winter 1999), Lisa Goodman, Lauren Bennett, and Mary Ann Dutton explore the reasons many domestic violence victims refuse to cooperate in the prosecution of their abusers.

Goodman, Bennett, and Dutton studied 92 abused women in Washington, D.C., whose partners had been arrested on misdemeanor domestic abuse charges, such as simple assault, threats, or destruction of personal property. Almost 90 percent of the women were African Americans aged 18 to 46 who had lived with their abusive partners for a little more than 3 years.

The participants generally reported high levels of physical violence during the past year with 90 percent reporting at least one instance of severe physical violence. More than half reported an instance of "minor" sexual assault and a comparable proportion reported severe injury from sexual abuse or physical assault.

The victims all struggled with a number of health and socioeconomic problems. More than half were unemployed, about three-quarters reported symptoms consistent with a diagnosis of clinical depression, and about one-fifth met the criteria for substance abuse. Despite these difficulties, Goodman, Bennett, and Dutton find that more than half of the women cooperated with the prosecution at the time of the defendant's first scheduled trial date, about 12 weeks into the case.

Goodman, Bennett, and Dutton find that the women who received tangible support, such as help with taking care of their children or an emergency loan, were about twice as likely to cooperate with the prosecution of their abuser. They cite several reasons for this finding. Although 82.7 percent of the participants were not financially dependent on the abuser, some indicated that the abuser provided other forms of support, such as child care or transportation. Goodman, Bennett, and Dutton find that when families or friends provided tangible support, the victims were more likely to seek help from the criminal justice system and cooperate with prosecutors. Surprisingly, the researchers find that the relationship between emotional support and cooperation with prosecutors was not significant. Similarly, institutional support, whether from police or victim advocates, was also unrelated to cooperation.

Interestingly, neither depression nor emotional attachment to the abuser was related to cooperation. This finding refutes the common perception that the battered woman is too depressed, helpless, or attached to the abuser to cooperate in his prosecution. Instead, Goodman, Bennett, and Dutton's findings show that many domestic violence victims persevere in the face of depression and the sometimes complex emotional attachment to their partner.

In contrast, women with substance abuse problems were less than half as likely to cooperate with the prosecution. Goodman, Bennett, and Dutton conclude that the women who used alcohol or drugs believed that the abuse was partly their fault or that a judge would not take them seriously. Some also feared that their substance abuse might negatively affect the court proceedings and possibly even lead to criminal charges or the loss of their children.

Consistent with findings from earlier studies, Goodman, Bennett, and Dutton find that the women who experienced more severe violence in their relationships were more likely to cooperate with prosecutors. Participants rearing children with the abuser were also more likely to cooperate, perhaps because these women hoped that the criminal justice system would force the abuser into treatment.

A victim's fear and ambivalence about testifying, and the importance of her behavior as a witness, have undoubtedly discouraged some prosecutors from taking action. Although many abused women have the courage to initiate legal proceedings against their batterers, some are later reluctant to cooperate with the prosecution because of their emotional attachment to their abusers, fear of retaliation, mistrust or lack of information about the criminal justice system, or fear of the demands of court appearances.

On the other hand, a victim might choose not to move forward with the prosecution because the violence ceases temporarily following the arrest while the batterer is in custody. Most women do not want their husbands to go to jail with the attendant loss of income and community standing. They just want their husbands to stop beating them.

Religious convictions, economic dependency, and family influence to drop the charges place great pressure on victimized women. Consequently, many prosecutors, some of whom believe abuse is a purely personal problem and others who believe winning the case is unlikely, test the victim's resolve to make sure she will not back out. This additional pressure drives many women to drop the charges because after being controlled by their husbands, they feel that the judicial system is repeating the pattern by abusing its power. Hence, the prosecutors' fears contribute to the problem, creating a self-perpetuating cycle.

Naturally, not all prosecutors and judges hold forgiving attitudes toward abusers. The *Santa Barbara County, California District Attorney Family Violence Prosecution Manual* advises prosecuting attorneys to keep in mind that the phrase "my spouse made me angry" does not excuse violence. Offenders tend to downplay violence and shift responsibility to the victim. The manual advises judges and prosecutors to follow the simple dictum that violence as a response to life's stresses is not legally an option. Commitment to prosecuting family violence, it stresses, must originate from both individual and policy-formulating prosecutors.

Mandatory Prosecution

A growing number of jurisdictions subscribe to mandatory prosecution policies. These policies require government attorneys to file criminal charges against domestic violence offenders. Though mandatory prosecution removes the burden of decision from the victim, it also removes the victim's control over the decision, especially when there is a no-drop policy in effect. With a no-drop option, no consideration is given to a victim's preference to drop the charges against the batterer.

Some research reports an unintended result of no-drop policies: battered women who were given the option to drop charges were at lower risk for subsequent violence than women who were not allowed to drop charges. Simply being able to participate in decision making with authorities served to empower the women. This finding is consistent with the observations of Carolyn Hoyle and Andrew Sanders in "Police Response to Domestic Violence: From Victim Choice to Victim Empowerment?" (*British Journal of Criminology*, vol. 40, 2000), who advocate for policies to empower, rather than to further disable victims of domestic violence.

LEGAL RESPONSE TO NONSTRANGER CRIME

The victim-offender relationship is an important factor in determining how the offender is treated by the criminal justice system. In general, strangers are treated more harshly because stranger offenses are considered more heinous and the true targets of the justice system. As a result, the criminal law is strictly enforced against them. On the other hand, the justice system has traditionally perceived nonstranger offenses as a misuse of the legal system to contend with strained interpersonal relationships.

Several studies confirm that while intimate partners are frequently charged with and convicted of more serious offenses, stranger offenders generally received longer sentences. It must be remembered that many intimate partner crimes never go to sentencing since victims drop charges or settle out of court. Those that do proceed through the judicial system are likely to be the more serious crimes.

PROTECTION ORDERS

A victim in any state in the nation may go to court to obtain a protection order forbidding the abuser from harming her. Also referred to as "restraining orders" or "injunctions," civil orders of protection are legally binding court orders that prohibit an individual who has committed an act of domestic violence from further abusing the victim. Although the terms are often used interchangeably, restraining orders usually refer to short-term or temporary sanctions, while protection orders have longer duration and my be permanent. These orders generally prohibit harassment, contact, communication, and physical proximity. Though common and readily obtained, they are not always effective.

All states and the District of Columbia have laws that allow an abused adult to petition the court for an order of protection. States also have laws to permit persons in other relationships with the abuser to file for protection orders. Relatives of the victim, children of either partner, couples in dating relationships, same-sex couples, and former spouses are among those who can file for a protection order in a majority of the states, the District of Columbia, and Puerto Rico. In Hawaii and Illinois, those who harbor an abused person can also obtain a protective order against the abuser.

In addition to violent physical abuse, petitioners may file for protection orders in other circumstances, including sexual assault, marital rape, harassment, emotional abuse, and stalking. Protection orders are valid for varying lengths of time depending on the state. In 30 states, the orders are in force for 6 months to a year. In Illinois and Wisconsin, the orders last two years and in California and Hawaii, three years. Furthermore, some states have extended the time during which a general or incident-specific protective order is effective. For example, a no-contact order issued against a stalker convicted in California remains in effect for 10 years. In Iowa, five-year protection orders are issued and additional five-year extensions may be obtained. New Jersey offers permanent protective orders and a conviction for stalking serves as an application for a permanent restraining order, and judges in Connecticut may issue standing criminal restraining orders that remain in effect until they are altered or revoked by the court.

Effects of Protection Orders

In the National Center for State Court Study *Civil Protection Orders: The Benefits and Limitations for Victims of Domestic Violence* (National Institute of Justice, Washington, DC, 1997), Susan Keilitz et al. report that most women who petitioned for a civil protection order had suffered physical abuse for some time. One-quarter of the women interviewed endured abuse for more than five years before obtaining a protection order.

The researchers find that temporary protection orders may be useful even when the victim does not follow through to obtain a permanent order. When victims were asked why they did not return for permanent protection orders, most said that their abusers had stopped bothering them.

Though abusers often violate the protection orders in some way, the orders generally deter repeated incidents of physical and psychological abuse. Keilitz et al. find that the majority of abuse victims felt that civil protection orders protected them against repeated incidents of abuse and helped them regain a sense of well-being. In initial interviews with women who had obtained protection orders, 72.3 percent of the participants reported that their lives had improved. At the six-month follow-up interviews, the proportion increased to 85.3 percent. More than 90 percent reported feeling better about themselves and 80.5 percent felt safer.

About 72 percent of participants in the initial interviews reported no continuing problems following the petition for protection orders, compared to 65.3 percent six months later. In some areas, however, the percentage that reported problems rose between the two interviews. The follow-up interviews showed that reports of stalking increased from 4.1 percent to 7.2 percent, as did reports of repeated physical and psychological abuse. Abusers with a criminal history of violent offenses were more likely to violate protection orders, prompting Keilitz et al. to observe that criminal prosecution may be required to stop abusive behavior in this group of perpetrators.

In contrast, restraining orders have been found to be somewhat less effective than orders of protection. Many victims questioned about the effectiveness of restraining orders said the orders were helpful to document that the abuse occurred, but less than half thought the abuser believed he had to obey the order. About 60 percent of the women with temporary restraining orders reported that the orders were violated in the year after they were issued and nearly 3 out of 10 reported that the violations were severe. Subsequent physical violence occurred as often for victims with permanent orders as for women with temporary orders.

The Strength of a Protective Order

Protection orders give victims an option other than filing a criminal complaint. Issued immediately, usually within 24 hours, they provide safety for the victim by barring or evicting the abuser from the household. However, this judicial protection has little meaning if the police do not maintain records and follow through with arrest should the abuser violate the order. Statutes in most states make violating a protection order a matter of criminal contempt, a misdemeanor, or even a felony.

The VAWA mandates that a protection order issued by one state for a domestic violence incident must be enforced in all states. The VAWA also makes it a crime to cross state lines to commit domestic violence or to violate a protective order. Courts and law enforcement agencies in most states have access to electronic registries of protection orders, both to verify the existence of an order and to assess whether violations have occurred.

The report from the U.S. Department of Justice *Enforcement of Protective Orders* (Washington, DC, January 2002) observes that while all states have passed some form of legislation to benefit victims of domestic violence, and 32 states have integrated these rights at the constitutional level, the scope and enforcement of these rights varies. The report calls for law enforcement agencies, prosecutors, and judges to be completely informed about the existence and specific terms and requirements of orders and to act to enforce them. John W. Gilles, the director of the U.S. Department of Justice, Office for Victims of Crime, asserts that "[u]nequivocal, standardized enforcement of court orders is imperative if protective orders are to be taken seriously by the offenders they attempt to restrain."

Nancy Loving, the program director of the Police Research Forum, observes that protection orders alone are unable to prevent domestic violence or safeguard the victims. To be optimally effective, the orders must be just one element of a comprehensive antiviolence strategy, along with shelters, police training, enforcement of legislation, and programs for batterers.

Lenore Walker, the author of *Terrifying Love: Why Battered Women Kill and How Society Responds* (Harper and Row, New York, 1989), endorses the advantages to obtaining protection orders that affect the entire spectrum of abuse situations because most batterers comply with the orders. Obtaining a restraining order not only acts to empower women, but also encourages police support because by obtaining the orders, the women are demonstrating the seriousness of their intentions to stop the abuse. Walker, who frequently serves as an expert witness, also observes that judges usually take an even dimmer view of the sanctions violation than of the assault itself, although spouse abuse is a misdemeanor or felony in every state. In addition, battered women who obtained previous restraining orders are more likely to be believed should they later injure or kill their abusers in self-defense, compared to women who had never taken any previous legal action.

Permanent Civil Protection Orders Reduce Risk

The results of research supported by the Centers for Disease Control and Prevention, the National Institutes of Health, and the National Institute of Justice, as part of the Interagency Consortium on Violence Against Women and Family Violence Research, are presented by Victoria Holt et al. in "Civil Protection Orders and Risk of Subsequent Police-Reported Violence" (*Journal of the American Medical Association,* vol. 2888, no. 5, August 7, 2002). Holt et al. report on whether obtaining a protection order acts to reduce the risk of subsequent police-reported intimate partner violence.

Holt et al. reviewed the cases of 2,691 female victims of intimate partner violence reported to the Seattle Police Department between August 1, 1998, and December 31, 1999. They looked at rates of police-reported physical and psychological abuse in the 12 months following the incident according to the victim's protection order status. Temporary protection orders were generally in effect for two weeks and permanent protection orders were usually in effect for one year. The researchers also followed those victims who chose not to obtain protection orders.

Holt et al. find that having a permanent protection order in effect was associated with an 80 percent reduction in police-reported physical violence in the 12 months following an incident of intimate partner violence. They also report that women with temporary protection orders were more likely than victims with no protection orders to be psychologically abused in the six months after the incident of intimate partner violence.

Holt et al. speculate that temporary protection orders may have restrained abusers from inflicting physical violence, producing a commensurate increase in psychological abuse. They observe that while temporary orders were linked to increased psychological abuse, the orders did not generate the increased physical violence that many victims and service providers fear will ensue. Holt et al. conclude that concern about increased physical violence after obtaining temporary protection orders may be unfounded and permanent protection orders may be more powerful deterrents to prevent violence recurrence than previously believed.

JUDICIAL RESPONSIBILITY TO PROTECT VICTIMS OF INTIMATE PARTNER VIOLENCE

Victims of domestic violence have historically sought legal protection from their abusive partners. This section summarizes the outcomes of several landmark cases that not only helped to define judicial responsibility, but also shaped the policies and practices aimed at protecting victimized women.

Baker v. The City of New York

Sandra Baker was estranged from her husband. In 1955 the local Domestic Relations Court issued a protective order directing her husband, who had a history of serious mental illness, "not to strike, molest, threaten, or annoy" his wife. Baker called the police when her husband created a disturbance at the family home. When a police officer arrived, she showed him the court order. The officer told her it was "no good" and "only a piece of paper" and refused to take any action.

Baker went to the Domestic Relations Court and told her story to a probation officer. While making a phone call, she saw her husband in the corridor. She went to the probation officer and told him her husband was in the corridor. She asked if she could wait in his office because she was "afraid to stand in the room with him." The probation officer told her to leave and go to the waiting room. Minutes later, her husband shot and wounded her.

Baker sued the City of New York, claiming that the city owed her more protection than she was given. The New York State Supreme Court Appellate Division, in *Baker v. The City of New York* (1966), agreed that the city of New York failed to fulfill its obligation. The court found that she was "a person recognized by order of protection as one to whom a special duty was owed . . . and peace officers had a duty to supply protection to her." Neither the police officer nor the probation officer had ful-

filled this duty and both were found guilty of negligence. Since the officers were representatives of the city of New York, Baker had the right to sue the city.

Equal Protection

Another option desperate women have used in response to unchecked violence and abuse is to sue the police for failing to offer protection, alleging that the police violated their constitutional rights to liberty and equal protection under the law.

The Equal Protection Clause of the Fourteenth Amendment provides that no state shall "deny to any person within its jurisdiction the equal protection of the laws." This clause prohibits states from classifying by group membership unless they have a very good reason. If a woman can prove that a police department has a gender-based policy of refusing to arrest men who abuse their wives, she can claim that the policy is based on gender stereotypes and therefore violates the equal protection laws.

THURMAN V. CITY OF TORRINGTON. Between October 1982 and June 1983 Tracey Thurman continually called the Torrington, Connecticut, police to report that her estranged husband was repeatedly threatening her and her child's life. The police ignored her requests for help no matter how often she called or how serious the situation became. She tried to file complaints against her husband but city officials ignored her.

Even when her husband was finally arrested after attacking her in full view of a policeman and after the judge issued an order forbidding him to go to his wife's home, the police continued to ignore Thurman's pleas for help. Her husband violated the order and came to her house and threatened her. When she asked the police to arrest her husband for violating his probation and threatening her life, they ignored her. She obtained a restraining order against her husband, which he violated, but again the police failed to take any action.

On June 10, 1983, Thurman's husband came to her home. She called the police. He then stabbed her repeatedly around the chest, neck, and throat. A police officer arrived 25 minutes later but did not arrest her husband, despite the attack. Three more policemen arrived. The husband went into the house and brought out their child and threw him down on his bleeding mother. The officers still did not arrest him. While his wife was on the stretcher waiting to be placed in the ambulance, he came at her again. Only at that point did police take him into custody. Thurman later sued the city of Torrington, claiming she was denied equal protection under the law.

In *Thurman v. City of Torrington* (1984), the U.S. District Court for Downstate Connecticut agreed, stating:

> City officials and police officers are under an affirmative duty to preserve law and order, and to protect the personal

safety of persons in the community. This duty applies equally to women whose personal safety is threatened by individuals with whom they have or have had a domestic relationship as well as to all other persons whose personal safety is threatened, including women not involved in domestic relationships. If officials have notice of the possibility of attacks on women in domestic relationships or other persons, they are under an affirmative duty to take reasonable measures to protect the personal safety of such persons in the community.

. . . [A] police officer may not knowingly refrain from interference in such violence, and may not automatically decline to make an arrest simply because the assailant and his victim are married to each other. Such inaction on the part of the officer is a denial of the equal protection of the laws.

For the federal district court, there could be little question that "such inaction on the part of the officers was a denial of the equal protection of the laws." The police could not claim that they were promoting domestic harmony by refraining from interference in a marital dispute because research had conclusively demonstrated that police inaction supports the continuance of violence. There could be no question, the court concluded, that the city of Torrington, through its police department, had "condoned a pattern or practice of affording inadequate protection or no protection at all, to women who complained of having been abused by their husbands or others with whom they have had close relations." The police had, therefore, failed in their duty to protect Tracey Thurman and deserved to be sued.

The federal court jury awarded Thurman $2.3 million in compensatory damages. Almost immediately, the state of Connecticut changed the law, calling for the arrest of assaultive spouses. In the 12 months following the new law, arrests for domestic assault almost doubled from 12,400 to 23,830.

Due Process

The Due Process Clause of the Fourteenth Amendment provides that "no State shall deprive any person of life, liberty, or property without due process of law," protecting against state actions that are unfair or arbitrary. It does not, however, obligate the state to protect the public from harm or provide services that would protect them. Rather, a state may create special conditions in which that state has constitutional obligations to particular citizens because of a "special relationship between the state and the individual." Abused women have used this argument to claim that being under a protection order puts them in a "special relationship."

DESHANEY V. WINNEBAGO COUNTY DEPARTMENT OF SOCIAL SERVICES. The "special relationship" and the gains for women achieved in *Thurman* lost their power with the Supreme Court case of *DeShaney v. Winnebago*

County Department of Social Services (1989). A young boy, Joshua DeShaney, was repeatedly abused by his father. Despite repeated hospitalizations, the Department of Social Services (DSS) insisted that there was insufficient evidence to remove the child from the home. Eventually, the father beat the boy into a coma, causing permanent brain damage. The boy's mother, who did not have custody, sued DSS for not intervening. The Supreme Court ruled that the due process clause does not grant citizens any general right to government aid and that a "special relationship" is a custodial relationship. The Court's decision noted, "The facts of this case are undeniably tragic" but "the affirmative duty to protect arises not from the State's knowledge of the individual's predicament or from its expressions of intent to help him, but from the limitations that it has imposed on his freedom to act on his own behalf, through imprisonment, institutionalization, and other similar restraint of personality."

The Court concluded, "It is well to remember once again that the harm was inflicted not by the State of Wisconsin, but by Joshua's father. The most that can be said of the state functionaries in this case is that they stood by and did nothing when suspicious circumstances dictated a more active role for them. The people of Wisconsin may well prefer a system of liability that would place upon the State and its officials the responsibility for failure to act in situations such as the present one. . . . But they should not have it thrust upon them by this Court's expansion of the Due Process Clause of the Fourteenth Amendment."

Although this case is about a child, it also applies to abused women. Following *DeShaney,* women have been unable to win a case on the basis of due process or equal protection. Jena Balistreri's case against the police department of Pacifica, California, began before *DeShaney,* but unfortunately for her, it was not finally decided until after the *DeShaney* precedent had been established.

BALISTRERI V. PACIFICA POLICE DEPARTMENT. Jena Balistreri first called police in February 1982 when her husband beat her. The police refused to arrest him and one of the officers stated that Balistreri deserved the beating. In November 1982 Balistreri obtained a restraining order forbidding her husband from "harassing, annoying, or having contact with her." Despite repeated vandalism that included crashing his car into her garage and firebombing her home, the police refused to take Balistreri seriously. She turned to the courts in an effort to force police to restrain her husband.

Two out of the three judges of the U.S. Court of Appeals for the Ninth Circuit, both women, found that Balistreri's case might convince a jury that the police were guilty either of "intentional harassment" or "reckless indifference to her safety." The police's conduct "strongly suggest[s] an intention to treat domestic abuse cases less seriously than other assaults, as well as an animus against abused women," and their behavior may "violate equal protection."

Regarding the due process claim, Balistreri argued that she had a special relationship with the state because the police knew she was being terrorized and had a protection order. Two judges ruled she might have a claim to a "special relationship" and the state might, after all, have "a duty to take reasonable measures to protect Balistreri from her estranged husband."

The third judge dissented, stating that the restraining order "heightens the state's awareness" of her risk of harm, "but the mere existence of the order" creates no "special relationship" to the state and imposes no constitutional duty to protect her. The case was initially returned to the lower courts for further proceedings. After *DeShaney,* however, the court reversed its decision and threw out Balistreri's due process claim.

MACIAS V. IHDE. During the 18 months before her estranged husband Avelino Marcias murdered her at her place of work, Maria Teresa Marcias had filed 22 police complaints. In the months before her death, Avelino Marcias sexually abused his wife, broke into her home, terrorized, and stalked her. The victim's family filed a wrongful death lawsuit against the Sonoma County, California, Sheriff's Department, accusing the department of failing to provide Marcias equal protection under the law and of discriminating against her as a Hispanic and a woman.

The U.S. District Court for the Northern District of California dismissed the case because Judge D. Lowell Jensen said there was no connection between Marcias's murder and how the sheriff's department had responded to her complaints.

Although a lower court had dismissed the family's claim, on July 20, 2000, the U.S. Court of Appeals for the Ninth Circuit reversed the earlier decision and ruled that the lawsuit could proceed with "opportunity to conduct discovery on the alleged constitutional motion, and to file any pretrial motions." Judge Arthur L. Alarcon of the U.S. Court of Appeals for the Ninth Circuit conveyed the unanimous opinion of the court when he wrote, "It is well established that there is no constitutional right to be protected by the state against being murdered by criminals or madmen. There is a constitutional right, however, to have police services administered in a nondiscriminatory manner—a right that is violated when a state actor denies such protection to disfavored persons."

CHAPTER 9

WHEN WOMEN KILL THEIR PARTNERS

Murder by an intimate partner is a relatively rare event for both men and women, but women do not kill intimates nearly as often as men. The National Crime Victimization Surveys estimate that intimate partner homicide accounts for just 4 percent of murders of men and about one-third of the murders of women.

In the *Special Report on Women Offenders* (Bureau of Justice Statistics, Washington, DC, 2000), researchers find that of the 60,000 slayings committed by women between 1976 and 1997, just over 60 percent were committed against an intimate partner or family member. In comparison, of the 400,000 murders committed by men during that same period, only 20 percent were against an intimate or family member.

According to the Federal Bureau of Investigation's (FBI) *Supplementary Homicide Reports, 1976–1999*, about 12.5 percent of all known murder offenders are female. But when a woman does kill, the victim is often her spouse or intimate partner. A 1994 Department of Justice study on "murder in families" analyzed 10,000 cases and determined that women made up more than 40 percent of those charged in familial murders.

In 1999, the latest year for which statistics are available, women killed 424 male intimates—in the same year men killed about three times as many of their intimate partners. Although these figures represent a decline from the previous year, they are also consistent with a 10 percent drop in violent victimizations from 1998 to 1999 and an overall decline in the violent crime rate.

Interestingly, there are regional variations in the rates of intimate partner homicide. When the National Center for Injury Prevention and Control of the Centers for Disease Control and Prevention (CDC), analyzed FBI data, southern and western states were found to have the highest rates of intimate partner homicide. Figure 9.1 shows the geographic variation of intimate partner homicide among white females by state and Figure 9.2 displays the rates of intimate partner homicide by state for black females. CDC researchers also report in *Morbidity and Mortality Weekly Report Surveillance Summaries* (vol. 50, no. SS03, October 12, 2001) that the risk of intimate partner homicide increases with population size, with rates in metropolitan areas with more than 250,000 persons 2 to 3 times higher than rates in cities with fewer than 10,000 residents.

Figure 9.3 shows that the number of males killed by intimate partners dropped by 69 percent since 1976. Researchers and advocates for battered women attribute this dramatic decline to the widespread availability of support services for women, including shelters, crisis counseling, hot lines, and legal measures such as protection and restraining orders. These services offer abused women options for escaping violence and abuse other than taking their partners' lives. Other factors that may have contributed to the decline are the increased ease of obtaining divorce and the generally improved economic conditions for women.

SPOUSAL MURDER DEFENDANTS

Female defendants are much less likely to be convicted or serve life sentences for killing their spouses than men. A 1995 Bureau of Justice Statistics (BJS) analysis found women were 7 times more likely than men to be acquitted at trial, while men were more likely to receive prison sentences and were sentenced to prison terms more than twice as long as those received by women. (See Figure 9.4.) With strong legal defense and detailed documentation of abuse, many women are able to successfully argue that after suffering years of mental and/or physical abuse at the hands of their victims they killed in self-defense. In fact, battered woman syndrome (BWS) has become a recognized defense in courtrooms throughout the country.

In the report *Spouse Murder Defendants in Large Urban Counties* (Bureau of Justice Statistics, Washington,

FIGURE 9.1

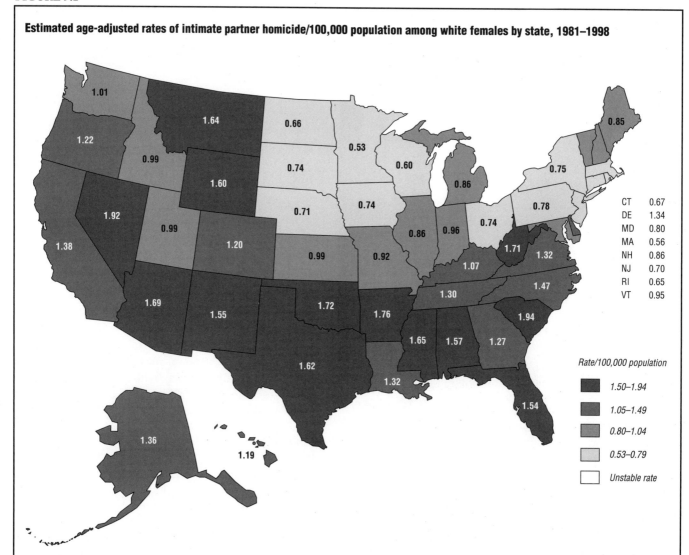

Estimated age-adjusted rates of intimate partner homicide/100,000 population among white females by state, 1981–1998

CT	0.67
DE	1.34
MD	0.80
MA	0.56
NH	0.86
NJ	0.70
RI	0.65
VT	0.95

Rate/100,000 population

- 1.50–1.94
- 1.05–1.49
- 0.80–1.04
- 0.53–0.79
- Unstable rate

SOURCE: Leonard J. Paulozzi, Linda E. Saltzman, Martie P. Thompson, and Patricia Holmgreen, "Estimated age-adjusted rates of intimate partner homicide/ 100,000 population among white females by state—United States, 1981–1998," in "Surveillance for Homicide Among Intimate Partners—United States, 1981–1998," in *Morbidity and Mortality Weekly Report Surveillance Summaries,* vol. 50, no. SS03, Centers for Disease Control and Prevention, National Center for Injury Prevention and Control, Atlanta, GA, October 12, 2001 [Online] http://www.cdc.gov/mmwr/preview/mmwrhtml/ss5003a1.htm [accessed October 31, 2002]

DC, 1995), BJS researchers Patrick A. Langan and John W. Dawson confirm that more husbands kill wives than wives kill husbands. The researchers examined 540 homicide cases in the nation's 75 largest counties and analyzed the defendants—59 percent were husbands and 41 percent were wives.

Nearly all the wives used weapons—95 percent of female suspects used a gun or knife. Men used those weapons only 69 percent of the time. Not surprisingly, in view of their generally larger size, strength, and body weight, husbands are far more likely than wives to strangle or beat their spouses to death.

Langan and Dawson also find that, proportionally, twice as many husbands (20 percent) killed in fits of jealousy. In addition, husbands were more likely to be sub-

stance abusers. Nearly one-third (31 percent) of the husbands had a history of drug abuse, compared to 9 percent of the wives. Almost one-quarter (22 percent) of the husbands were using drugs at the time of the crime and two-thirds, or 66 percent, were drinking alcohol, compared to 3 percent and 37 percent, respectively, for the women.

Wives on Trial

Although women in Langan and Dawson's study were about as likely as men to be prosecuted, stand trial, or plead guilty to killing their spouses, female defendants were less likely to serve jail time. In spouse murder cases, Langan and Dawson find that 41 percent of husbands were convicted of murdering their wives, while only 31 percent of wives were convicted of murdering their

FIGURE 9.2

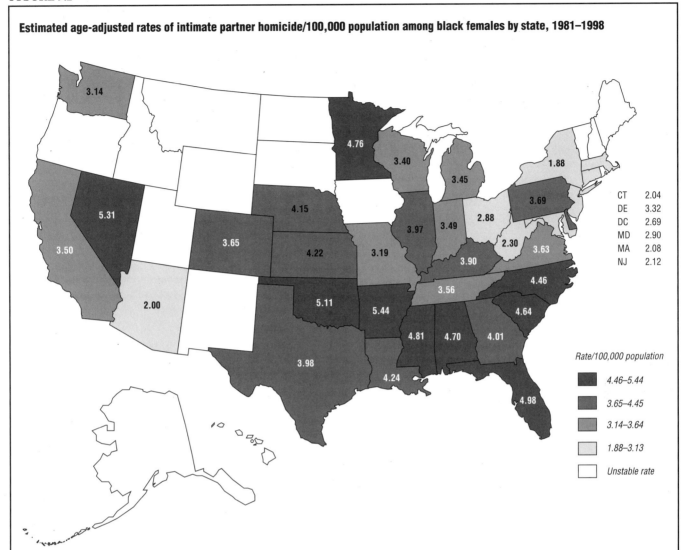

Estimated age-adjusted rates of intimate partner homicide/100,000 population among black females by state, 1981–1998

CT	2.04
DE	3.32
DC	2.69
MD	2.90
MA	2.08
NJ	2.12

Rate/100,000 population

- 4.46–5.44
- 3.65–4.45
- 3.14–3.64
- 1.88–3.13
- Unstable rate

SOURCE: Leonard J. Paulozzi, Linda E. Saltzman, Martie P. Thompson, and Patricia Holmgreen, "Estimated age-adjusted rates of intimate partner homicide/ 100,000 population among black females by state—United States, 1981–1998," in "Surveillance for Homicide Among Intimate Partners—United States, 1981–1998," in *Morbidity and Mortality Weekly Report Surveillance Summaries,* Vol. 50, No. SS03, Centers for Disease Control and Prevention, National Center for Injury Prevention and Control, Atlanta, GA, October 12, 2001 [Online] http://www.cdc.gov/mmwr/preview/mmwrhtml/ss5003a1.htm [accessed October 31, 2002]

husbands. It is worth noting that 46 percent of men and 39 percent of women pled guilty without a trial and were therefore not "convicted."

Women fared better than men both in jury trials and in bench trials. Juries acquitted 27 percent of the wives tried before them but none of the husbands, while judges acquitted 37 percent of the women and 17 percent of the men. Almost all men (94 percent) convicted of murdering their spouses were sentenced to prison time, while only 81 percent of the convicted women received prison sentences; wives received considerably shorter prison sentences than husbands, 6 years versus 16.5 years. (See Figure 9.4.)

Female murder defendants also received fewer life sentences. About half as many wives as husbands received life sentences (8 percent compared to 15 percent). Among wives

sentenced to prison, 15 percent received a sentence of 20 years or more, compared to 43 percent of the husbands.

In 44 percent of wife defendant cases, there was evidence that the wife had acted in response to a violent attack from her husband at the time of the killing. In contrast, just 10 percent of the husbands claimed that their victims had assaulted them at the time of the murder. The researchers observed that "[i]n many instances in which wives were charged with killing their husbands, the husbands had assaulted the wife, and the wife then killed in self-defense. That might explain why wives had a lower conviction rate than did husbands."

Even though Langan and Dawson analyze data from crimes and court decisions that took place more than a decade ago, they explain that "BJS knows from long experience with surveying courts that changes in case processing are quite gradual. The report's results are, therefore, likely to be applicable today."

FACTORS THAT INFLUENCE THE MURDER OF HUSBANDS BY WIVES

In one of the first studies of wives who murdered their abusive partners, *When Battered Women Kill* (The Free Press, New York, 1987), Angela Browne of the Family Research Laboratory at the University of New Hampshire compares 42 women charged with murdering or seriously injuring their spouses with 205 abused women who had not killed their husbands. Wondering why some women were unable to see that their partners were dangerously violent, she finds that some of the personal characteristics of men inclined to violent, abusive behavior were the same qualities that initially attracted the women to them. For example, the man who always wanted to know where his partner had been was initially viewed as intensely romantic. Only later, when the woman was unable to act or move without her partner's supervision, did the woman realize that she had become a virtual prisoner of her controlling mate.

Browne asserts that the intensity of these early relationships further serves to isolate the women. They may be denied contact with family and friends to the extent that a casual conversation with a neighbor may provoke abuse. The partner the woman once viewed as "protective" now is extremely jealous and possessive. This pathological protectiveness is communicated by an abuser's belief that his partner belongs exclusively to him and is a possession to be used as he pleases. Browne finds that many abusive husbands feared or believed their wives were sexually promiscuous and that these mistaken beliefs frequently prompted extreme sexual assault.

Rape

Browne's findings suggest a link between the frequency of marital rape and homicide potential. More than 75 percent of women who had committed homicide claimed they were forced to have sexual intercourse with their husbands, compared to 59 percent in the group of women who had not killed their husbands. Some 39 percent of the former group had been raped more than 20 times, compared to 13 percent of the latter group. Browne quotes one woman as saying, "It was as though he wanted

FIGURE 9.3

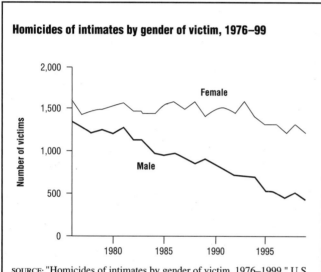

Homicides of intimates by gender of victim, 1976–99

SOURCE: "Homicides of intimates by gender of victim, 1976–1999," U.S. Department of Justice, Bureau of Justice Statistics, Washington, DC, September 2002 [Online] http://www.ojp.usdoj.gov/bjs/homicide/intimates.htm#intimates [Accessed October 21, 2002]

FIGURE 9.4

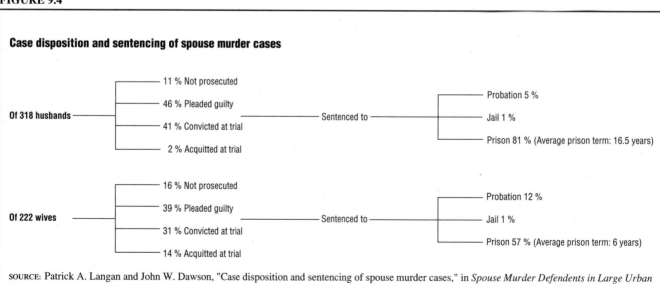

Case disposition and sentencing of spouse murder cases

SOURCE: Patrick A. Langan and John W. Dawson, "Case disposition and sentencing of spouse murder cases," in *Spouse Murder Defendants in Large Urban Counties*, U.S. Department of Justice, Bureau of Justice Statistics, Washington, DC, 1995

to annihilate me . . . ; as though he wanted to tear me apart from the inside out and simply leave nothing there." When sexual abuse escalates to extreme forms of sodomy, Browne speculates, it may be "the last straw," precipitating the woman's decision to kill her husband.

About 60 percent of the women who had been raped in their marriages reported that their husbands threatened to kill them, according to Raquel Kennedy Bergen in *Wife Rape* (Sage, Thousand Oaks, CA, 1996). Three of the women in the study reported that they were finally able to break free of their abusive relationships when they realized that they would kill their husbands if they did not leave. About half the sample confessed to thinking about killing their partners but did not believe they could actually follow through with their murderous plans.

Murder and Suicide Threats

Men murdered by their spouses had often threatened to kill their partners. In Browne's study, 83 percent of the men killed by their wives had threatened to kill someone, compared to 59 percent of the men whose wives did not kill them. Men killed by their wives used guns to frighten their spouses and were sometimes killed with their own weapons. Nearly two-thirds (61 percent) of this group also threatened to kill themselves. Many of the threats were made when women tried to leave the relationship or when the men were depressed. Browne questions whether the suicide threats were genuine expressions of wishes to die or whether they were used to manipulate the women in efforts to make them feel guilty and prevent them from leaving.

Many studies find that battered women often contemplate suicide because they see no other escape from the cycle of abuse. One woman in Browne's study expressed her wish to escape abuse when she decided not to seek help after a severe beating because she thought "[death] might not be so bad; like passing out only you never get beaten again."

Drug Use and Physical Abuse

When Browne compares abused women who had murdered their spouses and those who had not, she finds that in the homicide group, 29 percent of the men had used drugs daily or almost daily versus only 7.5 percent of the men in the nonhomicide group. There were even sharper differences in reported alcohol use. Twice as many (80 percent) of the men killed by their wives were reportedly drunk every day, compared to 40 percent of the abusive men who were not killed by their spouses.

In addition, 92 percent of the men killed by their wives had been arrested for crimes ranging from drunk driving to murder, compared to 77 percent in the group of women who did not kill their mates. A common feature of the marriages where the wife killed her spouse was that the wife did not know anything about her husband's criminal past, including his arrest records.

TABLE 9.1

History of physical or sexual abuse among women under correctional authority

	Women		
	Probation	Local jails	State prisons
Ever physically or sexually abused	41%	48%	57%
Before age 18	16	21	12
After age 18	13	11	20
Both periods	13	16	25
Ever abused			
Physically	15%	10%	18%
Sexually	7	10	11
Both	18	27	28

SOURCE: Lawrence A. Greenfield and Tracy L. Snell, "History of physical or sexual abuse among women under correctional authority," in *Woman Offenders,* U.S. Department of Justice, Bureau of Justice Statistics, Washington, DC, 2000

Lenore Walker, a renowned expert in domestic violence who is often hired as an expert witness in homicide cases, researches and testifies in cases where women killed their husbands soon after the men passed out from drinking. Convinced the beatings would resume when the men awoke, the women took the opportunities to kill their partners. Autopsies show that these victims had blood alcohol levels of up to three times greater than the measure normally defined as intoxicated.

Lawrence A. Greenfield and Tracy L. Snell, in "History of Physical or Sexual Abuse Among Women Under Correctional Authority" (*Woman Offenders,* Bureau of Justice Statistics, Washington, DC, 2000) find that 57 percent of women in state prisons had been physically or sexually abused in the past. Some (12 percent) of these women had suffered the abuse before the age of 18. (See Table 9.1.) More than one-third of abused women in prison had been victimized by intimates and just under one-quarter reported abuse from other family members.

LEGAL ISSUES SURROUNDING BATTERED WOMEN WHO KILL

In legal cases involving battered women who kill their abusers, the defendants often admit to the murder and reveal a history of physical abuse. The charge is usually first- or second-degree murder, which is murder with malicious intent either with or without premeditation. The outcome of these trials depends on three main issues: self-defense, equal force, and imminent versus immediate danger. Expert witnesses are crucial in an abused woman's trial to explain how these issues are different for cases involving battered women than for other homicide cases.

Self-Defense

Women often plead that they killed in self-defense, a plea that requires proof that the woman used such force as was necessary to avoid imminent bodily harm. Self-defense was originally intended to cover unexpected attacks by strangers and did not take into account a past history of abuse or a woman's fear of renewed violence. Traditionally applied, a self-defense plea does not exonerate a woman who kills during a lull in the violence, for example, when the drunken abuser passes out.

Many observers feel that self-defense law is problematic, inadequate, and/or not appropriate for use in self-defense cases of battered women, according to Diane Follingstad et al. in "The Impact of Elements of Self-Defense and Objective versus Subjective Instructions on Jurors' Verdicts for Battered Women Defendants" (*Journal of Interpersonal Violence,* vol. 12, no. 5, 1997). Traditionally, self-defense permits an individual to use physical force when he or she reasonably believes it is necessary to prevent imminent or immediate danger of serious bodily harm. Furthermore, a person must use only a reasonable amount of force to stop the attack and cannot be the one who provoked the encounter or initiated the violence. To justify the use of reciprocal deadly force, most jurisdictions require that the defendant reasonably believe the attacker is using or is about to use deadly force. Some jurisdictions further require that before resorting to deadly force, the defendant must make an effort to retreat, although this is not required in most courts if the attack took place in the defendant's own home.

Advocates of battered women have succeeded in convincing many courts to accept a subjective standard of determining whether a battered woman who killed her husband was protecting her own life. This concession allows the court to judge the circumstances of the crime in relation to the special needs of battered women and not according to the strict definition of "self-defense" as it has traditionally been applied. This is especially important for women who killed during a lull in the violence because a strict interpretation of "imminent danger" does not provide legal justification for their actions.

A subjective standard asks a jury to understand what is reasonable for a battered woman. Susannah Marie Bennett, in "Ending the Continuous Reign of Terror: Sleeping Husbands, Battered Wives, and the Right of Self-Defense" (*Wake Forest Law Review,* 1989), explains the critical difference as viewing the appearance of danger subjectively, from the perspective of one who saw and knew what the defendant saw and knew. An objective standard still governs whether a reasonable person, in similar circumstances and with the same perceptions, would also have acted in self-defense. This is the "hybrid" definition of self-defense that supporters of battered women encourage the courts to adopt.

In order for this hybrid definition to work, the court must first be subjective in understanding the woman's cir-

cumstances and then must be objective in deciding that, given the situation, she truly did act in a reasonable manner. Courts have already accepted the notion that self-defense does not require correctness in a situation, only reasonableness. Justice Oliver Wendell Holmes, in *Brown v. United States* (1921), said "[d]etached reflection cannot be demanded in the presence of an uplifted knife." Battered women and their advocates have asked the courts to revise their definitions of imminent danger and proportionate force.

Equal Force

Self-defense permits the use of equal force, which is defined as the least amount of force necessary to prevent imminent bodily harm or death. Women, however, who are generally physically weaker than men and who know the kind of physical damage their batterers are capable of, may justifiably feel that they are protecting their lives when shooting unarmed men. In *State v. Wanrow* (1977), the Washington Supreme Court ruled that it was permissible to instruct the jury that the objective standard of self-defense does not always apply.

Yvonne Wanrow was sitting up at night fearful that a male neighbor, who she thought had molested the child in her care, was going to make good on his threats to break into the house where she was staying. When the 6-foot-2-inch intoxicated man did enter, Wanrow, who was incapacitated with a broken leg, shot him. The court ruled, "The respondent was entitled to have the jury consider her actions in the light of her own perception of the situation, including those perceptions that were the product of our nation's long and unfortunate history of sex-discrimination. . . . Until such time as the effects of that history are eradicated, care must be taken to assure that our self-defense instructions afford women the right to have their conduct judged in light of the individual physical handicaps that are the product of sex discrimination. To fail to do so is to deny the right of the individual woman involved to trial by the same rules that are applicable to male defendants."

The court ruling also noted that women "suffer from a conspicuous lack of access to training in and the means of developing those skills necessary to effectively repel a male assailant without resorting to the use of deadly weapons."

Imminent versus Immediate Danger

Traditionally, self-defense required that the danger be immediate, meaning that the danger was present at the very moment the decision to respond was made, in order to justify the use of force. Accepting imminent danger, or danger that is about to occur, as justification for action permits the jury to understand the motivations and dynamics of a battered woman's behavior. A history of abuse may explain why a defendant might react to the threat of violence more quickly than a stranger would in the same circumstances. In *Wanrow,* the Washington Supreme Court found that when the jury considered a woman's actions based on immediate danger, it was required to focus only on the time immediately before the defendant's actions. "It is clear that the jury is entitled to consider all of the circumstances surrounding the incident in determining whether [the] defendant had reasonable grounds to believe grievous bodily harm was about to be inflicted," the court wrote.

Walker observes in *Terrifying Love: Why Battered Women Kill and How Society Responds* (Harper and Row, New York, 1989) that it is often hard for a jury to understand how a woman can be continuously afraid of a man with whom she lives. Walker insists, however, that her own research and others' repeatedly demonstrate that battered women know their abusers' potential for violence and live in constant fear, even when they have developed coping skills that enable them to continue living with their violent partners. Fully 85 percent of the 400 battered women Walker interviewed felt they could or would be killed at some time by their abusers.

Juries and Expert Testimony

Whether a woman will be convicted largely depends on the jury's attitude, or the judge's disposition when it is not a jury trial, and the amount of background and personal history of abuse that the judge or jury is permitted to hear. Juries that have not heard expert witnesses present the BWS defense are often unsympathetic to women who kill their abusive partners.

Regina Schuller et al., in "Jurors' Decisions in Trials of Battered Women Who Kill: The Role of Prior Beliefs and Expert Testimony" (*Journal of Applied Psychology,* vol. 24, no. 4, 1994), find that jurors who learned about BWS from expert testimony were more likely to believe the defendant feared for her life, that she was in danger, and that she was trapped in the abusive relationship. Equipped with knowledge and understanding of BWS, jurors handed down fewer murder convictions than were issued by a control group of jurors who were not given this specialized information.

Using mock jury trials, Schuller et al. examine whether a potential juror's belief in a "just world" would influence how he or she receives and responds to expert testimony. A strong belief in a just world says that a person deserves his or her fate. Persons holding strong "just world" beliefs would decide that when a woman is abused, she must be responsible for the beating in some way or she must deserve and share responsibility for the outcome. The study finds that women who did not accept the concept of a just world were especially receptive to, and influenced by, expert testimony. Men, however, independent of their beliefs, were generally more resistant to the influence of expert witnesses.

Walker believes that an expert witness is extremely helpful in educating a jury about issues that are outside of the realm of most jurors' experience and understanding. It is, however, up to the judge to determine whether an expert's testimony will be permitted. In Walker's experience, when an expert witness is not allowed to testify before a jury, a woman will not be acquitted on the grounds of self-defense.

When judges opt not to permit expert testimony, it is frequently because they do not wish the expert to influence jurors about the specific circumstances and details of the case. In some states, an expert witness is only permitted to speak generally about the phenomenon of BWS and may not comment about the individual woman on trial. On the other hand, some states permit the expert to express an opinion on the ultimate question of whether the battered defendant's behavior was reasonable in view of her circumstances.

A CASE STUDY: *STATE V. NORMAN.* In *State v. Norman* (1989), the North Carolina Court of Appeals overturned a lower court's verdict of voluntary manslaughter for a woman who fatally shot her husband while he was sleeping because the original court had failed to instruct the jury on self-defense. In the final appeal, however, the North Carolina Supreme Court reversed that opinion and reaffirmed the validity of the first court's traditional objective standard of self-defense, resulting in a conviction of voluntary manslaughter.

The defendant, Judy Norman, had been continually abused during her 25-year marriage to her husband, JT. He had beaten her with every available weapon, forced her into prostitution, and required her to eat dog food from a bowl on the floor. He had thrown her down stairs when she was pregnant with their youngest child, causing her to give birth prematurely, and often threatened to "cut her heart out." Dr. William Tyson, an expert witness at the trial, characterized her situation as "torture, degradation, and reduction to an animal level of existence where all behavior was marked purely by survival."

On this final occasion, JT was arrested for drunk driving and after his release from jail, he came home to vent his anger on his wife, beating her for 36 hours. In the past, Judy had sought help from Mental Health Services and the Department of Social Services, but her husband had always come to get her, reaffirming her belief that her husband was invulnerable to the law. In her mind, the only choices left were to kill him or die.

The defense relied heavily on BWS and the theory of learned helplessness. Bennett, in "Ending the Continuous Reign of Terror," applauds the court of appeals decision to accept the special circumstances of battered women, asserting that, by recognizing self-defense as a concern, the court validated the view that a defendant may reasonably fear imminent harm from a sleeping person. The court ruled that reasonable, deadly fear is not only theoretically possible, but also real, and may have been present in Judy's mind.

But Bennett argues that the court of appeals was wrong to claim that "therefore, a battered spouse who kills a passive abuser can satisfy the traditional elements of self-defense under an objective analysis." Bennett points out that the imminency requirement may stop the woman from employing the right of self-defense at the one time it would work: when the abuser is passive. Instead, the rule directs the woman to wait until she could be completely defenseless—during or just prior to a battering incident—before she can justifiably save her life. Thus, the court essentially recognized that the requirement of imminent danger may be met by events outside of an actual attack or a threat of attack, but only in the special circumstances of battered spouses. This recognition, Bennett contends, is a monumental exception to the general principle of self-defense.

By accepting this definition of self-defense, the court cannot claim to have used an objective standard. Bennett suggests that the reason the North Carolina Supreme Court overturned the court of appeals decision was because the latter court may have tried to mask its move to subjectivity and that it would have been better off to admit that it was relaxing its standard in order to accommodate killings that do not objectively meet traditional self-defense criteria.

Bennett concludes that instead of adhering to outdated concepts and a rigid interpretation of self-defense, the court of appeals made an honest effort to take up the legal aspects of spousal abuse. The court demonstrated significant insight by recognizing the plight of victims of BWS—a predicament created by the deadly combination of characteristics of the syndrome and strict judicial adherence to standards that were never intended to address such situations. Accordingly, the court ruled with a compassionate and insightful opinion that is part of a growing trend in self-defense law.

On July 7, 1989, Governor James G. Martin commuted Judy Norman's six-year manslaughter sentence to time she had already served.

SHOULD THE LAW BE CHANGED?

Some observers believe that by acknowledging the differences between men and women and accepting different conduct from each, the courts are moving perilously closer to providing two standards of justice. A woman can be permitted to use a gun in self-defense in cases where a man cannot and she may need the extra help of an expert witness to explain her motivation to a jury. Is this a step in the right direction for the courts? Are the courts

only now incorporating changes needed to resolve and adjudicate previously unconsidered situations? Have women been discriminated against and is society only now righting the wrongs?

Those opposed to changing the law claim that many domestic disputes are more complicated than battered women's advocates portray. Sonny Burmeister, the president of the Georgia Council for Children's Rights, an organization that lobbies for equal treatment for men in child custody cases, believes that women are trying to write a customized set of laws, depicting men as violent and women as victims, thereby absolving women from the social and legal consequences of their actions.

Incorrect Assumptions

There are those who object to revising the law, claiming that these modifications will permit women to kill their husbands indiscriminately. By allowing such change, they argue, the law is sending a message to society that revenge is acceptable, even permitted, under the law. Holly Maguigan, a defense attorney and law professor, argues in "Battered Women and Self-Defense: Myths and Misconceptions in Current Reform Proposals" (*University of Pennsylvania Law Review,* vol. 140, no. 2, 1991) that the law does not need to be changed. It needs to be properly applied.

According to Maguigan, the effort to change the law is based on two incorrect assumptions. The first is that juries convict battered women for killing in nonconfrontational circumstances, such as during a lull in the violence or when a man is sleeping. The second assumption is that the current definitions of self-defense apply only to men of roughly equal size and power. Some insist that the law ignores the social context of the battered woman's actions. Maguigan counters that reformers have not carefully examined the law as it stands and that when the reformers explain what they mean by "a fair trial" they are referring to a not-guilty verdict.

Studies show that a large majority of women kill their abusers during a confrontation and not during a break in the attack. Browne estimates that at least 70 percent of women killed their abusers during a confrontation. Other researchers estimate that as many as 90 percent of women kill under confrontational circumstances. Maguigan examines 223 cases and finds that 75 percent involved confrontations, 8 percent involved "sleeping-man" situations, and 4 percent were contract killings. In 8 percent of the cases, the defendant was the aggressor in a lull in the violence, and in the remaining 5 percent there was not enough background in the court opinions to establish the accurate details of the events.

Regarding equal force, Maguigan asserts that nearly every jurisdiction decides questions of equal force on a case-by-case basis and does not ban a woman from using a weapon against an unarmed man. Courts have recognized for years that use of a weapon by a battered woman against an unarmed man does not necessarily constitute disproportionate force. In *Kress v. State* (1940), the Tennessee Supreme Court reversed the conviction of a woman who shot her husband in the midst of an attack. "Where a great bodily violence is being inflicted or threatened upon a person by one much stronger and heavier, with such determined energy that the person assaulted may reasonably apprehend death or great bodily injury, he is justifiable in using a deadly weapon," the court wrote.

Furthermore, the law in every state permits a history of past abuse to be presented in court. Cases of abused women who have killed their partners and who claimed self-defense are not new. They date back at least to 1902, long before the theory of BWS. Maguigan concedes that jurisdictions that accept imminent danger as opposed to immediate danger are more likely to present the history of abuse to the jury to explain the reasonableness of the woman's conduct.

A Misapplication of the Law

Maguigan's analysis reveals that convictions of battered women usually resulted from a misapplication of the law, not from the unjust structure of the law. She finds that 40 percent of the guilty verdicts were later reversed in higher courts, a rate significantly higher than the national average rate of reversal of 8.5 percent in homicide cases in general. Problems arose when trial court judges interpreted the women's acts as vigilantism and did not permit instruction to the jury on self-defense or presentation of history-of-abuse evidence. In *State v. Branchal* (1984), the trial judge commented that the court "did not want to condone spousal retaliation for past violence."

Maguigan concludes that in most jurisdictions it is the failure of the trial judges to apply general standards of self-defense, not the legal definition of self-defense, that prevents battered women from obtaining fair trials. Neither current proposals for legal redefinition nor creation of separate standards will remedy problems resulting from a refusal to apply the law. If legal exceptions are made, there is a danger that trial judges will apply the law too strictly, possibly excluding some women. A trial judge in Missouri, for example, made a decision (subsequently reversed on appeal) that BWS did not apply to a defendant because she was not legally married to the abuser.

Maguigan cautions that when the law defines a special group of people, it eliminates others, and in this situation it could deny expert witnesses or special instructions on self-defense because an individual defendant's case did not meet the strict definition of a battered woman. She suggests that flexibility and general terms are more beneficial, citing the proposed rule of evidence for the New York State courts as an example, "If scientific, technical or other specialized knowledge will assist the trier of fact to understand the evidence or to determine a fact in issue, a witness qualified as an expert by knowledge, skill, experience, training or education, may testify."

According to Maguigan, the laws to provide women with fair trials are already in place. What is needed is for jurisdictions to understand and accept the legal precedents of imminent rather than immediate danger and to allow evidence of a history of battering and expert testimony to explain the reasonableness of a battered woman's reaction.

CALIFORNIA LAW FREES BATTERED WIFE WHO KILLED HER HUSBAND. On October 25, 2002, Marva Wallace, a 44-year-old high school graduate and mother of two, was freed after serving 17 years in state prison for the murder of her abusive husband. Wallace was the first person released under a California law enacted in January 2002 that allows inmates convicted prior to 1992, for whom evidence of BWS was not presented at trial, to file writs of habeas corpus (protection against illegal imprisonment) asking that convictions be overturned or sentences reduced and enabling them to petition for new trials.

The abuse began just two months into Wallace's marriage. According to court documents, her husband beat her and the beatings often left her bloodied and bruised. He refused to allow Wallace to work, isolated her from her family, and would not give her money to support her children. A substance abuser, Wallace's husband had previously abused his first wife.

On the day she killed him, Wallace asked her husband if she could take her two-year-old daughter to visit the girl's grandmother. Her husband became angry, slapped her, and forced her to perform oral sex in front of her daughter. Shortly after these events, she shot him with a gun that was in their home.

Although friends and family testified at the trial that Wallace had been abused, there was no expert witness to present the effects of abuse on Wallace's mental state. She was convicted of first-degree murder and sentenced to 27 years to life in state prison.

In an article that appeared in the October 26, 2002, *Los Angeles Times,* David S. Wesley, the judge who overturned the murder conviction, acknowledged that Wallace had been a battered wife and that she was convicted in 1985 when much less was known and understood about intimate partner violence. Judge Wesley said, "I am going to order a new trial in this case, and I am going to release the defendant on her own recognizance." The Los Angeles district attorney's office expressed the hope that the case would be resolved without a new trial.

CHAPTER 10

INTIMATE PARTNER VIOLENCE ISSUES AND ATTITUDES

Recent adoption and use of the term "intimate partner violence," instead of "wife battering," "spouse abuse," or "domestic violence," is one sign of changing views about violent relationships because intimate partner violence describes a broader range of abusive relationships, including psychological abuse and social isolation, and acknowledges that violence occurs among unmarried and same-sex partners as well as among persons who do not live together or maintain sexual relationships. Also, according to the American Medical Association (AMA) report *AMA Data on Violence Between Intimates* (AMA Council on Scientific Affairs, December 2000), the term is generally used to describe "a continuing pattern of behavior rather than a single violent act."

The Centers for Disease Control and Prevention (CDC) recognizes that use of consistent terminology is vital for researchers collecting data about the scope of the problem. In 1999 the CDC published *Intimate Partner Violence Surveillance: Uniform Definitions and Recommended Data Elements* (Linda E. Saltzman, Janet L. Fanslow, Pamela M. McMahon, and Gene A. Shelley, Atlanta, GA) in an effort to establish tracking systems, identify high-risk populations, and assess the results of prevention programs. The AMA report endorses the CDC effort to standardize the terminology, enabling researchers, health care professionals, and policy makers to use the same terms to describe comparable violent acts.

VIOLENCE ON OUR MINDS

Americans are worried about violence and violent crimes. Surveys find that violent crime, violence in schools and among young people, and the depiction of violence in the media are all worrisome trends. A 1999 nationwide ABC News poll asked adults: "And what do you see as the greatest remaining problem that people will have to deal with in the next millennium?" Although just 8 percent of respondents answered "violence," making it the fourth

most frequent response, arguably the top two responses, "racism/prejudice/hate crimes" (14 percent) and "learning to get along with each other" (9 percent), also reflect concerns about violence in society. Along with the more than 30 percent of survey respondents who considered the problems mentioned above to be the greatest challenge, an additional 5 percent cited "war," 3 percent named "crime," and 3 percent said "learning how to live in peace."

Fear of intimate partner violence is not foremost in the minds of most Americans, but an October 1998 Harris Poll found that 6 percent of respondents said they thought it was very likely they would be hit by a spouse or partner, an additional 8 percent felt it was somewhat likely, and 1 percent admitted that it had already happened to them. In view of the stigma associated with intimate partner violence and the reluctance to admit or disclose it, the finding that 15 percent of survey respondents thought it likely to occur in their personal relationships is significant.

A poll by Harris Interactive, Inc., which was published in the *Sourcebook of Criminal Justice Statistics 2000* (Bureau of Justice Statistics, Washington, DC, 2001), compares survey responses given in 1994, 1999, and 2001 about the factors Americans believe contribute to violence in our society. Although the most frequently named causes remained constant through each survey year—in 2001, 86 percent cited "lack of adult supervision" and 60 percent said "easy availability of handguns"—the percentage of respondents attributing violence to these factors declined from 1994 to 2001. The biggest drop was in the proportion of persons blaming television news media for encouraging violence—from 39 percent in 1999 to 30 percent in 2001.

Men and Women View Domestic Violence Differently

A 1997 survey commissioned by Women's Work, a program of Liz Claiborne, Inc., and conducted by the public opinion research firm Roper Starch Worldwide, found

FIGURE 10.1

Opinion poll on domestic violence being a widespread problem

DO YOU THINK DOMESTIC VIOLENCE IS A WIDESPREAD PROBLEM IN OUR SOCIETY?

	Respondents	
Domestic violence widespread?	Number	Percent
Yes	453	91.5%
No	42	8.5%
Total	495	100.0%

*Cases not applicable = 7

More than 9 of every 10 Floridians (91.5%) believe that domestic violence is a widespread problem in our society.

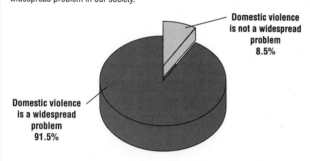

Domestic violence is not a widespread problem 8.5%

Domestic violence is a widespread problem 91.5%

SOURCE: "Question 1: Do you think domestic violence is a widespread problem in our society?" in *Florida's Perspective on Domestic Violence*, Florida Department of Corrections, Tallahassee, FL, 1999

FIGURE 10.2

Opinion poll on the increase or decrease of domestic violence in Florida

OVER THE LAST TEN YEARS, DO YOU THINK THE NUMBER OF INCIDENTS OF DOMESTIC VIOLENCE IN FLORIDA HAS DECREASED A LITTLE, DECREASED A LOT, STAYED THE SAME, INCREASED A LITTLE OR INCREASED A LOT?

	Respondents	
10 year change in domestic violence	Number	Percent
Increased a lot	219	48.9%
Increased a little	133	29.7%
Stayed about the same	69	15.4%
Decreased a little	23	5.1%
Decreased a lot	4	0.9%
Total	448	100.0%

*Cases not applicable = 54

The majority of respondents (78.6%) believe that over the past 10 years, the number of incidents of domestic violence in Florida has increased. Only 6.0% believe domestic violence has decreased over the past 10 years. Women felt that it has increased more (84.3%) then men (70.2%).

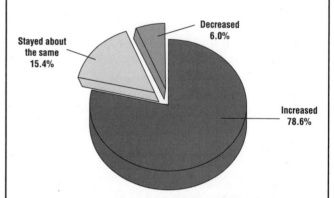

Decreased 6.0%

Stayed about the same 15.4%

Increased 78.6%

SOURCE: "Question 4: Over the last ten years, do you think the number of incidents of domestic violence in Florida has decreased a little, decreased a lot, stayed the same, increased a little or increased a lot?" in *Florida's Perspective on Domestic Violence*, Florida Department of Corrections, Tallahassee, FL, 1999

that men and women define domestic violence and abusive behavior differently. Interviews with a random sample of 1,011 adults nationwide revealed that while men and women basically agree that acts and threats of physical violence are abusive, they disagree about the behaviors that constitute psychological abuse.

Controlling behaviors, such as dictating the clothes a woman must wear, was considered by more than half the female respondents as abusive, but only 33 percent of men said it was definitely abusive behavior. Similarly, less than one-quarter of males thought that withholding money from a wife or girlfriend was abusive, while 37 percent of women felt it was definitely abusive and 74 percent thought it probably was.

More women (78 percent) than men (67 percent) viewed social isolation—preventing a woman from contact with family and friends—as abusive. Fully 85 percent of women and 75 percent of men thought that a man's cursing or insulting his partner in front of others constituted abuse.

About three-quarters of all survey respondents considered violence directed at women by their partners as among the major problems facing the country, and 21 percent thought it was a minor problem. A scant 2 percent said it was

not a problem at all. More women (85 percent) felt domestic violence was a major problem than men (69 percent).

More than half of all respondents reported that they knew someone directly involved in intimate partner violence, as either a victim or perpetrator. Slightly more women (59 percent) than men (54 percent) said they knew someone involved in an abusive relationship. Nearly one-third of respondents knew that about one out of four women is affected by domestic violence, but 37 percent admitted that they didn't know enough about the problem to estimate how frequently it occurs.

The State of Florida Weighs in on Domestic Violence

In June 1999 the Florida Department of Corrections surveyed state residents to learn how they felt about domestic violence. More than 9 out of 10 Floridians thought domestic violence is a widespread problem in

TABLE 10.1

Opinion poll on percentage of physically abusive men

WHAT PERCENTAGE OF MEN DO YOU THINK HAVE EVER PHYSICALLY ABUSED THEIR WIVES OR GIRLFRIENDS?

Percentage of men who have abused wives or girlfriends	Respondents	
	Number	Percent
0–10%	47	11.7%
11–20%	54	13.4%
21–30%	90	22.2%
31–40%	58	14.4%
41–50%	64	15.9%
51–60%	27	6.7%
61–70%	24	6.0%
71–80%	23	5.7%
81–90%	10	2.5%
91–100%	6	1.5%
Total	403	100.0%

*Cases not applicable = 99

SOURCE: "Question 2: What percentage of men do you think have ever physically abused their wives or girlfriends?" in *Florida's Perspective on Domestic Violence*, Florida Department of Corrections, Tallahassee, FL, 1999

FIGURE 10.3

Opinion poll on the witnessing of physical abuse by a man toward his wife or girlfriend

HAVE YOU EVER WITNESSED A MAN PHYSICALLY ABUSING HIS WIFE OR GIRLFRIEND?

Witnessed abuse?	Respondents	
	Number	Percent
Yes	219	43.7%
No	282	56.3%
Total	501	100.0%

*Cases not applicable = 1

Over 1 in 3 (43.7%) Floridians have actually witnessed a man physically abusing his wife or girlfriend.

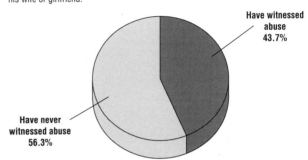

SOURCE: "Question 7: Have you ever witnessed a man physically abusing his wife or girlfriend?" in *Florida's Perspective on Domestic Violence*, Florida Department of Corrections, Tallahassee, FL, 1999

society, and the majority felt that their state had seen an increase in the number of incidents of domestic violence during the past decade. Only 6 percent felt the number of incidents of domestic violence had dropped. (See Figure 10.1 and Figure 10.2.) Official statistics from the Florida Department of Law Enforcement supported public perceptions—reporting that domestic violence crime increased by 9 percent—and the Florida Task Force on Domestic and Sexual Violence confirmed that only about one-seventh of all domestic assaults are reported to police.

Survey respondents were representative of the Florida population and ranged in age from 18 to 89 years—the average age of respondents was 45.5 years. The survey was composed of approximately 40 percent men and 60 percent women.

On average, survey respondents said they believed that nearly 40 percent of men have physically abused an intimate partner at some point in their life. (See Table 10.1.) Female respondents were more likely to believe that men abused their intimate partners (42.5 percent) than men (32.9 percent).

More than half (55.5 percent) the respondents knew at least one victim of domestic violence. Nearly 43 percent said the victim was a friend and more than one-quarter said an immediate family member had been a victim of domestic violence. One in three respondents (43.7 percent) reported that they had actually witnessed a man physically abusing his wife or girlfriend. (See Figure 10.3.)

The most frequently cited causes of domestic violence were women's reluctance to leave their abusers (89.8 percent), partners' inability to communicate and resolve differences (79.4 percent), drug and alcohol problems (78.4 percent), and the economic reality that many women are forced to choose between poverty and remaining with their abusers (76.7 percent). Respondents also thought that many men learned violent behavior in their homes during childhood and adolescence (73.1 percent), and they believed that the breakdown of the traditional family unit contributed to violence (67.6 percent).

Almost 65 percent of those surveyed said the courts did little to protect battered women, and 21.9 percent said they felt domestic violence persisted because police didn't do enough to stop it. (See Table 10.2.) More than 8 out of 10 respondents want police to arrest persons suspected of partner violence and more than 85 percent want to see offenders who caused serious bodily harm to their victims imprisoned. (See Table 10.3.) More than three-quarters believed that abusers should be both punished and forced to receive treatment, and less than 8 percent felt that punishment without treatment was sufficient.

To compare how survey participants viewed domestic violence in comparison to violence in the community, they were asked how a man should be punished who has beaten up his wife at home and how a man should be punished who has beaten up another man in a bar. Overall, the respondents did not view these violations as different in terms of their proposed punishments. Almost 70 percent favored imprisoning a man who assaulted a woman at

TABLE 10.2

Opinion poll on the causes of domestic violence, 1999

	Percent	
Causes	Agree	Disagree
Domestic violence continues because most women will not leave the men who abuse them.	89.8%	10.2%
Domestic violence is the result of a couple's inability to communicate and resolve conflicts.	79.4%	20.6%
Drug and alcohol problems are the primary cause of domestic violence.	78.4%	21.6%
Many women have to choose between living on their own and being poor or staying in the home where they are being battered.	76.7%	23.2%
Most men learn to be violent because they were beaten or witnessed violence in their home when they were growing up.	73.1%	26.9%
Domestic violence is caused by the breakdown of the traditional family.	67.6%	32.4%
The court system does very little to protect abused women.	64.9%	35.1%
Domestic violence is a result of unequal relationships between men and women.	54.3%	45.7%
Domestic violence exists because police won't stop it.	21.9%	77.1%
It's none of my business if a husband physically abuses his wife during an argument inside their own home.	14.8%	85.2%

*Those who neither agreed nor disagreed were not used to calculate valid percentages.

SOURCE: "Question 8: Causes of Domestic Violence," in *Florida's Perspective on Domestic Violence: A 1999 Survey of Public Opinion*, Florida Department of Corrections, Tallahassee, FL, 1999. [Online] http://www.dc.state.fl.us/pub/domestic/why.html [accessed on November 11, 2002]

TABLE 10.3

Opinion polls on police intervention in domestic violence cases/imprisonment of serious offenders

WHEN THE POLICE HAVE BEEN CALLED TO A HOME, DO YOU THINK AN ARREST SHOULD BE MADE WHEN THE POLICE SUSPECT THAT DOMESTIC VIOLENCE HAS OCCURRED?

	Respondents	
Arrest if police suspect domestic violence?	Number	Percent
Yes	397	86.3%
No	63	13.7%
Total	460	100.0%

*Cases not applicable = 42
More than 8 in 10 Floridians (86.3%) believe that an arrest should be made when the police suspect domestic violence has occurred. More women (90.3%) believed that an arrest should be made when the police suspect domestic violence has occurred, compared to men (80.1%).

DO YOU THINK IMPRISONMENT IS THE APPROPRIATE PUNISHMENT FOR DOMESTIC VIOLENCE INCIDENTS INVOLVING SERIOUS BODILY INJURIES?

	Respondents	
Is imprisonment the appropriate punishment?	Number	Percent
Yes	412	85.3%
No	71	14.7%
Total	483	100.0%

*Cases not applicable = 19

SOURCE: "Question 10: When the police have been called to a home, do you think an arrest should be made when the police suspect that domestic violence has occurred?," and "Question 11: Do you think imprisonment is the appropriate punishment for domestic violence incidents involving serious bodily injury?," in *Florida's Perspective on Domestic Violence: A 1999 Survey of Public Opinion*, Florida Department of Corrections, Tallahassee, FL, 1999

home, and 74 percent would jail a man who assaulted another man in a bar.

Most respondents said that not enough taxpayer money was being spent on preventing and treating intimate partner violence and enforcing laws against it. Eight out of ten would support a tax increase to pay for more counseling for victims. Nearly three-quarters would agree to a tax increase to fund more shelters for victims and more than two-thirds of respondents were willing to spend more tax dollars to treat offenders. (See Table 10.4.)

According to the respondents, the most effective strategies for reducing domestic violence were counseling for victims, public education, treatment for abusers, and placing restraining orders on convicted offenders. (See Table 10.5.) More female respondents (73.9 percent) than males (51.8 percent) thought treatment of abusers would be very effective. Similarly, 80.8 percent of women favored counseling for victims, compared to 58.8 percent of men.

When they were questioned about their willingness to help victims of intimate partner violence, 9 out of 10 respondents said they would call the police if they heard an assault occurring next door. (See Table 10.6.) Nearly all the woman surveyed (94.5 percent) said they would telephone police and 87.9 percent of men indicated they also would contact police. Furthermore, the overwhelm-

ing majority (93 percent) said they would testify in court about an assault they had seen. (See Table 10.7.)

To determine how they felt about the 1997 legislation that made it illegal for a person convicted of domestic violence to own a firearm, survey respondents were asked if they agreed or disagreed with this legislation. Most respondents (89 percent) agreed with the law, with women expressing more support than men (92.9 percent and 79.4 percent, respectively). Furthermore, 9 out of 10 respondents said neither law enforcement officers nor military personnel should be exempt from the legislation prohibiting convicts or subjects of an injunction from possessing a firearm. (See Table 10.8.)

Table 10.9 shows that only 40 percent of respondents were aware of batterer intervention programs and less than 8 percent said they knew of a man involved in one of the programs. Nonetheless, a full 91.8 percent of those surveyed felt that it should be mandatory for all men charged with domestic violence to attend batterer intervention programs. (See Table 10.10.)

Figure 10.4 shows that most respondents also believed the media has not directed enough attention to domestic violence issues.

TABLE 10.4

Opinion polls on spending taxpayer money/increasing taxes in regard to domestic violence issues

	Percent	
Do you think enough taxpayer money is spent on the:	Yes	No
Enforcement of domestic violence laws?	33.9%	66.1%
Prevention of domestic violence?	22.6%	77.4%
Treatment of domestic violence offenders?	22.0%	78.0%

	Percent	
Would you agree an increase in your taxes to:	Yes	No
Fund more counseling for victims?	83.1%	16.9%
Fund more shelters for abused women?	74.2%	25.8%
Fund more treatment programs for batterers?	68.0%	32.0%
Increase police enforcement of domestic violence laws?	66.7%	33.3%
Increase prison space for batterers?	60.8%	39.2%

SOURCE: "Question 15: Do you think enough taxpayer money is spent on the...?" and "Question 16: Would you agree to an increase in your taxes to...?," in *Florida's Perspective on Domestic Violence: A 1999 Survey of Public Opinion,* Florida Department of Corrections, Tallahassee, FL, 1999

TABLE 10.6

Opinion poll about reporting domestic violence situation at neighbors' home to police

IF YOU HEARD THE SOUNDS OF PHYSICAL ASSAULT FROM THE COUPLE NEXT DOOR, WOULD YOU CALL THE POLICE?

	Respondents	
Call police	Number	Percent
Yes	450	91.8%
No	40	8.2%
Total	490	100.0%

*Cases not applicable = 12

SOURCE: "Question 18: If you heard the sounds of a physical assault from the couple next door, would you call the police?," in *Florida's Perspective on Domestic Violence: A 1999 Survey of Public Opinion,* Florida Department of Corrections, Tallahassee, FL, 1999

TABLE 10.5

Opinion poll about how to decrease domestic violence

ON A SCALE OF 1 TO 10 WITH 10 BEING THE MOST EFFECTIVE, HOW EFFECTIVE DO YOU THINK THE FOLLOWING STEPS ARE IN DECREASING DOMESTIC VIOLENCE?

	Responses	
Most effective steps to decrease domestic violence	Number	Percent
Providing more counseling for the victim	357	72.0%
More education to the public	329	66.9%
Providing treatment for the abuser	318	64.9%
Placing restraining orders on those found guilty	284	57.4%
Sending more of those found guilty to jail or prison	262	53.9%
Increasing the number arrested	215	44.2%

SOURCE: "Question 17: On a scale of 1 to 10 with 10 being the most effective, how effective do you think the following steps are in decreasing domestic violence?," in *Florida's Perspective on Domestic Violence: A 1999 Survey of Public Opinion,* Florida Department of Corrections, Tallahassee, FL, 1999.

TABLE 10.7

Opinion poll about testifying in court after witnessing a domestic violence assault

UNDER WHAT CONDITIONS WOULD YOU TESTIFY IN COURT ABOUT A DOMESTIC VIOLENCE ASSAULT YOU WITNESSED?

	Percent	
Conditions would testify under	Yes	No
Would testify under any conditions	93.0%	7.0%
If it were a friend	56.0%	44.0%
Serious injury	61.6%	38.4%
No danger to you	44.8%	55.2%
Other	36.8%	63.2%

SOURCE: "Question 19: Under what conditions would you testify in court about a domestic violence assault you witnessed?," in *Florida's Perspective on Domestic Violence: A 1999 Survey of Public Opinion,* Florida Department of Corrections, Tallahassee, FL, 1999

How Do Women Feel About Mandatory Reporting of Domestic Violence?

There is considerable controversy about mandatory reporting requirements among health care professionals, patients, and advocates for domestic violence prevention. From 1991 to 1994 California, Colorado, Rhode Island, and Kentucky passed laws requiring health professionals to report cases of intimate partner violence to the police.

Proponents of mandatory reporting claim it increases identification and prosecution of abusers and improves data collection. Critics feel it compromises victims' autonomy, may increase the risk of further violence by perpetrators, and endangers patient-practitioner trust and confidentiality.

Michael Rodriguez et al., in "Mandatory Reporting of Domestic Violence Injuries to the Police: What Do Emergency Department Patients Think?" (*Journal of the Amer-*

ican Medical Association, vol. 286, no. 5, August 1, 2001), examine how female patients seen in emergency departments viewed mandatory reporting of domestic violence injuries to police. The investigators surveyed 1,218 female patients in 12 hospital emergency departments in California, where reporting is mandatory, and Pennsylvania, where there is no law requiring reporting. Twelve percent of the patients (140 women) reported physical or sexual abuse within the year preceding the study by a current or former intimate partner.

To determine patients' views about the mandatory reporting law, they were asked by female nurses: "Do you think the emergency department staff in hospitals should be required to call the police when they think that a husband, boyfriend, or partner (ex-husband, ex-boyfriend, ex-partner) has hurt or abused an adult patient?" Respondents could choose one of three answers: yes, every time; every time unless the patient objects; and never.

Rodriguez et al. find that more than half (55.7 percent) of the recently victimized female respondents supported mandatory reporting of intimate partner violence

TABLE 10.8

Opinion polls about whether domestic violence offenders (including law enforcement officers and military personnel) should be allowed to possess firearms

RECENT LEGISLATION HAS MADE IT ILLEGAL FOR AN INDIVIDUAL WHO HAS BEEN CONVICTED OF DOMESTIC VIOLENCE OR IS THE SUBJECT OF AN INJUNCTION TO POSSESS A FIREARM. DO YOU AGREE OR DISAGREE WITH THIS LEGISLATION?

Possess a firearm	Respondents	
	Number	Percent
Agree	431	89.0%
Disagree	53	11.0%
Total	484	100.0%

*Cases not applicable = 18

Overall, 9 of 10 (89.0%) of respondents are supportive of the legislation preventing domestic violence offenders from possessing a firearm. Women (92.9%) are more likely than men (79.4%) to agree with this legislation.

LAW ENFORCEMENT OFFICERS AND MILITARY PERSONNEL ARE EXEMPT FROM THE "POSSESSION OF A FIREARM ILLEGAL" LAW. DO YOU AGREE THAT THEY SHOULD BE EXEMPT?

Exempt law enforcement and military personnel	Respondents	
	Number	Percent
Agree	64	13.4%
Disagree	413	86.6%
Total	477	100.0%

*Cases not applicable = 25

SOURCE: "Question 20: Recent legislation has made it illegal for an individual who has been convicted of domestic violence or is the subject of an injunction to possess a firearm. Do you agree or disagree with this legislation?" and "Question 21: Law enforcement officers and military personnel are exempt from the 'possession of a firearm illegal' law. Do you agree that they should be exempt?," in *Florida's Perspective on Domestic Violence: A 1999 Survey of Public Opinion,* Florida Department of Corrections, Tallahassee, FL, 1999

TABLE 10.9

Opinion poll about awareness of Batterer's Intervention Programs

WERE YOU AWARE OF THE EXISTENCE OF THE BATTERER'S INTERVENTION PROGRAMS BEFORE TAKING THIS SURVEY?

Aware of programs	Respondents	
	Number	Percent
Yes	203	40.6%
No	297	59.4%
Total	500	100.0%

*Cases not applicable = 2

SOURCE: "Question 22: Were you aware of the existence of the Batterer's Intervention Programs before taking this survey?," in *Florida's Perspective on Domestic Violence: A 1999 Survey of Public Opinion,* Florida Department of Corrections, Tallahassee, FL, 1999. [Online] http://www.dc.state.fl.us/pub/domestic/batter.html [accessed November 11, 2002]

to police, while 36.4 percent thought physicians should report only with patient consent. About 44 percent of abused women opposed mandatory reporting. The women who opposed mandatory reporting tended to be younger and nonwhite.

Of the women with no prior history of abuse, 70.7 percent favored mandatory reporting and 29.3 percent opposed it. Women who were primarily non-English speaking were more likely to oppose mandatory reporting, perhaps because their experiences with police were different from those of U.S.-born women or because they feared deportation.

There were no differences between the opinions expressed by women in California and those in Pennsylvania. Similarly, opposition to reporting did not vary by relationship status or income.

Rodriguez et al. concede that one of the limitations of their study is that it very likely did not obtain the opinions of women who failed to seek care in California because they knew of the mandatory reporting requirement and did not wish to have their perpetrators identified. If abused women are choosing not to seek emergency department care because of reporting requirements, then this study may underestimate the extent to which abused women would oppose laws that mandate reports to police.

THE AMERICAN PSYCHOLOGICAL ASSOCIATION CONSIDERS THE ISSUES

In its *Report of the APA Presidential Task Force on Violence and the Family* (Washington, DC, 1996), the American Psychological Association (APA) outlines some of the issues that challenge researchers and professionals seeking to prevent and stop domestic violence. The APA Presidential Task Force identifies the 12 dilemmas faced by family violence researchers and mental health practitioners, including these concerns:

• Privacy—There is an inescapable tension between the right of individuals to privacy and the need to penetrate the isolation and secrecy that often shield intimate partner violence from public scrutiny. One example of how this concern affects research is the preponderance of data suggesting that more violence occurs among low-income families. Researchers speculate that these data may simply indicate that low-income victims who must rely on hospital emergency departments and battered women's shelters are less able to conceal the consequences of abuse than persons with greater resources.

• Expectations of law enforcement—There are differing expectations of the police response to violence. Many victims want the police to intervene to stop abusive behavior, but they do not want the perpetrators punished. On the other hand, researchers, health professionals, and law enforcement personnel contend that mandatory treatment and arrests are necessary to protect victims from further harm and safeguard the community at large.

TABLE 10.10

Opinion poll regarding whether male domestic violence offenders should be required to attend Batterer's Intervention Programs

DO YOU THINK IT SHOULD BE MANDATORY FOR ALL MEN CHARGED WITH DOMESTIC VIOLENCE TO BE REQUIRED TO ATTEND BATTERER'S INTERVENTION PROGRAMS?

| | Respondents | |
Should programs be mandatory?	Number	Percent
Yes	180	91.8%
No	16	8.2%
Total	196	100.0%

*Cases not applicable = 306

SOURCE: "Question 22: Do you think it should be mandatory for all men charged with domestic violence to be required to attend Batterer's Intervention Programs?," in *Florida's Perspective on Domestic Violence: A 1999 Survey of Public Opinion,* Florida Department of Corrections, Tallahassee, FL, 1999

• Conflicting attitudes about abuse—Although most people feel sympathy for victims, there are those who believe that society inadvertently encourages victims by allowing them to use a history of abuse as an excuse for all subsequent bad behavior and problems. This viewpoint is different from blaming the victim for the abuse because it is intended to help victims assume individual responsibility for their behavior, and to heal and recover, rather than remain in the role of victim.

• Effectiveness of mandated treatment—There are ongoing debates about the effectiveness of different philosophies and models of treatment, as well as the use of court-ordered treatment. While some abusers who complete mandatory treatment programs do change their behavior, many studies confirm that these perpetrators are the most motivated and that many other offenders fail to complete court-ordered treatment. The APA asserts that while the desire to change is linked to favorable outcomes of treatment, involuntary treatment can nevertheless be effective, especially when the perpetrator has been evaluated and enrolled in the most appropriate program.

PREVENTING RELATIONSHIP VIOLENCE

In 2000 the Working Group on Intimate Partner Abuse and Relationship Violence, a multidisciplinary group with members from five professional societies, published a curriculum for psychologists addressing issues related to researching, preventing, and treating intimate partner violence. The objectives of prevention were described as:

• Stopping the violent behavior from ever occurring

• Delaying the onset of violent behavior

• Reducing the impact of existing violent behavior

• Strengthening behaviors that promote emotional and physical well-being, thereby inoculating people from the negative effects of relationship violence

FIGURE 10.4

Opinion poll on domestic violence in the media

ON THE ISSUE OF DOMESTIC VIOLENCE IN THE MEDIA, DO YOU THINK THAT THERE HAS BEEN ENOUGH ATTENTION TO THE ISSUE?

| | Respondents | |
Media attention	Number	Percent
Not enough attention	271	56.7%
Just enough	122	25.5%
Too much attention	85	17.8%
Total	478	100.0%

*Cases not applicable = 24

Most Floridians (56.7%) believe the media do not direct enough attention to the issue of domestic violence. Only 17.8% believe that too much attention is being focused on the issue.

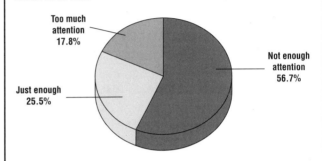

SOURCE: "Question 9: On the issue of domestic violence in the media, do you think that there has been enough attention to the issue?," in *Florida's Perspective on Domestic Violence: A 1999 Survey of Public Opinion,* Florida Department of Corrections, Tallahassee, FL, 1999

• Supporting institutional, community, and government policies that promote the prevention of relational violence

The APA recommends instituting violence prevention programs aimed at middle school, high school, and college students that are intended to heighten awareness and reduce rates of date rape. Furthermore, it is important that the prevention programs be repeated since there is considerable evidence that these education programs do produce measurable effects on knowledge and attitudes, though the effects are often not lasting.

Other special-needs populations that the curriculum targeted for prevention programs include immigrants, ethnic minorities, and persons who are gay, lesbian, or bisexual.

Levels of Violence Prevention

Many researchers believe that in order to effectively address the public health problem of intimate partner violence, health professionals, policy makers, educators, and women's advocates must intensify violence prevention efforts. There are three levels of prevention: primary, secondary, and tertiary.

Primary prevention of intimate partner violence aims to reduce harmful circumstances before they can produce violence and includes global educational efforts to promote nonviolent interactions and relationships.

Secondary prevention of intimate partner violence is intended to break the pattern of violent behavior before it becomes deeply ingrained. Examples of such efforts are early identification and counseling of first-time offenders—challenging and changing behavior as soon as possible after its occurrence. Unfortunately, few programs specifically targeting first-time offenders are available and programs for chronic perpetrators often alienate first-time offenders who feel they do not belong with severe batterers.

Tertiary prevention of intimate partner violence involves services for victims, counseling, and mandatory treatment of offenders, and may also involve justice interventions, such as arrest and incarceration.

The majority of efforts to date focus on tertiary prevention. However, changing attitudes about intimate partner violence and increasing recognition of violence as a societal problem that affects more than just the victims emphasize the need for primary prevention. Many researchers, health educators, and policy makers advocate community education that promotes a zero-tolerance policy. They contend that societal pressures exerted against intimate partner violence can reduce partner abuse in much the same way that antismoking campaigns have reduced both the overall prevalence and social acceptability of cigarette smoking.

Primary Prevention Theories

In *Primary Prevention of Intimate Partner Violence* (National Institute of Mental Health, Washington, DC, July 2002), researchers Martha Smithey and Murray Straus describe the environmental changes and educational approaches they feel will serve to reduce the risk of intimate partner violence for the entire population. Smithey and Straus assert that "the outcome envisioned as a result of primary prevention is that, although some individuals may continue to be violent, their number will be reduced."

Smithey and Straus feel primary prevention is consistent with the feminist approach to reducing intimate partner violence, since feminists view patriarchy and male dominance as the principle causes of violence. Societal change that promotes equality between men and women is viewed by feminists as primary prevention of partner violence. Underlying this view is the belief that the more humane a society becomes, the less likely that its individual members will resort to intimate partner violence.

Smithey and Straus find that while there are few programs specifically aimed at primary prevention of intimate partner violence, some programs offer both primary and secondary types of services. For example, in addition to aiding victims, battered women's shelters may offer community education and other programs to empower women. Furthermore, the presence of shelters in a community sends a clear message that victims have alternatives to remaining in abusive relationships and conveys the community's intolerance of partner violence.

Similarly, the justice concepts of "general deterrence" and "specific deterrence" have primary and secondary prevention objectives. Legal sanctions, such as arrest, prosecution, mandatory treatment, and incarceration, deliver the secondary prevention benefit of deterring an offender from further violence and may also perform a primary prevention function: deterring others from perpetrating violence by warning them of the consequences of their actions.

Though there are no data linking legislative changes, such as the enactment of the 1994 Violence Against Women Act and the criminalization of wife beating, to changing public attitudes about intimate partner violence, Smithey and Straus feel that the combination of legal reform and widespread access to and availability of services such as hot lines, shelters, and advocacy has resulted in social change.

Smithey and Straus present 11 criminal justice theories and their implications for primary prevention of intimate partner violence. The following theories have practical applications for prevention programs:

1. Deterrence Theory—Intensify formal and informal sanctions for abusive behavior by family, friends, and colleagues

2. Strain Theory—Create more opportunities for education and economic achievement, promote gender equality in the family, and foster realistic expectations of marriage and cohabitation

3. Social Learning Theory—Discourage corporal punishment of children and reduce celebration of violence in the media

4. Control Theory—Strengthen family ties by offering parenting education

5. Moral Justification Theory—Eliminate social approval of violence as a means of supporting moral standards, such as governments' use of capital punishment

6. Control-Balance Theory—Enhance gender equality in the family and reduce social isolation to enable social controls that condemn the use of violence to govern behavior

7. Conflict Theory—Promote economic, social, and political equality and increase access to and availability of marriage counseling

8. Feminist Theories of Criminal Justice—Treat all victims as reliable and truthful and strengthen criminal justice sanctions for intimate partner violence

9. Feminist Theories of Crime/Power-Control Theories—Eliminate male dominance in society and the home

10. Survival Strategy Theory—Increase the availability of escape options, such as shelters and safe houses, for victims of abuse

11. Convergence Theory—Eliminate differences between criminal justice treatment of victims by gender of victims and offenders and reduce cultural support and celebration of violence

Smithey and Straus also commend the United Nations' leadership role in global primary prevention of partner violence, evidenced by its adoption of the Domestic Violence Resolution in 1985 and its reiteration in 2000 that "[v]iolence against women and girls constitutes the single most prevalent and universal violation of human rights" (*Progress of the World's Women 2000: UNIFEM Biennial Report,* UN Development Fund for Women, New York, 2000).

Despite these promising observations about changing attitudes and reliable data indicating that intimate partner violence is decreasing, Smithey and Straus caution that there is no direct evidence demonstrating that declines in violence rates since the mid-1970s result from prevention programs. They offer other factors that may contribute to declining violence, such as an increase of three years in the average age at marriage from 1970 to 2000. Another possible explanation for the decline is that prevention programs have effectively stigmatized partner violence to the degree that there is even greater reluctance, on the part of both victims and perpetrators, to disclose it. Even if this explanation is true and actual rates of intimate partner violence have not dropped as much as the self-report data show, then there is cause for cautious optimism because greater reluctance to admit to abusive behavior indicates that society is less tolerant of violent personal relationships.

Primary Prevention Programs

A number of primary prevention programs are emerging to address the problem of intimate partner violence. Some began during the 1990s and others have been instituted as recently as 2000. There is no published research documenting their effectiveness, but researchers and battered women's advocates are hopeful that these initiatives will further reduce public acceptance and tolerance of intimate partner violence. Some examples of primary prevention programs follow.

The National Center for Injury Prevention and Control (NCIPC), an agency of the CDC, developed and implemented the Family and Intimate Violence Prevention Program to focus on surveillance, research, evaluation, and training and to fund community-based prevention programs at all levels of prevention. In addition to supporting community-based projects targeting the general public, such as the Milwaukee Women's Center and Georgia's Men Stopping Violence, Inc., the NCIPC also sponsors projects aimed at preventing intimate partner violence in specific populations, such as rural and Native American communities.

The National Crime Prevention Council offers school-based prevention programs that train teens to respond to hot line callers and perform peer counseling. The council focuses on violence in teen dating relationships and its dating violence intervention projects teach boys and girls not to accept violence in their earliest relationships, even before they begin dating. The students are taught how to identify and resolve conflict, recognize abusive behavior, and communicate respectfully with their peers.

The National Advisory Council on Violence Against Women was established in 1995 with the goal of eliminating social norms that support and condone violence against women. To achieve this ambitious goal, the council coordinates multidisciplinary efforts involving community leaders and representatives from health care agencies, the military, organized sports, the social welfare system, the justice system, the media, academia, businesses, and religious communities. The council also supports educating children about gender roles and stereotypes that condone violence against women.

The Family Violence Prevention Fund is a national, nonprofit organization that offers primary, secondary, and tertiary prevention programs. To admonish the general public that when people fail to speak out against partner violence, they perpetuate the problem with their silence, the Fund produced the media campaign "There's No Excuse for Domestic Violence." The Fund also provides services for abuse victims, offers community and professional education programs for the public at large, and actively seeks public policy reform.

IMPORTANT NAMES AND ADDRESSES

American Public Human Services Association (formerly American Public Welfare Association)
810 First St., NE, Suite 500
Washington, DC 20002
(202) 682-0100
FAX: (202) 289-6555
URL: http://www.aphsa.org

Center for the Prevention of Sexual and Domestic Violence
2400 N. 45th St., #10
Seattle, WA 98103
(206) 634-1903
FAX: (206) 634-0115
E-mail: cpsdv@cpsdv.org
URL: http://www.cpsdv.org

Center for Women Policy Studies
1211 Connecticut Ave., NW, Suite 312
Washington, DC 20036
(202) 872-1770
FAX: (202) 296-8962
E-mail: cwps@centerwomenpolicy.org
URL: http://www.centerwomenpolicy.org

Domestic Abuse Intervention Project
202 E. Superior St.
Duluth, MN 55802
(218) 722-2781
FAX: (218) 722-0779
URL: http://www.duluth-model.org/
daipccr3.htm

Family Research Laboratory
University of New Hampshire
126 Horton Social Science Center
Durham, NH 03824-3586
(603) 862-1888
FAX: (603) 862-1122
URL: http://www.unh.edu/frl/index.html

Family Violence Prevention Fund
383 Rhode Island St., Suite 304
San Francisco, CA 94103-5133
(415) 252-8900
FAX: (415) 252-8991

E-mail: fund@endabuse.org
URL: http://www.fvpf.org

National Clearinghouse for the Defense of Battered Women
125 S. 9th St., Suite 302
Philadelphia, PA 19107
(215) 351-0010
FAX: (215) 351-0779

National Coalition Against Domestic Violence
PO Box 18749
Denver, CO 80218
(303) 839-1852
FAX: (303) 831-9251
Toll-free: (800) 799-7233
URL: http://www.ncadv.org

National Council of Juvenile and Family Court Judges Family Violence Department
University of Nevada, Reno
PO Box 8970
Reno, NV 89507
(775) 784-6012
FAX: (775) 784-6628
Toll-free: (800) 527-3443
E-mail: info@dvlawsearch.com
URL: http://www.dvlawsearch.com

National Council on Child Abuse and Domestic Violence
1025 Connecticut Ave., NW, Suite 1012
Washington, DC 20036
(202) 429-6695
FAX: (831) 655-3930
URL: http://www.nccafv.org

National Criminal Justice Reference Service
PO Box 6000
Rockville, MD 20849-6000
(301) 519-5500
FAX: (301) 519-5212
Toll-free: (800) 851-3420
URL: http://www.ncjrs.org

National Institute of Justice
810 7th St., NW
Washington, DC 20531
(202) 307-2942
FAX: (202) 307-6394
Toll-free: (800) 851-3420
URL: http://www.ojp.usdoj.gov/nij/

National Resource Center on Domestic Violence
Pennsylvania Coalition Against Domestic Violence
6400 Flank Dr., Suite 1300
Harrisburg, PA 17112-2778
(717) 545-6400
FAX: (717) 545-9456
Toll-free: (800) 537-2238
URL: http://www.pcadv.org

National Self-Help Clearinghouse
Graduate School and University Center of the City University of New York
365 5th Ave., Suite 3300
New York, NY 10016
(212) 917-1822
URL: http://www.selfhelpweb.org

National Sexual Violence Resource Center
123 North Enola Dr.
Enola, PA 17025
(717) 909-0710
FAX: (717) 909-0714
Toll-free: (877) 739-3895
URL: http://www.nsvrc.org

Sexual Assault Recovery Anonymous Society (SARA)
PO Box 16
Surrey, BC V3T 4W4
Canada
(604) 584-2626
FAX: (604) 584-2888

**Stalking Resource Center National Center
for Victims of Crime**
2000 M St., NW, Suite 480
Washington, DC 200036
(202) 467-8700
FAX: (202) 467-8701
URL: http://www.ncvc.org

RESOURCES

A number of studies were conducted on domestic violence when spouse abuse first became a public issue during the 1970s and 1980s. Since that time, however, there has been little government-funded statistical research on domestic abuse. The pioneering work done at the University of New Hampshire's Family Research Laboratory in Durham, New Hampshire, has become an authoritative source of information and insight about family violence.

Chief among the University of New Hampshire researchers who perform the landmark studies and in-depth work on intimate partner violence are Murray Straus, Richard Gelles, David Finkelhor, and Suzanne Steinmetz. Studies released by the Family Research Laboratory investigate all forms of domestic violence, many based on the National Family Violence Survey and the National Family Violence Resurvey. Murray Straus and Glenda Kaufman Kantor published more recent data in 1994 in "Changes in Spouse Assault Rates from 1975 to 1992: A Comparison of Three National Surveys" (the Family Research Laboratory at the University of New Hampshire, presented at the 13th World Congress of Sociology, July 19, 1994). Martha Smithey and Murray Straus published the July 2002 report "Primary Prevention of Intimate Partner Violence" (National Institute of Mental Health, Washington, DC).

International data about violence against women is collected by organizations such as the Statistical Commission and Economic Commission for Europe and the United Nations Interregional Crime and Justice Research Institute. Private sources on abuse include *The Commonwealth Fund's 1998 Survey of Women's Health* (Commonwealth Fund, Baltimore, MD, 1998) and the World Bank's *Violence Against Women: The Hidden Health Burden* by Lori Heise (Washington, DC, 1994).

The National Academy of Sciences Institute of Medicine report *Confronting Chronic Neglect: The Education and Training of Health Professionals on Family Violence* (National Academy Press, Washington, DC, 2001), the American Medical Association (AMA) report *AMA Data on Violence Between Intimates* (AMA Council on Scientific Affairs, December 2000), the Centers for Disease Control and Prevention report *Intimate Partner Violence Surveillance: Uniform Definitions and Recommended Data Elements* (Linda E. Saltzman, Janet L. Fanslow, Pamela M. McMahon, and Gene A. Shelley, revised edition, 2002), and the Henry J. Kaiser Family Foundation report (*Violence Against Women,* Washington, DC, 2001) also provide information about medical and health care utilization by abused women.

National opinion poll research comes from Harris Interactive, Inc. (the Harris Poll) and from the 1999 Florida Department of Corrections' *Florida's Perspective on Domestic Violence.* These provide insight into attitudes and beliefs about intimate partner violence.

Research cited in this publication was drawn from numerous books including *Against Our Will,* by Susan Brownmiller (Simon and Schuster, New York, 1975); *For Love of Country: Confronting Rape and Sexual Harassment in the Military,* by Teri Spahr Nelson (Haworth Maltreatment and Trauma, September 2002); *Terrifying Love: Why Battered Women Kill and How Society Responds,* by Lenore Walker (Harper and Row, New York, 1989); *When Battered Women Kill,* by Angela Browne (The Free Press, New York, 1987); *Current Controversies on Family Violence,* edited by Richard Gelles and Donileen Loseke (Sage, Newbury Park, CA, 1994); *Legal Responses to Wife Assault,* edited by Zoe Hilton (Sage, Newbury Park, CA, 1993); *Wife Rape,* by Raquel Kennedy Bergen (Sage, Newbury Park, CA, 1996); *The Batterer: A Psychological Profile,* by Donald Dutton (Basic, New York, 1995); *Women At Risk,* by Evan Stark and Anne Flitcraft (Sage, Newbury Park, CA, 1996); *Do Arrests and Restraining Orders Work?* edited by Eve Buzawa and Carl Buzawa

(Sage, Newbury Park, CA, 1996); and *Abused Men: The Hidden Side of Domestic Violence,* by Philip W. Cook (Praeger, Westport, CT, 1997).

The federal government's Bureau of Justice Statistics in Washington, D.C., provides information on domestic violence from the National Crime Victimization Surveys in *Criminal Victimization 2001: Changes 2000–01 with Trends 1993–2001,* (2001); *Violence by Intimates, Findings from the National Violence Against Women Survey* (1999); *Intimate Partner Violence and Age of Victim, 1993–99* (2001); *Batterer Intervention: Program Approaches and Criminal Justice Strategies* (1998); *Women Offenders: A Special Report* (2000); *Extent, Nature and Consequences of Intimate Violence* (2000); *Special Report on Intimate Partner Violence* (2000); *Background Checks for Firearm Transfers* (2002); *Enforcement of Protective Orders* (2002); and *The Benefits and Limitations for Victims of Domestic Violence* (1997).

The U.S. Merit Systems Protection Board, an agency of the federal government, provides data on trends and responses to sexual harassment in *Sexual Harassment in the Federal Workplace* (1995).

Medical, psychological, sociological, epidemiological, and other types of journals publish useful articles on abuse. The journal articles cited in this publication were published in *American Sociological Review, The Psychology of Women Quarterly, Archives of Internal Medicine, American Behavioral Scientist, British Journal of Criminology, Crime and Delinquency, Current Opinion in Obstetrics and Gynecology, Journal of General Internal Medicine, American Journal of Public Health, Journal of Marriage and the Family, Violence Against Women, Violence and Victims, Journal of Comparative Family Studies, Journal of Research in Crime and Delinquency, Journal of the American Medical Association, Journal of Family Psychology, Journal of Family Practice, Journal of Emergency Nursing, Journal of Consulting and Clinical Psychology, Maternal and Child Health Journal,* and *Journal of Interpersonal Violence.*

INDEX

DEMCO